The Liberty Seekers:
An American Saga

The Liberty Seekers: An American Saga

A History of The Hughes' Family and Fortune
Book I

Howard Robard Hughes III

2009

The researches of the author here set down, that the deeds of men may not be forgotten, and the glorious and noble actions of the first Americans may not lose their fame; and, especially, the causes of their strife may be known.

TABLE OF
CONTENTS

CHAPTER I

THE LANDING

The queen of olde England died a goode death, in her bed, during the waning days of Winter, 1603. Witnesses, in her stately wooden chamber, saw Bess Tudor fall serenely and slowly asleep, forever. Eventually that fateful day, church bells rang the mortal message throughout England. All evening, and all through the rolling countryside, they clanged continuously. Flocks of birds flying high in the sky, above that verdant view, swept their broad gazes across a panoramic scene. Against the hard-blowing wind they heard the sound of bells roaring, minutely, from the distance far below. And to the humans on the ground, the sound of Sunday seemed to echo forever. The sad sensation flooded into the memories of English men and women. They would always remember, their country, the way it was that day.

At her funeral procession, men, women, and children overfilled the streets, houses, windows, leads and gutters, to see the obsequy. At the sound of heavy hooves hitting hard stone, they strained to see. Whence they beheld her statue lying upon the coffin, a loud long lamentable sighing, groaning, and weeping ensued as the like hath neither been seen nor known in the memory of man.

Everywhere, the English felt uneasy. In one another's faces they could see, presciently, into the future of their fate. All around, the topic of conversation turned reluctantly from the greatness of Queen Bess to concern for the kingdom. For, the queen was the daughter of the late Henry

Tudor, Duke of York, and founder of the autonomous Anglican faith. Indeed, she was the granddaughter of the first Henry Tudor, hero renown of the Civil War between North and South; between the Dukes of Lancaster and York, for whom would be king. The South won. Now, two kings and two queens later, the new king was the great-grandson of the old king's sister, allright, but he was also intimately related to powerful continental Catholics on his maternal side.

Unfortunately, Queen Bess had not given the people a popular heir. True, the crown passed to the king of neighboring Scotland. Nonetheless, King James was a Catholic sympathizer. Add, that his accession to influence came at a time of newfound national pride in England. The greatest English heroes, of late, were Queen Bess' illustrious knights. Especially admired, among all of the pirates cum heroes, were Sirs Walter Rawleyghe and Francis Drake, who sank the Spanish Armada invasion fleet, while the queen paced cold castle floors precariously, in fear for her very life, just fifteen years earlier. It was Bess' old beaus that held the hearts of the people.

In the months following the solemn day of death, desire waxed among the brave-hearted. They comprised those who loved and lived the traditions of liberty. The brave-hearted coveted the liberty that the law of *Magna Charta* guaranteed to the English. They adhered to that constitutional law made on one momentous day, in 1215, at Runningmeade. Through it, King John I recognized the autonomy of dukes and so swore to honour their local authority. In particular, he honoured the dukes' right to maintain their own armies that they needed to administer local law.

In fact, the liberty of Englishmen provided history with nothing new. Liberty itself had devolved to the English, through the republican Romans, from their original European ancestors, the ancient Greeks. It was they who established the cherished tradition.

As put forth by the philosopher, Aristotle, in *Economicus*, through which he describes the economy of Greece, liberty is that which distinguishes Europeans from Asians, including Africans. To him, the liberty of Greeks referred to their self-sufficiency. It did not, however, necessarily refer to their status as free persons. That is to say, Greeks had liberty because they owned their farms or practiced their own trades. Thereby, they provided their livelihoods themselves. All Greeks were thus self-employed. In Greece, only slaves gave the products of their labour to other men. Thus, a slave who owned his farm or trade, as did Aristotle himself, had liberty but no freedom. Indeed, in Greek life, a free man without liberty would likely have become a slave.

In contrast, Asians owned nothing. The emperors owned everything. In his famous example, Aristotle described the grain estate system in Egypt, bread basket of the ancient world, by which wealthy holders occupied lande as only life gifts from the pharaohs. At death, the lande did not transfer to their progeny. Moreover, they could and sometimes did, lose the lande by the ruler's political caprice. The philosopher thus described a political economy dependent on patronage. Accordingly, all Asians lived under slavery, whether in actual bondage or not, whereas all Greeks lived as free persons at liberty. Needless to say, Greek awareness of the singularity of their liberty kept them militantly vigilant to protect and strengthen it.

Therefore, the accession to the kingship of Queen Bess' catholic cousin, alarmed lovers of liberty. The foreign leanings of the new king made them vigilant to protect the liberty of Englishmen. Not surprisingly then, the fear of the New World that had spread, back in the late 1580's, by the mysterious disappearance of Sir Walter Rawleyghe's Roanoke Colony, subsided hastily now. The wilderness landes seemed less loathsome than theretofore. The foreboding salvage wilderness, far off across the raw waters, piqued the imaginations of the brave-hearted and adventurous once again.

In this bold atmosphere, risktakers confederated together to invest their fortunes, and their lives, in what would become England's second colonial venture. For many months, they diligently sought in and out of London, both those with and without royal favour, for subscribers to their colonial venture. Whence the group had gathered together sufficient investors, they approached the new king, reluctantly, to request approval of their charter.

Seeing a possible opportunity to establish an imperial power in the New World, like those of Spain and France, the king agreed to approve the charter. In Spring, 1606, the king signed the London Companie Charter. The subscribers, largely, referred to it as the Virginia Companie of London, nonetheless, in honour of their olde queen. For, where the would-be colonists sought liberty in the lande of Virginia; the king sought empire in the hallowed halls of London.

Upon approval, the king set down his signature and the royal clerk stamped the heavy parchment document. Dozens of stockholders invested in the companie including those, at last, whom the king bartered into it to promote his own interests. For the most part, the original investors expected dividends to get issued in the form of lande. There were those favoured few, that is, the king's cronies, however, who lusted for gold and silver. For too long, they had seen how New World mines added shiploads of precious metals to the Spanish Empire's treasury.

The king's government intended to establish English colonies somewhere between the French and Spanish in the New World. At the royal court, a position halfway between the two mighty navies and armies was thought prudent. Yet, fate would chose the exact location.

Finally, the king attempted to direct his own interests further. Deliberately, he sat down, dipped his quill, and penned a statement that named his suggestions for colonial officers. Naturally, he paid back favors that he owed for having gained the throne without civil war. The largeness of his intention for vast Virginia made these favors significant. She would not only be the first English colony in the New World but in the whole world.

Slyly, he rolled the names of the colony's officers in a scroll. They were to lie in sealed boxes, out of sight, until the landing. With the king's demands met, the venture got under way. It provided for the outfitting of three small ships of differing sizes, with crews, arms, powder, provisions, and parts for a small boat with which to explore, along with over one hundred mostly stockholders, to attempt a second colony. Just as Sir Walter Rawlewghe had named the lande itself, Virginia, after his virgin queen, the colonists would name the planned fort after the new king. The place would become known as Fort Jamestowne. The king would be appeased, hopefully.

Hereby, then, the author describes the setting in which the hardy companie set sail from the port of Blackwall, and thereby left England forever, on a cold windy December 19, 1606, in the Susan Constant, Godspeed, and Discovery, under the respective commands of Captains Newport, Gosnold, and Ratcliffe.

"If you want to go to the New World, then head south 'till thy butter melts and turn right," was the olde explorer's adage. Such a course pushed ships to the northwest coast of Africa where they caught the trade winds. Those lucky lusty winds sent ships sailing west across the ocean with swift ease. And, for those who would return home, the westerlies blew back from the northeastern shores of the New World to the olde. These were proverbial ocean highways.

Catching the trade winds was the trick. At the get-go, contrary winds and storms held the voyagers back. They yet hugged England's channel coast after seventeen days out. Delay frustrated anticipation for sunny southern seas. Winter's wet chill aggravated that damp frustration.

Dispositions became discordant. From deep within the mother ship's huddled galleys, months-long subaqueous rancour rose up to rivalry. It was a rivalry borne deep within history, and one that long before had claimed immortality. Indeed, it was a rivalry that would lead to revolution, one day, in the virgin lande.

On one side, stood those who the king had suggested for officer status. These were men who sought nothing less than an English empire. On the other side, stood the original investors. These were men who sought nothing more than liberty in the virgin lande. The king's godson, Mr. Edward-Maria Wingfield, one of those brought into the companie by his godfather's device, led the former. The soon-to-be famous soldier of adventure, Captain John Smith, veteran of wars, negotiations, and even slavery, led the latter.

Many months had passed since the original investors first felt the need to abandon their homeland, and strike out, without fear, on their own. During those months, however, they witnessed the gradual demise of their dream. For, the king turned their dream for liberty into a scheme for empire. They found themselves in a companie not of their choosing. The king's men had all but come to dominate the venture.

Those damp dreary days dead off the channel coast dragged, like a great heavy anchor, on already contentious tempers. The king's favourite, Mr. Wingfield, never happy with the ambiguous state of power within the companie, served as impellent for a return to Blackwall and reorganization of the whole situation. The initial colonists' hired choice for leader, Captain Smith, rallied the brave-hearted to stay the course of action.

If not for the intercession of the right goode and reverend Preacher Hunt, a regretful row likely would have wrecked and ruined the venture there and then. Fortuitously, all left the decision to him, on his authority from God. And, Preacher Hunt was a man of willpower and action.

So, after six weeks waiting, with unfavorable weather keeping England in sight, the mighty winds turned right, and the ships struck speedily out, into a pitch-black Winter night. As the days passed, the swelling waves grew ever larger and the humid air grew ever warmer. The prows pushed purposefully into every relentless rise. Then, one day, after a few weeks sailing, shining white sand, speckled with tiny green palms, flickered in sparkling sun on a distant horizon. Within a few hours, the three ships laid anchors at the Canary Islands.

Looking around the strange port, the colonists and crew could spot no other English ships. There were, predominately, Spanish and Portuguese ships at anchor, thereabouts. The African island stopover served the two mighty empire's naval and trading ships as a watering, supply, and maintenance stop mainly. So too, the procurement of fresh water drew the three small inconsequential vessels into port there. And, needless to mention, many landlubbers on board enjoyed a short break from the sickening sea.

One man was not a stranger to the African island. Captain Smith had once been at this tropical place. Some few years earlier, while he made passage on a French buccaneer's vessel, en route back to England from the Turkish Wars, the pirate captain made port here. Smith thus had gained firsthand knowledge.

From that encounter with the two imperial navies, Captain Smith knew the English would not be welcome. He warned the crew to this effect. He advised that the small ships should make themselves as inconspicuous as possible by sailing in after dark then out just after dawn. Thus, for the second time in the voyage, he undertook to earn the position for which the first investors had deemed him capable by virtue of his military experience with foreigners and his certain character.

The Susan Constant's crew took the advice of experience. The crews of the Godspeed and Discovery followed suit. The king's godson, however, did not take the commoner's advice respectfully. After dawn the next day, quickly back out to sea and happily heading west, Mr. Wingfield thought to nip the proverbial bud.

The man's merit would not be his qualification, he connived. Mr. Wingfield conjured up all the wiles he could wield. Enviously, he charged his would-be competitor with usurpation of governmental authority. He went so far as to claim that the man was dangerous and capable of murdering the colonial council. On the high seas, such an accusation goes by the name: mutiny.

After his manipulatory speech, he convinced the Susan Constant's legitimate legal authority, Captain Newport, to place Captain Smith in a makeshift brig below decks. Only the king's cronies felt satisfaction at Smith's imprisonment. As for the rest, resentment intensified. The venture was off course.

The voyage moved now into the trade winds. It gained speed. Atop decks, voyagers stood firmly facing a robust wind that blew umbrage off of their faces and into the invisible distance astern. The New World lay easily ahead.

Within a few weeks, on March twenty-third, the voyage sighted the Carib island known by Europeans as Martinique. It sailed on however, pass this nautical mile marker, in anticipation of a better port at which to replenish water and food. That they reached the next day at the island of Dominica. This was a place at which the Florentine sailors, under Spanish flags, Christofo Columbo and Amerigus Vespuciano, had landed one hundred fifteen years earlier. It was a place the Spanish claimed but could not take from the fierce natives.

The big anchors splashed down. The three wooden ships whined and moaned loudly at anchor ropes for the first time in weeks. Soon, a group of natives nimbly paddled their dugouts toward the decks full of apprehensive onlookers. This would be their first encounter with natives of the New World.

Once the Caribs were close enough to view, voyagers and crew quickly became concerned about their imminent approach, for they appeared menacing. Indeed, they were a strange sight to behold. The naked natives wore bones through their noses, ears, and lips. Their unfriendly faces bore the keen quick expressions of predatory animals.

"Wee'll be boiled in pots and eaten," someone cried out loudly.

Instead, the fierce-looking leader raised his hands in a gesture of no harm. So, with muskets loaded and pointed down at the dugouts that sat at port side, he was allowed to climb the boarding-rope ladder. Awkwardly, the Carib began to communicate his wonder. He was clearly unaccustomed to the English flag and language. He knew only those of imperial Spain. Through arduous communication, he conveyed the message that his men and he had driven the Spanish off many times. These proud Caribs would not be enslaved.

The English made him understand that they were not associated with Spain and did not intend to enslave them. Appeased, the Carib leader quickly overcame unfamiliarity and sought to trade. Thereby, the crew lowered rowboats and, well-armed, several men followed the dugouts ashore. Once standing on lande, the men found a fair island with trees full of sweet and goode smells. Unusual enough, they also found the men speaking one language and the women another one, alltogether.

Bartering thus ensued through all manner of sign language. The Caribs coveted knives and hatchets. The English promised to give wood-handled iron tools that yet remained on board the ships. In addition, the natives asked for copper and much esteemed beads. These too the men promised.

The deal thus made, the Caribs retrieved the empty water jugs from the rowboats and then replaced them full. They filled their own dugouts with fruits, vegetables, and surprisingly, French linen that they had liberated from a

Spanish ship. Finally, boats and dugouts headed out to the ships where the barter was consummated within hours of having dropped anchor.

Thereupon, the voyagers set out again. With renewed vigour, they maintained a northwesterly course across the warm Caribbean Sea. They made lande on the island of Guadeloupe. An eerie strange sense, in the seeming paradise, drew the landing party back to the ships and out to sea within an hour. In the early afternoon of March twenty-eighth, the ships anchored at the island of Nevis.

Captain Newport led a landing party on a mile march into the interior to search for whatever might be useful. In the thick of it, the men had to slash their way through the dense jungle. At one point, swords gashed into poisonous tree limbs that let loose squirts of acidic sap with all the vengeance nature uses in her defense. A few unlucky ones felt the sting. Within an hour, swelling and itching grew intense.

Luckily, the party sighted a warm spring. Without hesitation, everyone took off their sweaty clothes and plunged in to bathe with soap. All of the men lingered long in the salubrious spring for the sake of the few. While lolling about, all of a sudden, some of them caught sight of lurking natives looking on from the jungle, thereabouts. A mild panic ensued. All men made for the ships in just their shoes.

Refreshed with a night's rest, and with visions of the great stores of conies, sundry kinds of fowls, and great plentie of fish they had found on Nevis the previous afternoon, the party overcame fear and went ashore again in the morning. They kept themselves close to one another for offensive advantage. During the next six days of hunting and fishing, stores became stuffed. Meanwhile, the king's godson, thinking to issue the swift justice of strong government, directed the building of a gallows on which to hang the purportedly treasonous Captain Smith.

The time for tolerance, however, reached its end. Among the men, the better sort of characters did not need much discussion. They could read one another's feelings in their faces. Decisively, they gathered together in strength, walked purposefully, with eyes intent, and tools of destruction in hands, straightaway to the gallows. The carpenter labouring on the dreary device caught sight of the group just as it moved in on him.

"Draw nigh and thy souls shall burn in hell for ye crime," he coyly howlered.

Undeterred, and without a word, the men raised their heavy hatchets, swung them down, and struck the first blows. The strong timbers shook and shuddered in the sandy soil. The hacking sound of iron splintering solid wood invaded the tropical tranquility. Wide-eyed, the carpenter dropped his tools and ran for his rowboat.

The reverberating sound rushed across the main ship's deck and into the quarters astern where Mr. Wingfield sat, superciliously. Belligerently, he came atop deck. From the bow rail, he watched the cross beam fall down to the ground on the beach. He clenched his fists around the thick rail to steady his rage.

When the men onshore completed the job, the antagonists stood facing each other across the bay water. In the stare down, only the blowing breeze moved. Belligerence struck a standoff that day. Both sides vowed to have their ways.

Thereafter, no one broke the uneasy silence that surrounded the gallows on Nevis. At dawn, on the sixth day, the voyage got underway once again. The next morning,

Easter Sunday, the anchors dropped at Saint Croix. There, a few days of reverent celebration followed.

One day of pleasant sailing, due west, then brought the voyage to the island of Mona on Wednesday April seventh. Here, on an exploratory trek into the interior, fate brought the first fatality. The six mile trek, in tropical Spring heat, overwhelmed one Englishman. A lone makeshift crucifix marked his demise. On Friday, the voyage left the loss on a two hour sail to Monito.

Saturday morning the landing party encountered bounty the likes of which no one had ever laid eyes. That afternoon, when the rowboats pulled up to the ships, they were loaded down with barrels full of fowl. One man climbed aboard the first ship speedily and excitedly described the great sight to those gathered on deck.

He did not exaggerate, "Wee were drawn by the squawking of fowl to a field, where wee were not able to walk about the ground without wee set foote on fowls or eggs, for they lie so thicke in the grasse. Why, wee need only pluck the birds from the bushes and stuff them in barrels."

In that confident condition, the voyagers bid farewell to the tropical sea and headed north for the virgin wilderness. Their constitutions were now as for the first time, again, in both body and spirit. They had been eased by exposure to a hot sun, warm salt water, and bountiful nourishment.

Fortuitously, the tropical climate brought forth dispositions among them that were unlike any they had ever known back in England. A satisfied quietude fell over all like a long lull on the monotonously rising and falling waves of the water below them. Life seemed too peaceful. An ominous presentiment of the avaricious Spaniards kept their minds alert and their eyes focused.

Ten days north, and yet the virgin lande lay beyond them. The water that sprayed onto the decks turned cold again, and the passengers got out wool blankets at night. The trustworthy mariners, whom the companie had hired in England, were three days past their own reckoning, yet not the flight of a seagull could make the course right. A foreboding feeling of lost course crept in among the colonists. Signs of regret began to overcome the faces of those who took the habit of sweeping fearful glances across the treacherously churning water.

The navigators began hinting that the course seemed untrue. Intense concern arose among a few of the less hardy. Some thought they had sailed into the famous Northwest Passage, that the Italian explorer, John Caboto, had sought a century earlier. Thus, these doubters reasoned, lande lay ahead allright, but in the Orient months hence. Worse, the voyage might outlast its provisions.

However, praying to their Christian God for mercy on their hard task somewhat calmed those who neared panic. Other colonists tended less toward prayer. They mulled over maps based on Rawleyghe's nineteen-year old drawings from 1588. These stalwarts held firm to a belief in nature and geography.

Anxious days and nights passed on into the vast distance ahead of them. Captain John Ratcliffe, of the tiny trailing ship, Discovery, became concerned about the growing swells, and instigated heated discussion that caused the colonists to break into two groups. On one hand, there formed those who would return to England without further delay. On the other, there formed those who would stay the course. Neither the one nor the other group, however, planned for nature to usurp man in determining the course of the three small ships.

A sudden Spring squall arose from the desolate blackness of a lumberingly rolling sea night. The ships pitched and rolled right on into the wall of the squall. The unsteady decks became dangerous underfoot. Up in the flying riggings, the sailors furled the sails to ride out the vicious storm. Down in the tossing galleys, colonists took to the sides of decks, themselves, where they held hard to the hull boards. Miserable cold water poured in down the gangways, from the decks above, then swished around and out over and over again. After hours of this torturous tumult, the wild whistling wind and waves slowly subsided. Thereupon, sound sleep wrapped around all like a heavy wet wool blanket.

As the next dawn's sun slowly rose over tacking port sides, one colonist dreamed of the virgin forestlande. He dreamed that he could smell it. The taste of the smell swelled his tongue and made him swallow the green aura. Whilst the ship plunged and rolled with repetitious delirious monotony under him, a sudden whiff of lande brought him out of his delusion. Slowly, he stood up on his sea legs, ambled across the deck, and pulled himself up the passageway.

Startled, he took in the distant sight. He felt, at once, excited yet petrified. All the details of the Roanoke Colony's disappearance flooded heavily in on him. Everyone there had disappeared without a trace while Rawleyghe returned to England for supplies. According to Rawleyghe, he found the colony mysteriously abandoned. The only clues were a tree carved with the letters "CRO" and a post carved with the word "CROATOAN." Apparently, the savages had kidnapped everyone.

Those savages were not the same as those with whom the voyagers had traded, theretofore. They were more remote from contact with Europeans. In addition, explorers considered them more dangerous. Thus, as he thought of Rawleyghe's words, he feared the ships would not be welcome here, as they had been, somewhat, in the Carib Islands. The time to turn back had passed, however. Now, the ships moved straightaway into the same dense forbidding forests as had Rawleyghe twenty years earlier.

Suddenly, open but calmer water appeared. The forest receded away from the starboard side of the ship while open water lay ahead and on port side. His heart pounded.

"'Tis a cape," shouted a boatswain.

"'Tis a cape," echoed back and again from the sister ships.

"'Tis a lande made up o' capes by my judgement. First o' thy virgin lande sighted 'tis a cape, and wee shall name it for thy prince," shouted Captain Newport.

"Cape Henry" several shouts came back.

"Cape Henry," echoed back twice.

"'Tis ye shore 'twas chartered to our companie,' shouted the captain. "Take 'er in first place ye think to make lande," he shouted out the order.

"Aye ie captain," shouted back the mariners in unison, while the same order went abroad again.

Soon, the ships strained against strong current, as the pilots shifted their crafts. Yet, everywhere a mere rim of brown shore, betwixt blue water and black woods, strained the mariners' wits for a landing. Finally, after searching the shoreline exhaustedly, they spotted a beach and steered for a landing.

As a massive forest wall rushed toward the ships, the now wide-awake colonist scoured the thick denseness for any sign of movement. Straight ahead he thought he caught the glare of a pair of eyes for just a fleeting moment.

Perhaps they came from the eyes of a boar and not those of a savage human. He held himself steady.

With a hard splash, the boatswain threw in the anchor. The whining ship reared back and strained at the taut rope. Several men became impatient to make lande legs, but mixed emotions overwhelmed him. Circumspectly, he held fast to the rail, and waited, while watching the captain prepare a party to explore the sandy shore.

Cautiously, he joined the landing party. Then, standing solidly on the sandy beach, the strong aroma of wilderness intoxicated him yet once again. An easy pleasurable sensation overcame his physical senses. A rushing delirium immobilized him. His manhood seemed insignificant in this immense wilderness. Awe struck him.

The shout of another fellow brought him out of his dream. He focused on the foreground. There, in the distance, standing on the dunes, the fellow beckoned him with an arm gesture to catch up. After a moment's hesitation, he walked on toward the dunes and the forest beyond.

The Spring day was cool but sunny. Within a few hours, the explorers found faire meddowes and goodely tall trees. The virgin forest flourished with flora and fauna. They sighted no natives. Only the sound of birds could be heard.

Late in the afternoon the party began marching back to the beach. By twilight they reached it. The colonist that had lingered long in awe, on that beach, when the party set out in the early afternoon, felt relieved to be out of the thick forest and back in sight of the ships. His sixth sense had been warning him since the ships pulled in.

While waiting patiently, with the landing party, for rowboats to reach the beach, a brief breeze reminded him of the afternoon's intoxication. He turned his head back to take in, yet, another view of the strong aroma. In the shadowy twilight, his eyes admiringly followed the trunks of those tremendous trees to their very tops. And there, a flock of birds fluttered. Then, suddenly, an ominous dread pierced into the pit of his stomach like the quick lunge of a lance. In another moment, a screeching howling hoard of vicious red-painted savages descended upon the party from over the dunes.

A terrifying chaotic scene broke loose all around him. Instantly, the whizzing sound of a flying arrow just passed his left ear, and then plunged with a sickening thud, and splatters of blood, into the shoulder of a sailor.

"Make for ship," Captain Newport yelled.

He thought to run but gunpowder explosions, nearby, numbed him. Nonetheless, in a few deafening seconds he regained his senses and ran posthaste for the ship's haven. By the time he boarded her, the howling and shooting had stopped. The smoky shore turned silent.

"That 'ill put the fear o' God in 'em," cried the captain.

"They'll not be comin' out o' ye forest again anytime soon," one man mumbled, grudgingly.

But, he thought otherwise about the savages.

"Nay, I say. Our powder did not scare 'em off. Musket shot didn't even reach 'em. They aim their arrows accurately but from too great a distance. They just ran out of arrows is all."

Thereupon, the surgeon treated the two wounded men, while all around one heard much pitying and, again, regrets.

CHAPTER II

THE COLONY

By morning, everyone regained fortitude. The time had come to open the sealed orders. Most of the colonists came aboard the flagship, Susan Constant, to hear the reading. Once the group gathered together closely, the reader read the orders from the London council loudly. Obvious to all, the council had drawn up the orders straightforwardly. They named the seven men who would govern as members of the colony's own council and set forth a constitution, of sorts, for governance.

No one was surprised by the names therein. Mr. Edward Wingfield, the king's godson and investor; Captain Newport of the Susan Constant; Captain Gosnold of the Godspeed, an original investor; Captain Ratcliffe of the Discovery; George Kendall, a protégé of the Earl of Salisbury who was a major investor; John Martin, son of Sir Richard Martin, Lord Mayor of London, and brother-in-law of Sir Julius Caesar; and finally Captain John Smith.

The announcement of Captain Smith's name caused cursing from all the rest of the named council except Captain Gosnold. Promptly, they decided that Captain Smith would remain under arrest, for mutiny, and thus would be unable to assume his position. Quickly, the reader moved on to the detailed instructions.

The instructions derived from suggestions by explorers on earlier English missions. They read, take time in selecting a site, "for if you make many Removes, besides the loss of time, you shall greatly spoil your victuals and your casks, and with great pain transport it in small boats." Pick a site not heavily wooded since you lack enough labourers to clear a forest. The smallest ship, Discovery, should remain with the colonists for exploring, and when not in use, it should be tied close by and its sails and anchors taken ashore, "lest some ill disposed persons slip away with her."

The instructions revealed a stronger concern, in London, for the Spanish than natives. They commanded the colonists, "have great care not to offend the naturals" and begin trading immediately, "not being sure how your own seed corn will prosper the first year." When hiring natives as guides be cautious not to get stranded. Keep them intimidated by firearms, and never allow novices to shoot in their presence, "for if they see your learners miss what they aim at, they will think the weapon not so terrible, and thereby will be bould to assault you."

To reduce the threat of a Spanish attack settle the colony far from the ocean. Place an outpost at the mouth of the river with a light boat for the lookouts, "that when any fleet shall be in sight, they may come with speed to give you warning." And, do not allow natives to, "inhabit betwixt you and the sea coast," for they may serve as guides to the Spanish.

The instructions continued, that once a site were chosen the colony was to start seeking a return for investors right away. Captain Newport should take forty men upriver to seek a route to the "Other Sea" and even explore for minerals. Finally, the last two instructions struck a sinister note. The one stated that no man was to return to England except with permission of both president and council. The other stated that no one was, "to write any letter of anything that may discourage others."

The next morning, one group of men began to assemble a shallop from the various pieces brought over the ocean. The small boat would allow navigation in shallow waters, thereabouts. Meanwhile, another group took off hiking. It came across a small fire on which oysters roasted. No one was in sight.

In a few days, the colonists planted a Christian cross near the site of landing, and the three ships began heading upriver in search of a settlement site. At midday, on a western shore of the great bay, they spotted five natives carrying bows and arrows. Captain Newport took a small party toward shore in the shallop. He stood up and called to them in a sign of friendship, but at first, they were timorsome, until they saw him lay his hand on his heart. At that, they put down their weapons and gestured a welcome.

Trustingly, the party landed and followed the natives on foot to their village. The men learned that the village and tribe had the name, Kecoughtan. Their first sight was of natives laying their faces to the ground and making a doleful noise while scratching the earth with their nails. The party stood by and watched, uncomfortably. Once the ceremony ended, the natives spread mats on the ground.

The highest ranking of the tribe sat down, while the rest set out food or stood around. Some of the Englishmen grabbed for food. Hands reached out and stopped them. The natives wanted the Englishmen to sit, with them, on the ground, and then eat. The men complied.

The native men were naked except for a strip of deerskin leather hanging loosely from the waist. Some wore black or red paint. Birds' legs hung from their ears. Their shiny black hair was shell-shaved on the right and three or more feet long on the left. Dangling at the ends were knots with grey, blue, green, and red colored feathers.

The houses were made of reeds covered by tree bark. The rounded roofs were thatched. Hanging mats covered the entryways. There were no windows. They sat under groups of trees for shade and protection from foul weather. Each house was the same except for size.

After the meal, the natives gave a dance for their guests. A group formed a circle in which one man stood clapping to keep time. The rest shouted, howled, and stomped, in unison, while making faces and noises like wolves or devils each in his distinctive way.

When the dancing ended, the time had come to go. Captain Newport knew how to thank the chief. He stood up and dug some trifling jewels and beads from rucksacks. The English knew of native fascination with such items from accounts of the Roanoke expedition.

That evening, the few who attended the feast described the event to rapt audiences on board the ships. Captain Newport assured his cronies that the natives were simple-minded enough not to be of too great danger. Accordingly, the colony need only protect itself from surprise attack. His cronies agreed. Most of the men, however, remained skeptical.

The men spent the next two weeks sailing and scouting up a river known to natives as the Powhatan River. Along the way, they visited the villages of other tribes. These were the Paspahegh, Rappahannock, and Appomattoc.

The Paspahegh welcomed them. However, one tribal elder gave a long speech during which he made a foul noise accompanied by vehement utterances. The Rappahannock chief, himself, met the exploratory party at his shoreline. Ceremoniously, he held a majestical display as if he were meeting no one less than the king of England. At the Appomattoc village, warriors stood at the waterfront. Their leader held his arrow angrily notched in its bow. The English responded with gestures of peace. Reluctantly, the militant leader allowed them to lande, briefly.

After the close encounter with the Appomattocs, the colonists determined that the farther inland they explored, the more unfriendly the natives became. The encounter enabled them to make a decision on a site they had spotted, on their way upriver, several days earlier. All agreed that the site held promise. It sat considerably inland and thus a goodely way from the ocean and Spanish warships. It sat on a peninsula connected to the mainland by a narrow lande bridge that allowed for easy defense. It had deep water in which ships could pull up directly, tie to trees, and then load and unload. Upon reaching the site they laid anchors. Mr. Wingfield christened the place, Jamestowne, as expected. Yet, grumbling could be heard from many. These were those who had founded a private enterprise not a crown colony.

Ominously, the date on the calendar read, May thirteenth, sixteen hundred seven. Thus, many thought the settlement date boded bad luck. Indeed, that superstition would be proved.

The next morning, May fourteenth, they exhaustedly hauled the provisions ashore. Here is where Captain Newport's nautical authority ended and the council's authority began. London had directed the councilors to name a president from amongst themselves, for a one-year term. The councilors swore to be true to the king and, "faithfully and truly declare my mind and opinion according to my heart and conscience in all things treated of in that counsel." Then, not surprisingly, they voted Mr. Wingfield into the presidency. Predictably, they denied Captain Smith a vote.

Each councilor put forth his opinion about Captain Smith. That of President Wingfield was the most unflattering; that of Captain Gosnold the most flattering. He suggested that Captain Smith be released from the ship's makeshift brig because the colony needed his labour. This, the council agreed to do, albeit begrudgingly. It sought to appease the majority.

President Wingfield got in the last word on the matter. He reminded the council, and colonists, of London's order pertaining to colonial justice. It read, that on matters of moment a jury must deliberate. The majority of the council, however, and not peers, must have final determination over matters, with its president having not one but two votes.

On that ominous note from the president, the colonists fell about to work at various tasks. Some felled trees and burned stumps to prepare clearings in which to pitch tents and plant gardens. Others raked and hoed the forest floor.

Many colonists, led by Captain Smith, voiced their disagreement with London's orders in regard to the natives. The orders advised against martial displays so as not to offend them. However, those in close association with London, led by President Wingfield, responded that the orders were a rational response to the disappearance of the Roanoke Colony.

Nonetheless, many colonists considered the natives to be irrational in the civilized sense. Insistently, they voiced their belief in martial plans including fortifications. They reasoned, after all, the firing of muskets had helped halt the attack on the first landing party back at Cape Henry. These colonists swayed Councilor Kendall. He, in turn, persuaded President Wingfield to allow a small fence made of tree limbs.

On the third day, the stealthy savage natives circumspectly approached the colony. Paspahegh Chief Wowinchopunck sent messengers to announce his intended visit. The next day, Wowinchopunck arrived with an entourage of an hundred men, all of whom carried bow and arrows. The chief motioned for the English to put down their muskets. They refused. When one native feigned curiosity while picking up a hatchet a fist fight broke out. The chief left in a huff.

Two days later, the Paspahegh made another visit. This time, the chief sent forty men with a deer. The men sought to spend the night. The English denied the request. A few colonists thought to take advantage of the visit by making a show of force. They set up a wooden target and, with proverbial tongue in cheek, invited a native to take aim. Surprisingly, the arrow pierced the heavy target. So, the colonists set up a metal target. This time the native's arrow broke. They all left in another huff.

Nonetheless, the council ignored the obvious need for all to labour, at once, on more substantial fortifications. Meanwhile, Captain Newport thought to take the exploratory trip in search of minerals and the "Other Ocean" as ordered by the instructions. He gathered a group together, including Captain Smith. They returned after only ten days. They returned early because Captain Smith had a premonition that problems had developed at "fort" Jamestowne, as he derisively called President Wingfield's fenced-in camp. Upon the return, he explained that natives upriver had been helpful guides and hosts, at first. Then, they turned churlish.

Indeed, upon the return, Captain Smith found that his premonition proved prescient. Five days after the exploratory party had departed upriver, one hundred whooping warriors rushed on Jamestowne. The attack caught the colonists and crews toiling. Their guns lay packed away in dry vats. The makeshift fence proved useless. Seventeen were wounded and one, a boy, killed. If not for frightening fire from the ships' canons the colony might have perished then and there.

So, thereupon, the president conceded to allow the erection of palisades, mounted ordnances, and martial exercises. The new fort would be in triangular form. Palisades would be built of upright logs. Ordnances would be placed on artillery-like turrets at the three corners.

Now that Captain Smith vindicated his view of security, the original investors submitted an oration. Boldly, they demanded an explanation as to why he, their first choice for leader, should not get admitted to the council. In particular, they sought a justifiable explanation as to why he was charged with mutiny and imprisoned on the ship during the voyage. Many colonists believed that envy of his reputation for strong and courageous leadership provided true motivation for the arrest.

At first, the wily councilmen merely obfuscated the issue by responding with personal attacks against Captain Smith. Worse, they sanctimoniously repeated their charge that he treasonously conspired to usurp the governing body and rule the colony alone. Many colonists became dissatisfied and even disgruntled with this unfounded explanation. Thus, as they had once, back during the long wait off the coast of England put the question to Chaplain Hunt, they put it to him yet again, for unbiased deliberation.

The goode preacher, Master Hunt, brought the council to a compromise on the thirteenth day of June. Its members agreed to allow a hearing on the matter of Captain Smith's purported treason, rather than send him back to London for trial. At the hearing, the right honourable captain defended himself honestly and skillfully. He turned the accusers' accusations against them, claiming that they, not he, greedily coveted power. He claimed that this fact became obvious when they arrested him to prevent him from becoming president of the council.

When he spoke these wise words, a hushed gabble arose among the anxious colonists, for his statements had cast suspicion on the specious secrecy of the orders. Questions arose in all minds: Firstly, how could Captain Smith's accusers have known that the president of the council had to be elected by a majority of the same? Secondly, how could they have known that the governing body must consist of a council, unless they knew the contents of the orders beforehand?

The answers sat on the proverbial tips of all tongues. Suspicion quickly grew that the councilmen had known of the form of government, and their position in it, before the orders were ever opened. The colonists concluded that they conspired with President Wingfield to usurp Captain Smith's leadership.

Captain Smith's testimony portrayed President Wingfield as a sly and unethical character. In addition, the rest of the council appeared condescending. Thus, on this first matter of moment at Jamestowne, the jury of opinion deliberated earnestly but not long. Now, most of the men who made up the colony sought true justice.

The power of their opinion influenced the council. Therefore, they persuaded President Wingfield and his imperial cronies to recant their accusations of treason. Captain Smith took his oath of office and became a member of the council.

After the hearing, toasts of ale went around and kept going around. The councilmen, with the exception of Captains Smith and Newport, soon tired of toasting. They stood up and removed themselves from the table. Embarrassed, they sensed the time to go.

When they left, the remainder of the group talked more freely. Inhibitions fled. All agreed that the matter was resolved fairly. Thereupon, a lively toast to goode English justice went around. Thence, one of the colonists brought forth a serious query. It dampened the spirit of conviviality.

He said, "How are wee to 'ave goode and strong leadership 'ere in thy virgin lande through the form o' government thy London Companie has handed us? For it is too democratic, is it not?"

Another colonist responded, "Ye are on the mark, sir. The right amount o' democracy promotes representation for wee who are not on the council, but, oddly, too much democracy thwarts representation."

One strong-willed man saw the paradox inherent in democracy, "Ye talk wisely. Too much equality o' power places a handicap on leadership allright."

Someone else agreed, "Eh, says I, near makes leadership impossible, it does."

The first man continued, "Indeed, 'tis a lesson from history for us to heed. In olde Greece, when the Corinthians became too democratic, with the vote spread far and wide, they voted out the strong leadership o' oligarchs, who gave no favors for votes. Foolishly, they elected tyrants, because tyrants patronized the people. In effect then, the people used the vote to get something from government as opposed to electing those most qualified to govern."

"Aye," everyone, all around, agreed heartily.

"Government is meant to govern and nothing more," a colonist added.

Another man continued, "The olde Greeks taught us that too much democracy results in tyranny."

Yet another added, "Aye, wee should remember, just as the great poet Thucydides advised, in his *History of the Peloponnesian War*, he who does not learn history is bound to repeat its mistakes."

The second man continued, "Why yes, a true leader rises up likewise the cream o' thy barrel, but if all men be made equal in power, then no man can rise up."

"Aye," answered the first man. "Our Virgin lande will become leaderless like olde England, where parliament and king each are jealous o' the other's power, and no goode results except rabble rousing."

Indeed, after the Susan Constant and Godspeed pulled anchors and headed back to England, the first Summer simmered. It became obvious that strong individual leadership lacks among the equal. Most colonists criticized the London Council, fervently, for its covetousness from afar that had the effect of denying leadership at Jamestowne.

"How, ye might just like to tell me, could thy council in London know the way to do 'ere in thy colony?" one disgruntled colonist complained, while he hoed away on a sultry hot day.

His query was telling for its practicality. President Wingfield had taken a large number of men away from building and farming. He ordered them to produce clapboard for export to England, to show the economic promise of empire. For practical sake, however, the colony needed to know how to trade with the natives for food supplies with which to survive during the upcoming Winter.

On one such sultry hot July day, the native guide who had befriended the exploratory party, upriver, approached the fort door and called out for Captain Smith. The captain invited his small party through the gate. During the reunion, the guide drew a map that detailed the locations of various tribes strewn along the rivers of the Powhatan Confederacy. He advised that the tribes nearby were the unfriendliest ones, because they were the most intimidated, naturally. This was bad news for the food supply.

During hot afternoons, while colonists toiled sweatily at the makeshift fort and farm fields, criticism verged on the unholy. No leader could do more than the fear of Winter had already done to motivate hard work. Nonetheless, Winter did not supply the leadership needed to negotiate with the natives. Few admitted outright the truth that the London Company had overlooked. The colonists depended on friendship with the natives for survival in the forbidding wilderness.

Captain Smith's virtuous nature came to the fore concerning questions about the natives. His outward appearance, including his expression and demeanor, bespoke his honourable intentions. His character provided a great asset that could be drawn on against the natives' distrust for Englishmen. One stifling Summer afternoon as the colonists sullenly toiled, he eyed an opportunity in nearby woodland, whereat stood a native resplendent in his masculinity.

The native wore supple deer skin. Beads and various ornaments hung about him. A pouch swung from his shoulder that comprised the same material and held bright blue jay feathered arrows. His sinuous neck muscles bulged under his long straight black hair. He turned with curt apprehension toward Captain Smith's sure stride. The captain approached him, circumspectly, with an eye on his arrow hand all the while.

With prudence as his guide, the captain held his own hands fast at his sides while approaching the fearsome native with steadfast strides. Thereupon, slowly and prudently he began to communicate, in sign language, with the brave. He pointed to himself, his own eyes, and the sky above twice, all the while speaking English.

"I see your chief, I see your chief, wee have gifts, wee have gifts," the captain made himself understood.

The native responded through the same hand gestures. He bore a message from the chief of all Powhatans himself, Wahunsunakok.

"Sow and reap in peace," he communicated, in sign language, by bending over and pretending to plant and harvest. Then, abruptly, he turned and quickly disappeared into the thick dark forest.

"Well done Captain Smith," said one of the colonists, as the captain turned tacitly toward the hopeful group of on-looking labourers.

"Now it will be our pleasure to meet the chief of the great Powhatan Confederacy, and wee shall exchange gifts," the captain replied, hopefully.

Several days later, as the colonists toiled purposefully at their various tasks, the sudden presence of a stern-faced native standing nearby startled them. His stealthy approach alarmed several members of the group. Their faces betrayed fear. The native took great liking to their alarm. He grinned broadly for several long moments. Then, he got down to business.

Forthwith, he opened a deerskin pouch and withdrew a sample of its contents. With great intention of purpose, he held out a fistful of cornmeal. Concerned, a few colonists rushed off to find Captain Smith. On arrival, he approached the native confidently, held out his hand firmly, and received the gift with obvious pleasure.

Thereupon, the native gift-bearer commenced to communicate in sign language. He looked upward at the sky as he waved his hand at it. Then, he looked down and pointed toward the ground. The captain repeated the gestures and shook his head affirmatively. Thus assured, the native turned and strode away into the forested expanse.

Several more uneasy days passed. Suspicion mounted more each day. Everyone began to wonder just how far negotiations with the natives had progressed before the kidnapping occurred at Roanoke Colony two decades earlier.

"Wee should not trust the savages," warned one of the colonists. "'Tis a bad sign that one lurking up on us. Well it could be a trap," he added.

At this statement, all manner of chaos broke loose.

"'Ere, 'ere, indeed so, sir, defend for thy lives and trust them not," one loud colonist yelled out.

However, Captain Smith reasoned, "If wee do not negotiate, then the savage natives shall take of it badly. They are strongly superstitious. Why, they might take it as an omen. 'Twould, in effect, show our bad faith. They bring cornmeal because they want hatchets and ornaments. I say, wee are lucky they're giving and taking gifts. Wee 'ave no choice but to trust 'em."

As Summer progressed, Captain Smith's reasoning proved itself. During July and August, bugs infested the cereal supply. Fresh water that had flowed downriver in Spring became briny in Summer. Bothersome mosquitoes bit night and day.

Worse, without warning, an epidemic of illnesses swept through the sultry air. The number of men able to labour and stand sentry fell continually. Unluckily, in just eight weeks, by the beginning of September, half the colony lay underground. A mere fifty remained.

Plague sent the political fate of the place in a promising new direction, none too soon, when Captain cum Councilman Gosnold died. He was President Wingfield's strongest supporter on the council. Indeed, the Gosnold and Wingfield families were intermarried back in England. The president's support weakened further with arrest of Councilman Kendall who was caught committing a "heinous" act. A few colonists caught him writing a report of the colony's dire condition for the Spanish ambassador in England. Finally, the fickle finger of fate pointed at the king's godson himself.

Captain Smith accused President Wingfield of hoarding private stores for his cronies and himself. The remaining councilors, John Martin and John Ratcliffe, followed the captain to the hoard. In front of all the colonists, they uncovered beef, eggs, oatmeal, liquor, and wine. Thereby, the three removed Wingfield from office, according to and in keeping with the orders. The men placed him in the brig, on board the remaining ship, the little Discovery, for return to England with Kendall.

Ratcliffe became the new president of the council. With an open mind, he took Smith's advice that survival depended on learning the natives' alliances, methods of war, language, and customs. He placed the seasoned soldier in a position of leadership. Smith now sat on council in charge of stores, building, and natives.

CHAPTER III

THE FIRST THANKSGIVING

For the next several weeks, an uneasy feeling crept slowly into the fort from the surrounding dark forest. The disease lurked about stealthily in shadows. It harbored unseen under bunks, during daylight hours, only to jump out, with wild screams, at sweating sleepers during dark nights.

Dread brought the colonists to an understanding of native ways. In the past, natives had always welcomed explorers and traders, because by their passing they gained gifts. Contrarily, colonists did not pass through.

Nothing less than the dread of death could counter apathy. Fear motivated men to work at the hard tasks and tedious toil. By it, minds sharpened and hands quickened. Now, they laboured with more purpose over postholes and the wood saw.

As a result, construction work on the palisades strengthened those substantial protective walls. Some even found strength to gather twigs, rushes, and brush from the surrounding forest floor with which to make thatch for hut roofs. The hardiest worked sod into the crevices of their cabin walls for warmth. When they awoke to find the first frost glimmering off the ground one October morning, substantial palisades of heavy thick timber posts and boards, matted by sod, surrounded the minuscule fort at Jamestowne.

So dire were their straits that whence a day's work was done, appetites were denied. Desperate for more stores, President Ratcliffe and Captain Smith deemed possible what was once thought to be a long shot. Smith took gifts back downriver to the friendly Kecoughtans. He reasoned that the tribe had received them well, once.

The Kecoughtans rebuffed Smith. The natives knew that the English were near starvation. Without proverbial tongue in cheek, their chief offered pieces of bread and handfuls of beanes for tomahacks or mattassin, hatchets or copper. Smith, the skilled survivor, thought quickly. He bolstered the English image by spreading strings of beads, and like toy trinkets, among excited youngsters. Within a day, the Kecoughtan Chief got down to business. He gave quantities of fish, oysters, bread, and venison for tomahacks and mattassin.

While rowing back upriver, the trading party encountered inquisitive natives rowing downriver in dugout canoes. Since the English hoard made them appear prosperous, the natives led them to their village, Warraskoyack. There, Smith gained even more grain. Upon the return to Jamestowne, the men unloaded thirty bushels of grain in all.

Heartened, Smith and a few chosen men made gift-giving trips to the Rappahannock and then Paspahegh villages. At the former, the natives ran into their huts in fear before greeting the party timidly. At the latter, they boldly tried to take muskets and swords without offering any gifts in exchange. Upon return from this trip, the men unloaded many more bushels.

The morning after, Captain Smith sat nimbly thinking, on a fresh-smelling tree stump, in bright sun. His fist propped up his strong chin. His eyes focused forward. His feet sat firmly on the ground. The ways of Powhatan royals consumed his thoughts.

Through his travels, Smith had garnered not inconsiderable knowledge of the Powhatan Confederation. He learned that it comprised a loose amalgamation of surrounding tribes. The Powhatan people knew their highest-ranking chief as the Great Powhatan. He functioned as the patriarch, by blood or marriage, to a large extended family of men, women, and children.

He patronized the various tribes scattered about in numerous river villages. These tribes allowed him the deference that subject peoples allow emperors. Indeed, they paid him gifts that sometimes amounted to the major portion of their crops. In exchange for this loyalty, he provided security from powerful hostile outlying tribes.

Wahunsunakok held court at his primary residence, Werowocomoco. The location of the place was a closely-kept secret. Smith surmised, from bits of evidence that the capitol, of sorts, sat somewhere on the Pamunkey River. That river lay between the Powhatan and Toppehannock Rivers. His secondary or Summer residence sat on the great ocean considerably north of Cape Henry. The capitol required a one-day rowboat trip from the site of Jamestowne.

Among the confederation's tribes, the most independent were those whose chiefs were Wahunsunakok's younger brothers. For, they paid no part of their crops to him. Smith concluded that the colony stood to gain the greatest amounts of grain from these tribes. In addition, he concluded that, through the brothers, he stood the best chance of gaining an audience with the Great Powhatan,

Wahunsunakok, and perhaps a permanent peace, by honouring him with gifts.

The Chickahominy was the nearest such tribe. The Chickahominies lay up the Chickahominy River. To reach its delta required rowing up the Powhatan River of which it was a branch. The Chicahominy would be found beyond the Paspahegh. The tribal chief was the most revered of the brothers. His name was Opekankano.

"What has ye in such deep thought, captain?" asked a colonist who caught the captain's trance-like gaze.

"Methinks wee need make a trip up the Chickahominy River. The chiefs there are brothers of the Great Powhatan. 'Tis said, they have much store o' grain among them," Smith responded.

"Seems a wise plan," the man agreed.

"Perhaps, wee should gain an audience with the Great Powhatan, thereby, through his brothers," Smith added.

"Aye, indeed," now all agreed.

"'Tis decided, then. Let preparations begin," Smith ordered his most trusted men.

The next day, Smith took eight men in the shallop to the villages of the Chickahominy. The Discovery was to follow. The ship would serve as a cargo-taker. It would take the contents of the shallop after each loading. That way, Smith could lande at the several villages, with an empty shallop, yet not show too great a need.

Unfortunately, poor seamanship foiled the plan. The Discovery ran aground, thus allowing Smith just two brief visits. Undeterred nonetheless, he would spend the next few weeks organizing another Chickahominy River expedition.

During those temperate colorful early November days, when the mind falls into complacent delusion, the danger of Winter seems somehow far off. Thus beguiled, a wearied assemblage of colonists whiled away the days waiting for Captain Newport's return from England, with supplies aplenty to support them. A few, however, were growing weary, themselves, of complacency.

Since the first frost, sickness had subsided. The sky overhead had become filled with squawking flocks of geese, and sundry other fowl, flying south for the season. Huge droves rested in the water to be shot at, close up, with ease of aim. In the cool weather, wild boars were wont to snort about the forest intent on fattening up for the cold season coming.

The self-assured few spent these days turning the grindstone. Crushing the gifts of golden grain into brown flour brought reality home to them. After milling, exhausted, they placed the wooden lid on the last barrel of that precious commodity.

When they completed the grinding, their attention turned to hunting. Well-armed, they hunted the river and forest, nearby the fort, in packs several men strong. When their sacks became full, they returned, cleaned the carcasses, and hung the fresh meat for smoking.

When not hunting nature's bounty, they built up fuel supplies. Thus, the gathering of kindling from the forest floor, the strenuous toppling down of yet more trees, and the chopping of firewood out of fallen trunks ensued. Only the hardiest men maintained sufficient energy for this most strenuous of tasks.

After a week of mild November weather in the virgin lande, the colonists awoke, one dank dreary morning, to the season's first bluster of cold wind as it whistled through the cracks and into their cabins. The colony's lack of preparedness, for a long Winter, sent attitudes around the fort toward pessimism.

That very afternoon, the hardy ones set about the task of preparing more wood fuel with renewed vigour. The founders of the Virginia Companie had not removed to the virgin lande merely to subsist on the king's largesse. Their intention, from the beginnings of the companie, remained unchanged. They had planned to plant themselves down on the virgin lande and by it live lives of liberty. The strong-willed among them remained true to their belief in themselves.

During November, with the fruits of their labour ripened, the colonists celebrated a thanksgiving to their heavenly father and earth mother. They thanked him for their propitious fate and her for their bountiful sustenance. Everyone took part in the preparations.

The men hunted down and shot the largest grunting boar they could find. The hardy hunters hauled the carcass back to the fort, skinned it, removed the entrails, and then skewered it onto a long iron rod. They secured the ends of the rod to the top sides of a tightly built stone pit and started a fire under it. Meanwhile, as the smell of sizzling succulent boar meat permeated the brisk Autumn air, bakers placed several loaves of bread doe and pumpkin pies into an iron oven box and hauled it to the cooking pit.

In the middle of the day, the cooks laid out the fabulous feast. Natives espied the festivities from perches in trees outside the palisade. Innocent enough, they merely had wont to satiate their interest in the ceremonial customs of Englishmen. The holiday atmosphere eased the colonists' suspicion of the natives that day. Thereby, all of the colonists, together, invited the natives to partake of the feast that was getting laid out on the big wooden table.

Uncertain at first, the natives refused to sit down. Instead, they stood reluctantly around and watched. Of course, having savage natives standing behind them made the colonists uneasy. They proffered the invitation with more insistence. The extra effort broke the awkward stalemate. Gradually, the natives made their ways to seats at the table.

The feast began with a solemn prayer of thanks. It continued with a toast to everyone's effort in its preparation. The prayer filled the gathering with emotion and brought home to the diners, both English and native, a sense of the event's propitiousness.

As the diners filled their stomachs with food, they filled their souls with inspiration. A vision of potential life in the virgin lande inspired the Englishmen. The natives sensed the afflatus and became spiritually affected by it, themselves. The simple goodewill, and trust, of the merrymakers moved the silent savages to doubt their own emotions. For, in their hearts, they admitted that the Englishmen did not fully feel the duplicity, and brutal ways, of native culture.

They knew more than they let on. They knew, for example, that the Great Powhatan admired the English people. He believed his own people would benefit from the greatness of their inventions and technical knowledge. Moreover, they also knew that many braves, especially the Great Powhatan's brother, Opekankano, felt threatened by those very inventions and knowledge. Unlike the chief, he could foresee no benefits to the Powhatans from English culture.

After the great feast, the most senior brave pulled out his deerskin smoking pouch and ceremoniously laid it on the table. He meant it as a symbol of goodewill. Nimbly, he removed green leaves from it, stuffed them into his pipe, and lit them up. With great intention of purpose, he slowly inhaled the thick odoriferous smoke and then passed the pipe.

The meticulously carved wooden pipe went around the table, with refills, several times over. Most everyone heartily partook of the native's smoking plant. Within a few minutes, the smoke induced a relaxed revelry among the merrymakers. The effect of the smoking plant awed the Englishmen.

One among them voiced his sentiment at the uncomprehending but, nonetheless, understanding brave.

"The ambrosial smell o' thy smoke, sir, 'tis worthy o' the pagan gods themselves. 'Tis like a tribute to Apollo the healer," he believed.

Thence, he paused and looked around at his fellows, all of whom felt a strong sensation, of pure awe, at the natural wonder of the massive green virgin forest that surrounded them.

Another agreed, cautiously, "Methinks it the very same plant ancient Greeks smoked for health and spirit. They grew it in plenty, I've heard."

"Aye," commented another. "The Greeks loved nature. They felt themselves a part of it. Accordin' to the poet-historian, Hesiod, in his *Theogony*, humans derived from the gods whom, in turn, came from earth, water, fire, and air. They believed that nature governs man as opposed to the supernatural governing him. They served neither gods nor men, but nature."

The natives grinned knowingly at one another. Several long moments passed in peaceful contemplation.

"Reminds me o' the hemp that country folks smoke at harvest festivals in me Suffolk," one man began again, from the far end of the table.

"'Tis the same stuff, allright, but much a bit stronger, me knowest," added another.

One man shouted out, with a pound on the table, "'Tis pagan practice in the eyes o' thy church."

"Sure 'nough, 'tis outlawed under the pope, because 'tis pagan practice," added a man at the table corner, apprehensively, with guiltily lowered eyes.

"Thy Church strikes down all that's pagan simply because 'tis Greek," yet another spoke up, boldly.

"Aye, I say, 'tis against the ways o' Greeks because 'tis Roman. Imperial Rome conquered and enslaved Greece," a fellow next to him countered.

"'Ere, 'ere, long live the liberty of Greeks," the first man bolted out.

Everyone at the table burst out in a roar of laughter at the man's veracity. One of the companie stood up, raised his mug, and suggested a toast.

"To the liberty of Virginians," he yelled out.

"To the liberty of Virginians," everyone shouted, loudly, in unison.

The divine aroma had an especially profound effect on the man who had dreamed, back in April, that he smelled lande before sighting the cape they named Henry. An end to a hard year, he thought to himself. He remembered, as the ships approached lande that fateful day, he felt a premonition of impending attack. Sure enough, his premonition proved true. The savages hid in ambush behind thick tree trunks. Then, a torrent of arrows drove the landing party back on board the ships.

Yes, he remembered well. Now, a truce, of sorts, kept an uneasy peace. The companie had gained the ability to farm the lande for which it had paid such a large sum back in England. His thoughts came to an uncanny pause. Wonder grabbed hold of him. He excused himself from the table, stood up, and meandered away from the crowd to a solitary bench.

The man's close companion watched him and wondered what might be on his mind. In curiosity, he too excused himself, stood up, and followed his fellow colonist. He situated himself down next to him. For several minutes, both men slowly sipped from their mugs, while taking in the austere wonderment of awesomely strong-smelling nature. Without willing it, both became wonderstruck by a tremendous sensation of insignificance in the midst of the magnanimous forest. They had been surrounded by it for several months now. Yet, they saw it as if for the first time.

"Well Jesse, has not been an unfortunate outcome for our companie," his friend said.

"'Tis true John," Jesse replied.

"The natives do not claim to own the lande 'ere, but methinks they'll not allow settlement on it without compensation, of sorts," John said.

"'Tis true John," Jesse replied again. "Native culture 'tis not what it seems ya know. 'Tis not so much that they seek to protect the lande itself from us English. Rather, 'tis the honour of their braves they seek to protect."

Jesse paused, gazed up at the tall tree trunks in trance-like thought, and continued to ponder the philosophy of property and pride.

"Ye know John, this America, as the Italians call it, 'tis not the first new world in history," he said.

"Aye, America 'tis called," John added. "Back in 1492, Spain's King Ferdinand named this new world after Christofo Columbo's sailing partner, Amerigus Vespuciano, as compensation for having appointed Columbo commander of the voyage."

"True, America 'tis an Italian name," Jesse agreed, then paused and continued. "England itself was once a wilderness. England comprised unsettled lande in plenty then. In time, the Celtic tribes grew in the wilderness. Later, Romans, Vikings, and Normans came each in their turn.

"Aye, so it 'twas," John agreed.

Jesse continued his discourse.

"Thy Celts lived in desolate wilderness there. Many centuries later, the Roman Army invaded the still primitive place. In 62, the descendants of the original Celts fought them fiercely under the leadership of Queen Boudica. The Romans had come with better weapons and greater discipline. But, the Celts saw them leave, eventually" he explained.

"'Tis all true so far, Jesse," John agreed.

"A few centuries after the Romans pulled their army out of Britannia, in the second century, to defend Gaul against Germans, Viking invaders nearly overwhelmed the Celts. Those Angles, Saxons, and Jutes fought the Celtic survivors for centuries. The long conflict reduced numbers of families. Thus, when the Normans invaded olde Anglelande in 1066, they found it a place of much lande," Jesse explained further.

John looked up with intense concentration and thought about Jesse's historical reasoning for several minutes. He came to the same conclusion.

"Anglelande 'twas the lande of anyone who could survive it, then," he responded.

"Aye," Jesse concluded. "Just as there's lande in plenty 'ere for to settle without depriving anyone of their birthright."

"Whence the Norman Army invaded olde Angleland, the Angles, Saxons, and Jutes retreated to their settlements. Thence, the Normans cultivated the wilderness," Jesse looked over to John, for further agreement.

"Aye, thy ancestors and mine, both, go back to those Norman days," John interposed.

"Aye, at that time, there were but few persons in a large lande," Jesse reasoned.

"These natives, too, are small in number compared to this massive wilderness," John opined.

Both men pondered the comparison. They began to study the strong braves, among the revelers yonder, with a new perception. They respected the proud Powhatans and their culture, notwithstanding its brutality.

"Well, I say, if wee are to prosper 'ere, then wee must gain the ways of those who are native to this lande," John reasoned.

"Many there are among us who harbor dislike and distrust for the natives. They'll never live peacefully with 'em," Jesse responded.

"Aye, me sees it meself. What's the worse is thy deceitful council ya know. Even now, some councilmen begrudge our goode captain for his favourable way with the natives. Methinks there's too much influence from London on thy council, yet. Thy captain stands to the fore among self-serving men," John continued.

"Aye, badness could come to pass. Sure 'nough, there could be trouble during the Winter. Wee companie might meet the fate o' Rawleyghe's colony, yet," Jesse feared.

"Captain Newport returns from England soon. Whence he does, wee'll 'ave an advantage with the Great Powhatan. Wee'll not 'ave need for his gifts," John predicted.

"Aye, unless Newport brings less than enough stores. Regardless, wee need make the expedition to Werowocomoco Captain Smith plans. If wee are to survive in this lande, then wee need gain the great man's welcome 'ere. Wee need to greet him with gifts more than those given the chiefs," Jesse stated.

"Aye, indeed wee should," John believed.

"I 'ave a mind to give him muskets and powder. He would esteem them high. As high as lande. Wee could live on the lande then, with them, without fear," Jesse stated, firmly.

Both men pondered the dangerous idea for a few fortuitous moments.

"Methinks thy council will arrest us for arming the savages," John knew.

"Thy council is concerned more for its own benefit than for that of us colonists, notwithstanding thy goode Captain Smith," Jesse knew.

"'Ere, 'ere," John agreed.

The friends passed several more minutes in deep ponderous thought.

"Ye know, I'd like to go it on me own. Just choose a goodely sight to farm a far way from the colony," Jesse thought aloud.

"Would the natives allow us to live amongst 'em, Jesse?" John doubted.

"I shall prove my honour to them as they like," Jesse answered.

"Wee'll go it alone together, Jesse," John added, enthusiastically.

CHAPTER IV

THE INITIATION

In early December, while Captain Smith made the final plans for a second expedition up the Chickahominy River, he sought advice from the few trusty natives nearby. From them, he learned much. They warned him about Wahunsunakok's brother, Opekankano, chief of the Pamunkeys.

Bravely, the natives advised Smith that Opekenkano harbored jealousy toward his wise older brother, Wahunsunakok. Jealousy prompted Opekankano to propagate resentment toward the English colonists, among Powhatan braves, just to empower himself. Moreover, the crafty Opekankano, in past, obstructed braves from neighbor tribes, who strove to settle among Powhatans. In his lust, he seized on any opportunity to propagate prejudice among the braves and thus gain power. Opekankano, the trusty natives warned, might harm the captain and his men.

Nevertheless, Smith took the warning in stride, because he knew the Great Powhatan welcomed Englishmen in his confederacy. The wise olde royal thought his culture would benefit from English technology, especially that of iron. Confidently, Smith called on his staunchest supporters. Without hesitation, Jesse and John volunteered for the expedition, making a small party of men. The expedition departed with confidence. They packed substantial gifts for Wahunsunakok and his brothers.

Out on the broad Powhatan River, the intrepid men rowed and sailed the shallop strenuously upstream. At the Chickahominy delta, they came starboard into the whirling flow. Then, up the narrow Chickahominy, they rowed. Along the way, they passed farm fields and wigwam villages larger and better cropped than any they had yet seen. By late in the day, the river had become little more than a fast-flowing shallow stream. The villages along its banks had dwindled in frequency and size. When rowing became rough, they turned back downstream, toward the last little village they had hastily passed, to ask for guides.

Upon approaching the settlement in the trickishly flickering shadows of a late-day sun, the expedition's eyes rested on an astoundingly marvelous sight. There, on the riverside, sat a luxurious leather lodge sitting majestically on a substantial clearing. The domain's heavy timber posts and A-frame roof formed a rectangular structure with its long side running along the rolling river. Several trees, thick with dense dark-green fir, provided heavy shade for the royal residence. The awesome site immobilized the Englishmen for several mesmerized moments.

Eerily, no one seemed to be around the place. A sultry breeze blew, barely perceptibly, through massively winding barren branches. The invisible breeze stealthily rustled fallen leaves. Sensing mystery, the landing party kept a distance. They thought that attempting a landing, without a greeting, would likely be too risky. The men strained their eyes, while turning in all directions, searching for signs of life. They thought that, surely, several braves must be on guard at such a place.

Seemingly out of nowhere, several fierce unfriendly looking braves began gathering on the larboard side of the lodge. Menacingly, they began whooping and shouting strange-sounding Algonquian words at one another. Without hesitation, they gathered up their weapons and ran toward the shore. Fearing a rain shower of arrows, the boatswain shouted retreat, loudly, at the rowers. Smith, however, threw up his arm and yelled out.

"Hoe," he hollered, in an effort to gain the attention of the loud braves on shore.

"Hoe, hoe," the leading brave yelled back, in confused apprehension.

The awkward greeting continued long enough for the boatswain to pause.

"Very well then men, come ye ashore," he ordered the rowers.

With a twisting and straining of the oaken oars, the creaking wooden shallop began making its laborious way toward the line of unfriendly braves blocking the shoreline.

During exhaustive communication between Smith and the leading brave, the party concluded that this was a lodge of Opekankano known as Apokant. No one, it seemed, except these few braves were around. Smith offered gifts and made known his need for guides. The natives refused the gifts and made motions to the sky, in sign language, as if to say wait until sun up. They would escort their chief back at dawn. Thence, they turned and made their way into a forest pathway.

"Very well then," Smith turned and shouted to the boatfull of men. "Wee shall make camp for the night on thither shore," he commanded the crew.

The braves did not need to know the English language to understand the looks on the Englishmen's faces. They disapproved of the intentions they saw in them. Likewise, the Englishmen sensed the braves' disapproval. Nonetheless, they held to their plan. They had come this far and so they continued to hold out hope for meeting the royal brothers. Adamantly, they turned the boat in the opposite direction and rowed off, in search of a campground.

The party landed and then set up camp, for the night, at what seemed a safe distance. By the next morning, the party began to comprehend the braves' unspoken message. One of the men spoke up.

"What make ye of the weird behaviour, captain?" he asked.

"Methinks Opekenkano knew of our coming and removed purposely," Smith answered.

"Perhaps wee be too light with gifts to gain his welcome," said another man.

"Let us pray it is so simple a thing, sir," Smith roared back.

Meanwhile, Smith swallowed hard. For, he had failed to negotiate with Opekankano's braves. Deep down, he felt a foreboding, for the party's security, in the shadowy thick wilderness. Indeed, he knew that security could be merely tenuous, at best.

As the captain opened his mouth to suggest a return to the fort, the whistling of two natives, from a canoe at the riverbank, caught his attention. The two were whistling and motioning with their arms to come on.

"'Twould be two guides, captain," one fellow spoke, suspiciously, for all.

"'Tis a five-man dugout. Who shall volunteer to accompany me?" the captain asked.

"Iye, Iye," two of the men where first to answer.

"Very well, then. You other men wait 'ere. Give me a fortnight. Then make a speedy retreat. And, staye near the shallop, for sure," the captain ordered the rest.

"Will do, captain," the loyal men responded.

Thereafter, all the long day, whilst the men sat closely around a campfire, they watched the village across the water and waited for signs of life. At mid-afternoon, life appeared. A half-dozen, or so, young native squaws came to the village carrying baskets.

"They 'ave no children with 'em," one man noticed.

One squaw laid her eyes on the shallop and then lifted them at the men around the fire. She began squealing and pointing in their direction. In no time, all of the squaws were giggling and looking across the river.

"What say wee row over and offer some ornaments," one smiling man suggested.

"Methinks their men might not like our approaching them in their absence," another said, in a cautious tone.

"Well, wee'll keep to the shallop and stay safe thataway," the first man insisted.

At that, he strapped his sack on his back and boarded the shallop. When he turned and saw his fellows, on shore, hesitate, he tried to encourage them.

"Well, come on y'all," he grinned.

With various degrees of reluctance, the rest boarded the shallop and pushed off for the other shore.

The squaws became more excited as the shallop approached them. When the bow smashed into the mud bank below the surface, the man who had suggested the row stood up, thrust out a fistful of shiny ornaments, and beckoned to the smiling squaws. Nonetheless, they hesitated. They came not quite near enough to reach his hand. He stepped out of the shallop onto lande.

The squaws backed off shyly but smiling all the while. In this aura of innocence, some of the men felt lured ashore.

A few remained in the shallop. Cautious, they watched the scene on shore closely.

In an instant, shrill-screeching whooping warriors appeared from seemingly nowhere. They rose from under piles of dead leaves, behind trees, and the lodge door.

"'Tis a trap," yelled the men in the shallop, as they pushed urgently away at the oars.

The distracted men on shore turned on their feet, for their very lives, and rushed headlong to the shallop. At the bank, they took leaping jumps into safety. All made it, save an unlucky one.

"Ye savages 'ave Cassen," one man yelled.

Gazing back at the receding shore, the men watched helplessly, as savages tied one of their own.

Posthaste, the oarsmen rowed downstream. The shallop made a swift getaway. At the end of the day, now in the lande of the Paspahegh, and with a Winter night quickly descending, the survivors made camp.

Two men took sentry duty. The other four gathered firewood and kindling, built a roaring warm fire that threw light on shadows, pitched the tent, and heated food. The sentries ate first, so as to avoid the group getting caught unprepared to fire muskets, in event of attack. Warmed and secure, taking turns on guard; the men wrapped themselves tightly against the cold night and settled in to sleep. In fact, all of them, including the sentries, wrapped themselves so tightly against the cold that they sunk into satisfying slumber.

Stealthily, Opekankano watched from afar. The scheming usurper knew he must capture the party this night before they would reach their fort the following day. His braves used their warrior wiles to the utmost. Without rustling a dry dead leaf on the forest floor, they crept up to the camp.

One sentry thought he sensed a presence, perhaps. His nostrils caught the smell, of something out of the ordinary, in the thin cold air. He turned his head around carefully, both in curiosity and to calm his fear. The fire flickered.

Suddenly, the open hand of a stealthy brave smothered his scream to a snuffle. Panicked, he struggled with all the might he could muster. Fiercely, he fought for his life in those fleeting moments of dark cold night. He prepared for the certain blow of a tomahack. Yet, he remained alive.

In another instant, a second brave nimbly tied the terrified sentry's hands tautly behind his back, while a third shoved a leather strap into his mouth. Immobile and muted now, he turned toward the tent. He wondered, where is the other sentry?

He summoned his strength, inhaled all the breath he could pull through his nose, and let out a hard scream. His neck muscles bulged. Blood went rushing to his head. In a fury, he sighted his mate in a similar predicament.

"Ugh!" came the first shout out of the tent.

A ruckus of fists filled the forgotten peace of night. Startled, the four men succumbed to the sly surprise. In a few minutes, the braves pushed the tied men into the open air. While the prisoners stumbled forth, they wondered about fate and wished for freedom. Thence, more braves nimbly tied them to one another.

In the shadowy flickering fire light, Opekankano stood in front of the strapped men with neither word nor expression. In his view, he need not communicate anything. He had achieved his intended goal. In the morning, he had captured the English chief, Captain Smith. In the afternoon, he had skinned and burned one symbolic

Englishman at the stake. Now, at the end of the day, he held the rest prisoners. He would take them to Werowocomoco. His older brother, Wahunsunakok, could not release them without dishonour.

Unbeknownst to Opekankano, however, his brother awaited the showdown. A spy, loyal to the great chief, had brought him news of Opekankano's scheme. The messenger's news set Werowocomoco bustling with activity.

In preparation for what would be, after all, a family gathering, braves hunted down fresh game and prepared the roasting. Squaws prepared sauce, ground cornmeal for baking, and shelled nuts for snacking. More squaws erected a wigwam in which the prisoners would sleep. A convivial spirit spread throughout the place.

Wahunsunakok prepared his wives and children for a stately event. He foresaw a great test of power between his brothers and himself. The chief and his wives donned their most majestic clothes, feathers, and pearl beads. Wahunsunakok donned his raccoon-skin robe. They gathered their entourage around themselves, readied their places in the great long lodge, and awaited the arrival of the brothers with the captured English ruler and his men.

Opekankano, triumphant and mean, led his braves, with the English in tow, into Werowocomoco. Defiantly, he strode to the front of that greatest lodge of all, with his brothers, Opitchapam and Kekataugh behind him. Thereat, with his arms folded, he stood in expressionless aplomb.

Wahunsunakok's native herald entered the hall and announced the arrival of the brothers. The chief ordered let them enter and set his own face into a stern scowl for the greeting. Opekankano's legs trembled slightly as he started forward across the threshold. His braves noticed the false start.

When Smith and his men walked through the door, the chief's attendants let out a loud yell, in unison. Once seated, a curt greeting, among the brothers, lasted just a few moments, whenat two royal aides opened up the gathering. They flung open the large door and allowed everyone waiting outside to enter the lodge. Once the spacious interior filled to its limit, the chief ordered all to cease chattering and sit down.

Court came to session. On one side, the chief's braves flanked him. Opposite, his brothers' braves flanked them. In between, Smith and the Englishmen sat. The royal entourage scattered throughout the place.

Once everyone became situated and quiet, all eyes landed on the chief.

"Welcome to Werowocomoco, Captain Smith. Wee are honoured by your presence and that of your men," he began forthrightly through both sign language and his native aide's very simple English.

"The honour is ours, Wahunsunakok," Smith responded, confidently.

The chief and captain understood each other, intuitively. The chief called to one of his aides for bowls of water in which the guests could wash their hands. Then he called another for juice.

"Take this," he ordered his guests. "Our finest drink for you," he said, as he sent mugs into the men's hands.

Likewise, Smith bid him thanks by the gift of a ring.

"Take this ring as our gift to you," Smith offered.

The chief's eyes widened at the sight of the perfectly round and smooth brass bauble.

"The ring gives me great pleasure captain," he communicated. "Now, let us smoke pipe," he ordered another of his aides.

Many minutes of suspenseful silence passed, as several pipes made their ways around the group.

"I have more gifts for Wahunsunakok," Smith spoke up as he reached into his leather pack and pulled out more brass baubles.

He laid the shiny hoard in front of the chief to the sound of 'ous' and 'ahs' from the admiring court crowd. The chief reached over, picked up each piece separately, and studied them intently. Pleasure filled his face.

"Your gifts please me much," he said, with sincerity.

"There is more at our fort," Smith added.

The chief's mouth fell open slightly. Then he got down to business.

"Why have you come to my lande?" Wahunsunakok queried Smith.

"Wee had great sea battle with our enemy, the Spanish. Their force drove us to retreat. Their guns struck a large hole in one of our ships. Then, as luck would have it, the weather drove us into the big bay of the Powhatan. 'Ere wee plan to make repairs and wait for our countrymen to take us away," Smith lied.

"Why so far from fort? What you look for in small boat upriver?" Wahunsunakok wondered.

"Wee look for another great sea and a lande beyond. The people there slew our chief. Wee seek to avenge his murder," Smith explained skillfully.

Wahunsunakok's eyebrows rose, just slightly, at the thought of musket-toting Englishmen seeking revenge. Several suspenseful minutes passed in silence, again, while the pipes made their ways around. Finally, he motioned to an aide to hand him the stones of justice.

The aide stepped forward and placed a small deerskin pouch into the olde man's hands. Wahunsunakok chanted a short prayer to the spirits, untied the pouch's knot, and turned it upside down. The stones plopped out onto the ground. All eyes riveted on the shiny stones. No one knew for certain how to read them. Only the chief could interpret their fall. Without a word, he clapped his hands and called for the feast to begin.

That night, after the banquet, the Englishmen slept uneasily. About their fate they had not a clue. Dawn delivered a dreary day. The first uneasy hour seemed an eternity. As light strengthened within their wigwam, footsteps grew purposeful, and voices certain, without. By their sixth sense, the men sensed life's end.

Soon enough, the smack of the door flap startled them. Reality reached in and pulled each of them out. The short walk to the executioner's stone would be blacked out of their memories, forever. Wahunsunakok's speech lasted only a short time. Opekenkano's grin never ended.

Finally, one strong warrior pushed Smith's head down on the stone slab. The executioner, with a mad face, a headful of bright-red feathers, and brass baubles ringing his bulky body, raised his club high to gain aim and force on the captain's skull. The Englishmen, solemn, lowered their sad eyes.

The smash of skull went unheard. For, at that very moment of death, fate intervened. Confidently, a young squaw threw herself down onto Smith. The large crowd gasped loudly.

"No!" Pocahontas raised her royal hand.

The executioner, perplexed, dared not move. He looked to Wahunsunakok. Would the chief have his daughter removed or spare the Englishman at her desire?

"Pocahontas why you want to save them?" her father asked the princess in Algonquian.

"It is my hope to wed with an Englishman one day," the girl answered.

The chief raised his hand. He ordered the executioner off. He sent the prisoners to their wigwam. Carefully, he placed his hand on Pocahontas and led her to his lodge. The royal entourage went along. The villagers disassembled.

At the end of the day, the clouds exposed a setting sun. Captain Smith broke the silence.

"Are wee to live or die?" he asked himself out loud.

"Aye, that wee could get it over with one way or t'other," one man expressed himself.

"'Twould suit me," another added.

"Aye, Aye," the rest joined in.

The happenstance of the day consumed Jesse's thoughts.

"Methinks, perhaps Pocahontas was a ploy," he thought aloud.

"Aye, seems a dramatic twist o' fate," John agreed.

"Wahunsunakok, at once, saved his honour, in his brothers' eyes, and kept us alive, thanks to the princess," Jesse reasoned.

"Ye mean to say, 'e put 'er up to it. 'Twas planned between father and daughter?" John asked.

"Aye, he's a wise one, 'e is," Smith added.

"The olde chief thinks much but says less. He knows wee mean to staye. And more be comin'. 'E knows 'e cannot forever fight off our canon and muskets with bows and arrows. He'll offer lande, Jamestowne, for iron weapons.

Methinks even 'e tries for us and our iron, as allies, against his enemies. 'E faces the Monacan and Mannahoac Siouans to the West and the Massawomeck Iroquois to the North," Jesse believed.

"Wee nay give 'em guns, Jesse. He'll use 'em against us," Smith warned him.

"For a few guns, we'd 'ave a treaty," Jesse reasoned.

"Thy council, in London, would 'ave me hanged for arming 'em," Smith knew.

"Aye, thy chief knows not that," Jesse reminded him.

On that practical thought the men pondered for several long minutes.

Again, the door flap smacked back. The executioner stood waiting without.

"The chief see you," he communicated to Smith in sign language.

Smith left with the man, and then returned forthwith.

"Well?" Jesse queried him.

"Wahunsunakok says wee staye. Make tomahacks, bells, and trinkets," Smith answered everyone.

Two more days went by at Werowocomoco in this precarious way. No one dared say anything to the prisoners, nor they to the natives. Everyone stayed out of one another's ways. Wahunsunakok and his brothers were nowhere about. Only the playful glances of Pocahontas assuaged the prisoners' doubts.

On the third day, the great chief summoned the men to his lodge once again. This time, the court greeted them, not with a shout, but merely cordially. Nonetheless, the chief displayed his power by having one hundred warriors standing about. He gave many minutes over to silent smoking so as to sharpen his sagacity. Then, he sat back on his mats and communicated through his interpreter.

"Captain Smith, your men and you are my friends. Return now to your village. My men take you there. They return with your gifts, a canon from your big canoe and a corn grindstone," the chief, subtly, demanded.

Smith hesitated inwardly but did not betray it. He turned to his fellows in distress and searched their expressions for agreement. Dammed if he would and dammed if he would not, he knew. The council would arrest him for arming the natives. The natives would kill him for withholding the gifts. The sharp look in Jesse's eyes caught his thought at that dilemma. Jesse's knowing expression betrayed it. Of course, the grindstone. But, how would the natives ever move the heavy canon off the ship?

"The gifts are yours, Wahunsunakok," Smith said.

Satisfied, the chief ordered his warrior braves to take the trip to the English village. Everyone began to get up and head for the door.

At that point in negotiations, premonition caught Jesse in excited courage. He nudged John in the thigh with his bended knee.

"Wee too 'ave gifts for Wahunsunakok," he spoke out, boldly.

Thence, he reached down deep into the folds of his heavy wool clothes and pulled out his musket. John did not hesitate to do the same. They laid the muskets, along with small bags of powder, down in front of them.

The chief betrayed no emotion. Jesse reached down into his deep pockets for more. When his hand came out, it held a compass encased in shiny silver. For a few moments, exuberance overcame Wahunsunakok. He had demanded canons for their symbolic power. Nonetheless, he prized muskets for their usefulness. Now, he sat in possession of the promised canon plus these muskets. He concealed his delight. His hand reached for the odd-looking instrument instead of a musket.

Perplexed, the chief turned the funny gift to-and-fro. He placed it back on the ground and then picked it up again. Without expression, he asked Jesse to explain it to him. To do so, Jesse found it necessary to take him on a meandering zigzagging walk around the lodge while the needle jumped about. Jesse was hard-pressed to explain the purpose of a compass. Once seated again, the chief's expression betrayed seeming disinterest in the gift. He placed it back on the ground, glanced over the muskets, and looked askance in pretended boredom.

Jesse reached into his rucksack for the last item he thought could break the stalemate in negotiations. The bright brass bugle, that he carried during the expedition, elicited quick interest for its unusual shape and shine. The chief held the front of the bugle up to his face and peered into the dark circumference. He shook his head in consternation.

Jesse held out his hand for the bugle. The chief handed it over to him for an explanation. Jesse blew a short melodious tune into the mouthpiece. The royal gathering roared and applauded approvingly. The chief grinned broadly, took the bugle back, and blew into it hard. His blowing went on for many minutes to the near hysteria of those gathered around. Then, abruptly, he put the bugle down.

The gathering had begun to get merry from smoking. The chief needed several more minutes to bring everyone to quiet attention.

Finally, his right hand went up and he yelled, "Agh."

Slowly, he turned his domineering gaze toward his brother, Opekankano.

"My brother does not welcome English in Powhatan Confederacy. In his heart, he knows his reason. He claims it is because some moons ago, our Shaman warn us of new settlers, on the great bay, who would overwhelm us one day. My brother believes you English are the people in the prophecy," he began. "English not the first foreigners to staye among us. In past, wee had Shawnee, Iroquois, and others come with intention to staye. Those wee welcomed became one of us. Do you want to become one of us?" he asked with a discerning eye.

Jesse and John sat forward in anticipation of what the chief meant.

"Yes, Wahunsunakok," they both answered, with a detectable note of uncertainty.

Diplomacy continued.

"You two Englishmen must prove that you are worthy to be werowances," the chief informed them.

"Wahunsunakok, what is a werowance?" Jesse asked.

"A werowance is a chief. If you prove your honour among the braves, then you will become chiefs and my adopted sons, besides. Then all will be well. Powhatan lande will be your lande," he explained.

A ripple of assent crossed the gathering, like the deliberate roll of a slow wave, as the assembled crowd voiced their approval of the chief's great justice. The chief smiled broadly in benign acceptance of the accolades. Then he spoke once more.

"Tomorrow wee shall have the initiation. Today, wee feast," he ordered.

At that, the crowd began talking amongst themselves and milling about. The chief conversed with Jesse and John about England, their only one god, and their science. In a few hours time, squaws brought in a feast. The rest of the day went by in a largely jocund atmosphere of eating, drinking, and smoking in spite of Opekankano's rudeness.

After feasting, the chief spent more time with Jesse and John learning about the gifts. They taught him how to load, shoot, and clean the muskets. Interest drew many natives to the two newcomers. They asked numerous questions in an effort to get to know more about English culture. The jovial crowd wore itself out with gusto.

By the time the sun sank, one found most of the natives fast asleep under a starry sky. At the end of the day, the Englishmen found themselves once again alone together. In the privacy of their wigwam, they wondered aloud about the initiation ceremony. What does initiation by the braves and adoption by the chief mean? What might Opekankano do to sabotage it? Would they live through it?

Notwithstanding their doubts, they felt confident. In their dealings, the chief had been sagacious and they had been brave. The agreement favoured their future in the virgin lande. The final outcome remained uncertain, however. The agreement needed consummation by an initiation ceremony. The initiation ceremony must take place, according to the chief, to prove their honour. What did honour mean to the native people? The chief had explained that initiation is the way of all boys who become braves. In addition, it guarantees approval of native gods and acceptance by the tribe. They hoped that, perhaps, honour means simply proving one's ability to survive the initiation itself.

Thus, it came to be that Jesse and John found themselves with painted faces the following morning. The two initiates were dressed in the deerskin of native braves around their loins. Moccasins wrapped their feet. Having barren chests made them self-conscious, so they sat awkwardly stooped over until they, slowly, overcame their Christian awareness of themselves. Bows in satchels, filled with arrows, hung from their shoulders. Tomahacks hung from their waists. At completion of the preparations, they looked the part of dignified braves, save for their light skin.

Thence, the initiates arose and strode off boldly into the forest to prove their mettle. But, as they penetrated the forest beyond Werowocomoco, a premonition of impending doom overcame them. They thought that the braves had the tactical advantage in this hunting game, for they knew these woods. In the deepest part of their guts, they felt the impropriety of their situation.

They sensed that this initiation would not be a usual one. Opekankano's braves relished the pair's failure. His braves might even kill them, even though traditional rules of the ritual held otherwise. Pride, they reasoned, took precedence over custom. They feared that a bloody death would be theirs before sundown. Therefore, they mustered all their courage and made themselves as imperceptible as possible. They strove to even the odds.

"Be confident. All men are equal against nature," Wahunsunakok had advised them.

Earning honour among natives proved an arduous task. The braves pursued them vigorously and relentlessly. Whenever they encountered braves, they shot arrows their way. That is to say, all those braves except for the ones inclined to sneak up and assault them from behind.

Careful forethought went into tactical planning. They trudged not straightaway from the village, but rather in a great arc, so as to return to the safety of the place when need would arise. They hid in any cache they could find so as to preserve their energy. They ate wild berries for sustenance throughout the ordeal. Nevertheless, they nearly did not survive.

By the time shadows lengthened, close-pursuing braves had separated them. One pack of braves harassed John with arrows. He climbed into the lower branches of a tree to get a shooting advantage. There, he at once took cover and leveled his aims. Not far off, an unseen few ambushed Jesse. One pack attacked him from behind. The other came out of brush ahead. Although the two eluded capture, they did so with sheer luck. Determinedly, they made their separate ways back to the village, taking advantage now of the arc tactic.

But, as the thick trees absorbed the setting sun, Jesse lay in vague awareness of his whereabouts. Wet bloody mud chilled him. Nonetheless, he had stayed alive. Disoriented, he stumbled up onto his feet. All his will power could not make him stand without faltering.

Like images in a dream, first a few girls and then a few boys, appeared in his misty sight. They gawked at him as if they looked at a deformed man. He tried to look down at himself. A blur is all he saw. The ground receded and returned, over and over again, under his weak wobbling legs. Once again, he mustered willpower and continued on resolutely.

It seemed to take forever to make any forward progress at all. Then, more natives began to appear in the foreground of his sight. Alarmed squaws, olde men, and a few teenagers moved slowly closer. Finally, he came upon them. They stood at his front and sides. Cumbersomely, as if in a heavy stupor, his eyes followed their turning heads until locking onto John who approached him with a broad smile.

"Wee seem to 'ave made it, Jesse," he boasted.

"Thought I lost ya for a time there, buddy," Jesse responded, with relief.

Just at that moment, Jesse felt the verge of collapse. His legs wobbled as light flickered into a black void. Then, he fell heavily into the arms of three teenagers with a subdued moan.

In his next memory, he awoke to the light of the rising sun, while lying in the wigwam, surrounded by young natives, and safe. My God, I am alive, he thought. He looked down to find his body in one piece without significant wounds. The ordeal had ended. He savored the moments of life for a long time. Eventually, the village outside the wigwam began to stir. John began to awaken next to him. Jesse saw John's eyes open and looked over at his friend.

"Wee 'ave a great story to tell o' thy virgin lande, do wee not," he bragged.

"Indeed so, Jesse, indeed so do wee," John agreed, wholeheartedly.

"Wee proved our brave honour. Wee survived their rough game in the wild," Jesse continued.

"Aye, wee 'ave honour to live on now," John added.

"Wee'll be honoured this day in Werowocomoco. Wee need be prepared for Wahunsunakok," Jesse said.

The ceremony that followed, that afternoon, impacted the course of their lives forever. The royal entourage came together for the ritual. In the festive atmosphere, the two Englishmen partook of the rite by which they became sons of the Great Powhatan. After much talk, dancing, smoking, and feasting the ceremony began.

Teenage boys led Jesse and John to Wahunsunakok's ceremonial seat. The olde chief stood up briskly, put his hands first on ones and then the other's shoulders, and spoke to each in turn.

"Jesse, brave man, my son" he said in practiced English.

Then the chief ordered him to kneel down. Jesse knelt laboriously. Once on his knees, the chief took a small deerskin pouch from the outstretched hand of an aide. Majestically, he opened it with a slight tug, reached inside, and pulled out a fistful of white powder. Thereupon, he sprinkled the powder on Jesse while chanting to the gods in the sky above. John's turn under the magic spell followed.

Through the powder, the great chief cast a perpetual spell on the two. The spell protected them and their progeny, forever, from harm anywhere in the Powhatan Confederacy. For, the gods assure that any brave who would dare break the spell would die. The natives truly believed this, for the Powhatans always avenge insults to the honour of their chiefs. The threat of revenge, not might, kept them safe from their enemies.

The chief had been secretly hoping for just this end. He believed the presence of English colonists benefited his confederacy. Their technical knowledge could strengthen his power and improve the lives of his people. And, this end rendered his brother less obstructive. The outcome thus empowered the chief in matters relating to his own people. His word commanded greater respect now. Opekankano lost power by the result.

Indeed, many natives admired the English people. However, some natives did not want them to farm the lande, hunt the game, and fish the waters. Although the English did not compete for honour against braves, their alien culture made no difference to Opekankano and his warriors. For, in their minds, the English posed a political threat. Opekankano meant to be the great chief at his aging brother's impending death. Therefore, his tribe did not intend to share the lande with Englishmen.

Nevertheless, in the meantime, an uneasy peace governed the royal family. All of the braves respected Wahunsunakok's rule. For the rest of the day, the two Englishmen mingled congenially with natives. The ordeal strengthened their view of native culture. Now, they were able to set aside its savage aspects and admire its civilized ones. Jesse and John especially admired Wahunsunakok. He proved the term "savage" to be a misnomer.

Wahunsunakok adopted the two bold Englishmen because they proved their honour, among braves. He gave them lande in exchange for muskets, powder, a compass, and a bugle. Caution moved him to give them lande far upriver. Thereby, he felt more certain about the safety of their lives. A great deal of distance would separate them from any trouble Opekankano might cause in the future. The braves far upriver would respect the honour, and thus security of the two Englishmen under risk of revenge. The chief called for braves who wished to volunteer to take the two upriver in canoes, and once there, to help them clear lande, build a cabin and shed, plant corn, and harvest it.

And so, it would come to pass, that these two Jamestowne colonists would remove upriver, to the remote edge of the Powhatan Confederacy, under safety of the magic spell. They had become tribesmen and chiefs. Even more, they had become sons, by adoption, of Wahunsunakok.

CHAPTER V

THE LANDE

Jesse and John remained at Werowocomoco for a few more months. Through Winter and into Spring, they became more familiar with native culture. They gained first-hand knowledge about customs, habits, and values. The two colonists became well-acquainted with two braves who volunteered to accompany them to their lande. Each pair of men grew to trust and admire the other pair.

At Jamestowne, skeptical colonists thought Jesse and John's lives would be short-lived. Meanwhile, at Werowocomoco, Jesse and John accepted their fate without misgivings. They grew accustomed to living among the natives. They came to enjoy the adventure of it, actually. Wahunsunakok treated them like members of the royal entourage. However, they had little time to become complacent. For, at the end of Winter, 1608, they prepared to depart the place.

The canoeing party boarded the boats at the foot of Werowocomoco and crossed the river to the thither shore. Thence, they portaged overlande for two full days until reaching the North shore of the Powhatan River. There, they began rowing along the shoreline against the weakest current. Several days passed in this slow-moving way.

On one unseasonably cold, windy, and rainy day in April, as the canoeing party progressed northwestwardly up the narrowing river, the damp weather chilled the hard-rowing men to their aching bones. It seemed to Jesse and John that the forbidding forest held their deaths at every deepening bend in the river. A week west of Werowocomoco, when the canoes encountered their first obstruction in the river's rocky rapids, they came to the last Powhatan village.

"Powhatan," the native in the leading canoe called out to his fellow in the trailing one.

"Why's 'e yelling? They cannot hear our name from 'ere?" John asked, confusedly.

Jesse and John's hearts beat harder. They thought this would be their first encounter with unfriendly natives. Silent tense moments passed. Only the sounds of nature could be heard. Then, the stalwart brave spoke.

Powhatan, they learned, means "Falling Waters." Ergo, the tribe of Falling Waters. Here, in the Powhatan's oldest village the party would lay over for two days. The natives at Powhatan hesitated at the Englishmen. Thence, the braves explained that they were not only fellow Powhatans but sons of Wahunsunakok. At that, the natives became comfortable with the two and welcomed the entire party like brothers. They treated Jesse and John as equals.

Indeed, the friendships made there, in the remote wilderness, would come to last forever. And, those friendships would prove beneficial in time. Native ways would transcend unto the twosome. So, two days later, with sentiment, and long looks astern, they left the tiny village behind.

Thenceforward, the party portaged the canoes and heavy cargo laboriously along the riverbank. Above the rapids, they replaced the canoes in the river. A short time upriver from Powhatan, the native guide threw up his left arm, with his palm facing outward, and shouted loudly. He recognized the place. At his command, the rowers rowed toward the steep riverbank on the shore.

"'Tis the lande Jesse," shouted John.

"Aye, and goode rich soil 'tis, too, John," Jesse shouted back.

Thereupon, the two canoes smashed into hard mud, at the bottom of the bank, with a smash and thud. The second native pulled down a low-hanging branch and secured a rope line to it. Both newcomers, at once, skewered vigorously up the steep bank, strenuously grabbing vines with which to pull themselves, while scattering rocks underfoot into the water below.

Upon reaching the top, they caught sight of the lande on which they would spend the rest of their lonely lives. Once on their feet, awe struck them deeply. Immediately in front of them lay a thick dark forest. It ended only at the very edge of the riverbank upon which they stood.

"'Tis a propitious place, John," Jesse predicted.

"'Tis deep in the wilderness, Jesse. Jamestowne is a long journey back downriver. Wee are desolate," John feared.

One of the braves, now standing behind them, spoke and pointed west toward a creek, in the distance, that flowed into the Powhatan River. He motioned to both men. They followed him as he walked to the edge of the muddy creek, easily descended down its gradient, pulled off his buckskin trousers, squatted, and defecated into the water. Thereafter, the men returned to the canoes and rowed them strenuously into the creek. Once in shallow water, they pulled them onto broad flat rocks.

The group unloaded their cargo, removed the canoes from the water, and turned them upside down to absorb the sun. They pitched a big buckskin wigwam at the edge of the wooded bank. Thence, they piled the leather bags packed with tools, cooking equipment, and gear into the inside of the shelter. Crowded in, all four fell into an exhausted deep sleep without taking time to eat.

The following morning came with but a moment's warning. Yet, the men knew just what to do with that day. They meandered about the forest to find a suitable site on which to plant a corn field. Once everyone agreed on the best site, they began at its center taking turns with the large heavy-handled tools. They became exhausted by felling just the first few trees. By mid-afternoon, they had stacked a sizable pile of firewood and kindling next to the wigwam. Before the early Spring sun sank into the onrushing river, they removed their clothes and bathed in the muddy creek. Cold and shivering, they built a fire with the freshly cut wood. After warming themselves, they prepared hot stew of venison meat and cornbread.

The warming weeks of Spring passed into hot Summer. During these labouriously lengthening days, tree cutting and stump removal required a tremendous amount of work. The natives practiced their long-proved tree removal method. First, they took turns chopping down one tree at a time. Every evening they spent an hour sharpening the dulled tomahacks with a stone. Second, they dug about the felled trees and stripped off the numerous small branches for kindling. Third, they chopped off the larger branches and split them into small logs. Following these procedures, they put tomahacks to the massive trunks themselves to make large logs. Fourth, they set aside the best logs for building and split the remainder, again and again, into firewood. Fifth, they meticulously formed the building logs into pieces suitable for construction purposes. Sixth, they bored holes into the stumps. Seventh, they gathered poisonous plants, cooked them, and poured the sludgy solution into the holes. After a few weeks, the stumps became molsh and required just a shovel to remove.

In the end, the clearing seemed small in the midst of the massive forest. Yet, the sense of accomplishment seemed big. Jesse, John, and the natives proudly admired their hard work. They envisioned a field of corn grown tall, in the neat clearing, by Autumn. The virgin field imbued a sense of self-worth into them all. It filled them with a pride like that of young husbands. Emboldened with confidence now, they thought they could accomplish anything.

Meanwhile, they nearly allowed the season for plowing and planting to slip away into Summer's heat. It required many full workdays to craft a wooden plow, search and pick around the river rocks for bits of ore, make charcoal, melt the ore, and forge a piece of iron into a cutting edge, then attach it firmly onto the cutting board. The crafters worked diligently to turn out a well-built sturdy tool. It cut deeply into the heavy moist virgin soil, though with the aid of torturous manpower. Finally, they planted the little corn field. The plowing put calluses on their hands and feet, but it also intensified an ever growing sense of self-satisfaction into the husbandmen.

May Day had come and gone in the wilderness with little notice. However, memories of England began catching up with Jesse and John. They succumbed to melancholy in evenings. The natives sensed the change in mood and became perplexed. For their part, they felt enthusiastic about the next project at hand. They had become quite enthused about constructing a building of wood.

They tried to raise the Englishmens' spirits. They talked to them, in Algonquian, sign language, and simple English, at length, about construction plans. Another clearing required the felling of more trees and removal of stumps. The building logs required a great deal of close chopping and working. A chimney required the gathering of stones of various sizes. In addition, the cabin would require rudimentary furniture. A complete cabin includes beds, tables, chairs, and cabinets. They reminded them that much important work lay ahead.

However, the natives had minimal success in spreading their enthusiasm to Jesse and John. The hardy natives did not comprehend the homesick mood at hand. For, they had never removed from their own homelande. Even more, they were happy men for having been chosen by the chief to live with the Englishmen, because the honour boosted their status among native peers. The consummation of the planting task had acted as a time-marker for Jesse and John, however. The respite brought home to them the solitude of their situation. Subconsciously, they knew that they had the time to pine for England and they used it. Once construction work began, they came out of it. In the days following, the melancholy mood abated.

The motley group of Englishmen and natives performed the task of construction with renewed energy. They turned their attention to the shed first. The plan called for a structure sizable enough to accommodate not only the harvested crop but also a few farm animals that they planned to obtain. Thus, once finished, the intended shed became something more akin to a small barn.

Meanwhile, the men hoped to spend the first Winter in a warm wooden cabin. They decided to build it close enough to the riverbank to catch breezes off the water in Summers. Thereby, the clearing of a third parcel of lande got under way. By October, a sturdy one-room cabin with a wooden floor, shingle roof, and stone chimney stood out, in the wilderness, above the river. Roofed porches extended off the front and rear to shield the place against sun and rain. Open front shutters revealed the river flowing through thick tree trunks. Soon they would learn that the resolute cabin rivaled any in Jamestowne.

Completion came too late in the season, however, to allow any time for furniture making. Early Autumn dawns came with brisk reminders of frost any morning. In October, some of the corn stalks reached heights above the men's heads. Harvest knows its time. Thus, harvesting began according to nature's demand.

The corn, wrapped with beans and bedded in squash, grew so thick that it swallowed the men as they took turns chopping and resting. After several days of back-bending labour, the bountiful crop filled more space in the shed than they had anticipated. They felt, at once, satisfied with the crop but dissatisfied with the shed. Nonetheless, the season called for rest. Thoughts of enlarging the shed went unspoken until another year.

The serious hard Summer thus ended more than a month after the solstice introduced Autumn. The work pace ratcheted down, in fits of built-up energy, to near leisure. As the cool days of November turned into the cold days of December, the men slept longer. They slept away blissful nights on stuffed quilt mattresses in front of the warm wood-burning fire. The first Winter went by tranquilly. Without hurry, they carefully chopped logs into board planks, split some for legs, and then meticulously worked wood into several pieces of useful furniture.

Wet Winter days, in the virgin lande, kept the men indoors. The group spent these easy days playing card and table games. Sometimes, Jesse and John read, with the aid of exhaustive sign language, to the natives, from books beginning with Sir Thomas Malory's *Le Morte D'Arthur.* The early days of English history begot the natives' close attention. The knight's honour was the same as the brave's honour. Common to both cultures, it was a measure of wealth and means of economic exchange, besides a code of law.

On sunny days they charily taught the natives use of the one firearm the two yet possessed. The natives habitually became quite excited by the loud bang, jerk, and recoil when the musket fired off. The thrill of shooting so excited them, in fact, that their excitement grew as they shot. Thus, they consumed all the gunpowder the first time they hunted alone. They did not think to conserve powder, because they reasoned that they could substitute bows and arrows as usual.

Providentially, some weeks later, a brave arrived from Werowocomoco on horseback. The traveler carried gunpowder and medicinal supplies from Jesse and John's friends at Jamestowne. He carried a message of goodewill from Wahunsunakok, too. But, unhappily, he brought no farm animals yet. Therefore, the men resigned themselves to the fact that plowing, planting, and harvesting promised more back-breaking work during the upcoming season.

The traveling brave broke the isolation of four seasons in the wilderness. The men wanted him to answer many questions from back at Werowocomoco, Fort Jamestowne, and England. From him, they learned that the situation at Jamestowne had worsened. Although more colonists had come from England, and more supplies, Opekankano felt no obligation to honour his brother's bargains. He had made the most of the colony's lack of enterprise to cause trouble for the colonists.

The bad news strengthened Jesse and John's resolve to continue building their homestead way deep in the wilderness. They accepted their fate with less remorse, now. After having relayed so much news, fatigue overcame the traveling brave. But, before dawn, he left as abruptly as he had arrived.

That day the season's work started just as unexpectedly as the native's visit. The field needed plowing and planting. The barn needed enlarging. The expected livestock would need a fence to keep them from straying into the surrounding wilderness.

The men set about to work on more trees and stumps with renewed energy. Thereby, the corn field grew larger. By the end of Summer they had enlarged the small barn and prepared many dozen fence posts and boards. They planned to put up long rows of fencing the following Summer. Sunburned and exhausted, the men turned their attention to harvesting. Nature's timetable allowed for no delay.

After the harvest that year, another cold Winter descended, quickly. Tired, the men slowed down. Just as quickly, it seemed, the air warmed. A slight bit less inclined than the previous year, the hardy husbandmen went to work in the field.

Nonetheless, during that third Summer, they accomplished nearly as much as in the first two combined. They had gained work organization, and thus pace, that raised their productivity. By the next Winter, the enlarged barn housed a larger corn crop. Plus, fencing stretched from the barn, into the woods beyond, and returned back.

Passed exhaustion, they welcomed the respite Winter brought to their cozy little cabin in the wilderness.

The arrival of Summer, 1611, brought propitious news. While the two pair of Englishmen and natives toiled rigorously under a newly hot sun, a brave suddenly jolted out of the dense forest on horseback. Excitedly, the sweating men put down their tools and greeted the brave. He dismounted, and followed the others onto the shaded porch for a drink of cool river water. The brave betrayed his surprise at the apt appearance of the homestead.

"Hard-working men," he grinned in Algonquian.

Everyone laughed heartily. They gathered up chairs and sat down as one of the natives served up mugs of water. Generously, the brave brought a gift for them. He reached into his saddlebag and pulled out a pouch of smoking weeds. They sat smoking the green weed, commenting on its qualities, and feeling somewhat dazed when, unannounced, an Englishman burst through the forest door.

"Englishman follow me. Fall behind," the brave stated in English.

The happy fellow rode up to the porch and dismounted.

"Well, what a great pleasure 'tis to see a fellow colonist, sir," Jesse got up and loudly greeted him, as salutations went around.

"I had to see for meself the lande on which Jesse and John planted themselves down," the excited colonist blurted out, whilst he refused the offer of a hard wooden chair.

"Give us news from the fort," Jesse and John blurted out, themselves, in unison.

"Well sure 'nough, wee had a rough time of it a few Winters past. Low food supplies, cold, and troubles with thy natives made us long for olde England. Oh, woe for us, a starving time wee had. Nevertheless, wee came through it. Lord de la Warre landed to lead us. He brought ample supplies too," the excited colonist informed them.

"No woe 'ere," Jesse proudly stated.

"Aye, you lucky men," the colonist responded.

"Indeed so, sir," John interjected.

"In the middle of all our woe, there's goode news," the colonist added.

"Let's hear it, sir," Jesse demanded.

"Well, wee been plantin' tobacca at the colony. Smokin' is all the rage 'round London now, ye know. It puts all in great revelry. It 'ill make our livelihood some say," he explained excitedly.

He strode over to his horse and retrieved a saddlebag. He laid it on the porch and opened it, in front of the five men. Then, he scooped out a fistful of seeds.

"These are tobacca seeds from Jamestowne. Ye plant 'em. Ye will 'ave a goodely crop by 'em," he offered.

The men sat silently pondering the thought for several moments.

"Ye could plant a crop of it and send it downriver with natives. In Spring, wee could send you supplies upriver on pack horses," the colonist continued.

"Wee can plant tobacca allright, but to do so would require our clearing more lande, and building more barn space," Jesse hesitated.

"Indeed, wee must grow it if wee are to 'ave supplies from England. No doubt, England will take no other crop from 'ere," John reasoned.

Jesse looked intently at John and the two natives.

"Wee 'ave yet to enlarge the barn enough to accommodate our corn and animals," Jesse said, with one eyebrow crocked up.

"Wee work harder. Build bigger barn," Moose Hunter stated flatly in English.

"Me second motion," Brave As Bull added.

"The matter's settled then. Wee'll plant tobacca," John said.

"A toast o' thy goode river water all 'round," Jesse said, loudly.

"And, a bountiful crop it 'ill be," John added.

At this, everyone raised their water mugs to the toast and drank heartily. Then, after a few lusty days of smoking and sport, the travelers departed on the trip back downriver.

The Summer of '12 passed much the same as had the first ones. The husbandmen cleared a new field to accommodate the intended tobacco crop. The wood cutters left a stand of forest, between the two fields, to maintain the integrity of the lande from erosion. The new field that awaited the tobacco crop thus stood apart from the corn field. The barn became even larger to accommodate the growth of crop production and herd. Livestock began arriving piecemeal, from Jamestowne through natives, that Summer and Autumn. As usual, Winter called for stocks of firewood.

In late Winter '13, the husbandmen scattered the tobacco seeds on seedbeds fertilized with wood ash, to bring about their germination. They covered the beds with branches to protect the young plants from frost damage. By early May, they had dug numerous holes in the new field and transplanted the plants into them. During the burning heat of Summer, the plants required attention repeatedly. They would sprout shoots, at the joints of leaves and stalks, that sucked energy away from the maturing leaves. Such shoots necessitated succoring. In addition, they sprouted flower clusters, at their tips, as well as at the tips of remaining shoots. Like the shoots, the flowers sucked energy away from maturing leaves. Leaves necessitated topping. At harvest time, the men used big curved knives to cut off the stalks at the ground. They hauled piles of the cut plants to the airy barn and hung them to cure. After a few weeks of curing, they stripped the leaves off of the stalks and onto a building pile on the barn floor. Finally, they packed the leaves, as tightly as possible, into heavy wooden hogsheads, that they would roll to the river, for transportation on a raft. Indeed, tobacco farming involved iterative digging, bending, and lifting that bore down hard on them.

The exhausted husbandmen realized they could not farm tobacco without additional labour. In November, when Moose Hunter returned from Powhatan, with braves, to take the crop downriver, Jesse and John made a verbal contract with them. The braves agreed to live on the homestead, during the following planting season, and labour along with the two pair of men. With the agreement consummated, the group of six men gathered on the porch to smoke, drink, and eat.

"Ah, wee forgot something," John blurted out in mid-meal.

"What's that John?" Jesse asked.

"Wee 'ave overlooked the obvious. The bundles must be marked with our own identification, so as to keep our crop separate from the rest, after it arrives in Jamestowne," John cried out.

"Ye are correct, sir, wee need to think of a name for thy place 'ere," Jesse responded.

"Aye, what shall wee name it?" John wondered aloud.

"Wee shall name it for thy muddy creek. The place shall be known as the Muddy Creek Plantation," Jesse offered.

"The Muddy Creek Plantation it be then," John shouted.

Thus, the next morning, the men proudly marked all of the hogsheads with the initials MCP and then loaded them onto the raft.

The next year, natives brought supplies upriver via pack animals. The plantation had sent the order for supplies, with the tobacco, to a merchant in Jamestowne the previous Autumn. The merchant had forwarded the order, with the tobacco, to his factor in London. After having gained possession of the tobacco, the factor in London purchased the supplies. Once purchased, he had them shipped to the merchant in Jamestowne. The merchant then held them for transshipment to the plantation. Thus, nearly a year passed between shipment of tobacco and receipt of supplies.

The supplies included gunpowder, medicinal items, nails, various tools, paper, ink, books, rolls of wool and cotton, plus a surprise for Moose Hunter and Brave As Bull. Unbeknownst to them, Jesse and John had ordered muskets. The guns thrilled them so much that they went off hunting, right away, and did not return for a day. Thereafter, Jesse and John found it difficult to prevent their wasting gunpowder in their excitement.

That Summer the men worked less diligently than during the six previous ones. The hardest work lay behind them now. The corn field yielded crop ample enough for immediate needs, including beans and squash. The barn and pasture allowed just enough space, presently, for both crops and a growing herd of farm animals. The tobacco field yielded crop ample enough for necessary supplies.

The small cabin became cluttered and easily crowded, but served its purpose well enough. No pressing needs presented themselves. The homestead made them self-sufficient.

In Summer '14, after planting, the men set about enlarging their cabin. The wood came from forestlande bordering the tobacco field. Late one hot afternoon, John stood sweating in the setting sun, hammer in hand. He glanced forlornly at the fast-flowing river beyond and below the trees. Exhausted, a long lonely life passed through his mind's eye in a sudden flash.

"What wee need, Jesse, are rocking chairs on thy porch, right 'ere, in the shade. Then, wee can rock on 'em, in our olde age, and watch thy river flow," John dreamed.

Both men turned toward the river and envisioned the view.

"Wee 'ave to cut down these trees to get a clear view of thy river," Jesse said, reluctantly, as he stared into the dense stand of untouched nature.

"Wee 'ave to cut down these trees, Jesse, to get some river breeze," John quipped.

"If wee cut down these trees, John, then the riverbank will erode," Jesse reasoned.

"Well then, wee shall cut out just the ones in the middle," John reasoned.

"Methinks, wee must not get too bolde about cutting down trees, anywhere. 'Tis a way to keep thy lande from sliding away. Ye cannot 'ave goode lande without plenty o' trees to keep it goodely, my father used to say," Jesse looked away, in reminiscence.

"Aye, your father managed well his lande, Jesse," John agreed.

"Indeed so," Jesse added.

"Now, he would be taken aback if 'e were to be standin' 'ere in the sight o' such thick nature. Would he not?" John asked.

"Aye, truly overwhelmed," Jesse answered, as he looked up to catch a commotion of chirping in the trees.

A large flock of noisy birds fluttered and flew off. In the next moment, the men heard the ramble of hooves echoing from the dense thickness.

"'Tis the sound o' horses wee hear, yonder," John yelled, softly.

The ramble became a patter and with it the unmistakable drawl of an Englishwoman. Then, a native on horseback came through the swishing brush. A few moments later, a woman rider emerged from the forest door, on another horse, followed by two packhorses. John stared up, incredulously, into the face of the smiling women.

"'Tis my sister Anne come from England, Jesse," John exclaimed, in disbelief.

Upon approaching the homesteaders, the riders received a stunned greeting, dismounted, and were invited into the cabin.

Embarrassed, John seated Anne in the midst of male surroundings. Moose Hunter stumbled as he went out the door to fetch up a bucket of cool river water. Brave As Bull sat in mute confusion. Jesse took a seat carefully. The visiting brave solemnly reached into his bag and brought out his smoking weeds.

"What a surprise 'tis for me to lay eyes on thy lovely face Annie," John flattered her.

"What a relief 'tis for me to lay eyes on ye, handsome brother. I did not know whether or not you were alive,"

Anne responded, before taking a few puffs on the circling pipe.

"Dear Anne, when last wee spoke in England, I told you that I would send for you, from Jamestowne, when the time came. Jesse and I, as ye see, 'ave planted down up 'ere instead. 'Tis no place for the delicate sex," John explained.

"I come prepared to pioneer, brother John," Anne responded, forthrightly.

"Pioneer you shall indeed, mam. Wee lack as much as a bathin' tub," Jesse added.

Anne proved to be as sturdy a pioneer as any man. Her feminine presence had a domesticating effect on life in the wilderness. Daily, she bathed vigorously in the rushing creek. Her smell reminded the men of their sex. She not only freed them from the drudgery of clothes washing, but caused them to change clothes more often. Meals became less a chore and more a pleasure. Her kitchen smells brought out their more thoughtful side. Even the animals responded to her soft voice and gentle hand with liking. The wilderness itself became as tame as an English farm. Everyone adored her, especially Jesse.

On the first cool rainy morning of Autumn, the five member household sat at the cramped table over breakfast.

"'Tis become a bit of a crowd in 'ere on a rainy day. Might be time to think 'bout building another addition," John began, as he looked around the table for agreement.

"'Tis a goode idea and wee 'ave the time to do it, too. After harvest, wee can spend the rest of Autumn clearing more lande for wood. By planting time wee could 'ave another addition," Jesse responded.

"Thy cabin will be twice as large as when wee started out," John said, enthusiastically.

"Aye, wee could add a second-floor instead of an addition," Jesse said.

"Goode idea. Need quiet place to sleep," Moose Hunter said.

"Me second idea," Brave As Bull added.

"'Tis resolved then. Wee'ill add another floor to thy cabin by Spring," John stated.

Jesse got up, went to the cabinet, and removed the writing equipment. Anne cleared the table. Jesse returned to it and began drawing a construction plan. They passed the greater part of that dreary day, outside, in inspired discussion and drawing, inside. By evening, the group had drawn up a viable plan for a second-floor down to every detail. The next morning, however, they constrained their enthusiasm, for harvest time called them to the fields. Throughout the harvest, their attention centered on the cabin. Thereafter, they undertook the task readily. By springtime, the little cabin in the remote wilderness became a farm house.

The two-story house now stood much larger than its original size. The plantation grew, likewise. In a few subsequent years, planting expanded. A golden crop of wheat grew adjacent to the corn field. A green vegetable garden grew too. The barn grew larger and higher. A shed housed equipment and tools. The family of livestock multiplied. They required fencing that stretched far. Plans got underway for a cabin, to house the new natives whose labour became a permanent necessity.

Moreover, the house became a home. Wilderness isolation drew everyone together more closely with each passing year. The five-member family grew stronger in feelings for one another. Although, nothing could weaken the strong bond between Jesse and John, something could strengthen it. Jesse's love for John's sister strengthened the bond between the two men. Anne's heartfelt emotion for Jesse maintained that strength. The two sought each other's company whenever possible. Together, they took long walks in the forest's massive solitude. On one such occasion, Jesse made a bold move.

"'Tis the house big enough for yet another, think ye Annie?" Jesse posed his riddle.

Anne smiled knowingly and thought of a similar response.

"'Tis big enough for another and then some," she responded, with a knowing wink.

And so it came to pass, that on a sultry Spring morning, John administered marriage vows to his sister, Anne, and his partner, Jesse. The two consumed their vows in a breeze on the front porch, while the river flowed onward beyond and below the trees. Moose Hunter and Brave As Bull stood grinning in attendance. Within a year, the smack and scream of new life shattered serenity.

"Ye are a hardy man of honour, Jesse. He must continue the legacy ye 'ave begun in this virgin lande o' liberty," Anne suggested in new-found seriousness.

"Very well, his name 'ill be Jesse too," Jesse agreed.

"I would not think to 'ave it any other way, Jesse," Anne demanded.

"Jesse Junior 'tis then," Jesse affirmed, blithely.

CHAPTER VI

THE MAGIC SPELL

John grew lonelier by the days but hid it always. Outwardly, he showed nothing but friendship and affection toward everyone. His true emotions led his mind elsewhere. Thereby, when an opportunity for travel presented itself, he volunteered to take the trip. Moose Hunter and he planned a trip to Jamestowne to attempt to establish a contract with a new agent. The agent with whom they did business, theretofore, dealt with British shippers exclusively. Dutch shippers, however, paid a higher price for tobacco. Thus, he sought to establish a contract with an agent known to deal with the Dutch.

As John and Moose Hunter mounted their horses at the barn door, Jesse slapped and squeezed John's thigh firmly.

"Goode luck, John. Keep a low profile. A dozen years is a long time. But not so long that someone won't recognize ya," he looked up squinting into the sun, his left hand thrown out to cover his eyes, and his voice betraying trepidation.

"Been too long to arrest us now," John assured him.

"Eh, but the law is for the few," Jesse warned him.

At that moment, Anne rushed up.

"Don't forget to ask Wahunsunakok for a squaw to help me with the baby, when ye pass through Werowocomoco with our gift and greetings, John," she reminded him.

"I shall not forget thy squaw," John turned to assure her, as Moose Hunter and he started off toward the river trail.

Witnessing John's departure from the lande, for the first time since their arrival twelve years earlier, caused just as many years worth of memories to flood in on Jesse, at once. Anne and Brave As Bull trundled behind him as he walked briskly to the riverbank. There, they caught sight of the riders again, at that point downriver, where the trail came out of the trees to meet the edge of the riverbank. Thence, with choked throats, they watched the riders slowly fade away far out of sight.

That Summer passed absent of John. Sometimes, without warning, worry would jab Jesse. The company of natives, Anne, and the baby notwithstanding, Jesse felt strangely alone. He remembered when John and he kept each other company in the English language. He fought off false premonitions.

On a sunny September day, Anne sat on the front lawn, atop a thick dark-grey wool blanket, reading William Shakespeare's play, *Tempest*. The poet's allegory of the Jamestowne colonists brought her world home to her. Upon reaching the end of the last page she sighed, set the book on the blanket, looked out over the water, and down the river that led to that colony. The poet's poignant sarcasm of colonial leadership made her feel lucky to live upriver. She walked to the river's edge and gazed thitherward toward the trail. The balmy Summer breeze blew benignly from the river below. The breeze bent the tips of trees, in unison, down the long stretch of rushing river, like a chorus bowing, over and over again, in encore.

Steadfastly, the pioneer woman stood, in nature, against the blowing breeze. As she gazed, her eyes caught a speck of color far downriver. She watched it closely as it disappeared, and then reappeared, at another point in the trees. It came to her. There are horsemen riding up the trail along the riverbank. She became excited, scrambled across the lawn, lifted the baby out of its wooden cradle, and then searched for Jesse and the natives.

When Anne reached the barn door she spotted Brave As Bull working inside.

"Brave As Bull, there are horsemen coming," she shouted out.

Brave As Bull came out of the barn, walked to the river's edge with her, and looked toward the east.

"There 'tis thither, can you see? she asked him.

"I see feathers," he answered flatly.

"I'll find Jesse," Anne said, as she bolted off across the lawn. She spotted him, in the distance, stacking firewood, with the natives at their cabin. She cupped her mouth with her hands to amplify her voice.

"Horsemen coming," she strained to be heard.

Jesse looked up in alarm, for he could not hear her clearly. He rushed toward her, but she turned and ran away. Perplexed, he rushed to follow her. He caught up with her, on the expanse of lawn, just as five horses emerged from the forest trail. In the lead, came John followed by a woman. Next, came Moose Hunter followed by a squaw. Finally, a young brave followed them all.

John tilted his head back, slightly, with almost imperceptible pride, pulled in the reins, dismounted, and ceremoniously held out his hand to assist the woman rider down.

"Allow me to introduce my wife, Bessie," John said, with great dash.

He dumbfounded Jesse, Brave As Bull, and Anne with astonishment. They stood, open-mouthed, and stared up at Jesse's sister, in awkward hesitation. Then, they turned their eyes toward Moose Hunter and the squaw.

"My wife, Harvest Moon," Moose Hunter said, proudly.

"Bessie and Harvest Moon. What a pleasant surprise! Welcome to the Muddy Creek Plantation," Anne greeted them both, with a broad smile, and outstretched arms.

"My nephew, Freebird," Moose Hunter introduced the young brave.

"Freebird," Jesse said, as he grabbed him firmly by the shoulders.

The first sight of other females in years lifted a dormant spirit from deep within Anne's bosom. Without hesitation, the three walked straightforwardly into the house, where they began talking about Jamestowne.

The men took seats on the porch, where Jesse began relaying the events of the Summer season. When Brave As Bull appeared, with the other natives, and a wooden bucket full of water, the women removed from the house. John and Moose Hunter introduced Bessie, Harvest Moon, and Freebird to the natives. Then, the impassive native men sat down on the edge of the porch, at both sides of Moose Hunter's nephew.

Jesse went into the house and returned with a tobacco pouch and pipe. He stuffed the finely chopped brown burley leaves into the pipe and lit it up. He filled his mouth with a thick draw and passed the pipe to his sister, Bessie.

"Y'all gonna love the hardy life 'ere," Jesse began.

"'Tis sure a lovely place," Bessie commented.

"'Tis so indeed, mam," Jesse responded, as Bessie passed the pipe to Harvest Moon.

"Harvest Moon excited to live on plantation," Moose Hunter said, with a grin.

"Plantation goode place," Harvest Moon responded.

"Freebird tired of hanging around Jamestowne. He want to live on plantation too," Moose Hunter added, as Harvest Moon sat forward to pass the pipe to Freebird.

The young brave held up his hand, in refusal.

"No smoke tobacco," the young brave scowled, as he reached into his pouch and retrieved smoking weeds. "Smoke weeds. They give me strength," he said, bluntly.

"'Ave as you please, Freebird. I do not disagree. Yet, wee must grow tobacca, on the plantation, to 'ave supplies," Jesse explained.

"Indeed, thy weed 'tis goode for body and mind. But, in Europe, thy Church outlaws it 'cause 'tis pagan. Thy Christian Church cannot 'ave power without putting paganism underfoot," John knew.

"Ye can add, that Europeans are prejudice against all things native. They'll not smoke your weeds. They'll smoke only tobacco, because the Spanish brought it to them," Jesse reasoned.

"The Arawak of the Carob Isles gave tobacco to Spanish. It native plant," Freebird retorted.

"'Tis not so goode for health, as smoking weeds," Jesse reasoned further.

"European has strange way of thinking. He thinks his God made nature at one time and he at another. False pride make him weak to smoking weeds. Weed too strong for his mind." Freebird quipped.

Jesse put the tobacco pipe down, when it came back around.

"Ye are right. Smoking tobacca when one has weeds is like eating rye when one has wheat," he quipped back.

"Rye, what is rye?" Freebird asked.

The Englishmen and women laughed.

"Rye is what the poor peasants in Europe must eat," Jesse answered.

Thereafter, the three new members of the plantation settled into the routine of pioneer life. Bessie and Harvest Moon both became pregnant that first Autumn. The next Summer, they gave birth, a few months apart, to a girl and boy respectively. John and Bessie named the blue-eyed baby, Bonnie. Moose Hunter and Harvest Moon called their son, Deerslayer. Now, three children lived on the plantation.

Jesse Junior and Bonnie, double-first cousins, shared the same bloodlines. His father, Jesse Hughes and her mother, Bess Hughes, were siblings. Likewise, her father, John Tarleton and his mother, Anne Tarleton, were siblings. They grew up more as brother and sister than cousins, actually. In fact, as youngsters, they shared the same bed. They would share a larger one again, one day. Their play imitated their parents, aunts, and uncles, until the time came when they no longer played.

In the 1620's, the crowded four-room house underwent another enlargement. This time, instead of adding rooms only, the rooms themselves became larger. Thereby, the front porch became longer and wider. Plus, a two-story addition went up, to accommodate two more large rooms, both down and upstairs.

The original cabin thus disappeared, forever, into the greater structure. Moreover, the natives' cabin became larger and a second-floor added to its height. Plans for a second cabin got underway. The barn became huge to accommodate a proportionately growing crop production. A great deal of wood went into these construction projects.

In late Spring '22, Jesse, John, and Moose Hunter left the plantation to the care of Brave As Bull. Times had changed. Wahunsunakok died in 1620. His brother, Opekankano, now ruled the Powhatan Confederacy. In addition, the colony lived under a new form of governance. Upon his return from Jamestowne, back in Autumn '20, John had described that new system.

The royal governor, Sir Edwin Sandys, reorganized the Virginia Companie in '19. The colony now enjoyed self-government, under a parliament known as the House of Burgesses. The colonists elected its members, popularly. The house legislated under authority of the governor and his council.

Thereafter, intermittent news of the government's success piqued the pioneers' interest, especially as it related to the tobacco trade, and native relations. They wanted to witness the house in session, and judge the new governor and his council for themselves. They discussed the trip more and more, for a couple of years.

The opportunity came in June '22. At the end of planting season, Jesse, John, and Moose Hunter took off down the river trail on a trip to Jamestowne. At Powhatan, they found an atmosphere of unease. Word had reached the village, just a few weeks earlier, that Opekankano no longer withheld his resentment for the colonists. Rumor had it that his braves played tom-toms at night.

"Maybe not safe to travel farther," Moose Hunter warned them.

"If there's trouble, then perhaps wee can avoid it," Jesse hoped.

"Wee cannot stay anyway. Harvest season 'ill call us back soon," John reasoned.

"Wee go with caution then," Moose Hunter, reluctantly, agreed.

The three men rode on with sharper senses. A half-day before Jamestowne, they passed a plantation. The sight of a plantation, in the wilderness, took Jesse back a bit. He became even more amazed, thereafter, as they passed a succession of them.

"You're right, John. We're no longer the only pioneers in thy virgin lande," Jesse said, as the group rode along.

"'Tis what I told ye, Jesse. Jamestowne is spreading out," John responded.

"'Twas hard to believe without me own eyes," Jesse said.

"Wait till ye see Jamestowne, itself, ole buddy," John bantered.

Upon arrival, Jesse knew the long hard ride was worthwhile. Fifteen years had completely changed the place. He became amazed at the bustle in town. Dozens of houses, shops, and buildings lined the several streets. Government buildings stood out amongst the rest.

"Ye can sure spot thy governor's house easily enough," Jesse noticed.

"Thy House of Burgesses too," John added.

Moose Hunter rode on silently, beside them, with his mouth hanging slightly open, in wonderment.

Upon reaching the inn, the men checked in, bought mugs of ale, to show their goode will, and slept a day away. On the second morning, the house sat in session. The three men walked to the hall, and took seats in the small spectator's gallery. Quickly, rowdy colonists filled the seats around them. The clerk's gavel could barely subdue their boisterous commotion. Finally, the crowd calmed down. Governor Sandys stood up and began speaking.

"Gentlemen, let it be known, that I am just as concerned as anyone gathered 'ere 'bout the defense o' thy colony," Sandys assured the crowd.

The governor's words, however, met with disregard from one angry man. He promptly stood up and yelled out.

"Opekankano will go on the warpath before this house ever acts in defense of thy colony," he roared.

At that statement, the crowd broke loose again.

"'Ere, 'ere," came loud shouts in response.

The governor held up his hands to calm the crowd, without avail.

No sooner did the clerk begin pounding the gavel again, to subdue the uncontrollable commotion, than the doors burst open, with a boom! A wild-eyed man rushed in, with sheer terror on his face and a bloody chin.

"Man thy barricades! Man thy barricades! It's a mad massacre," he screamed.

"To arms, to arms," shouted one spectator.

Thence, a wild uproar broke loose. Chairs began banging and crashing against one another, as the place turned topsy-turvey. A hasty rush for the doors emptied the gallery. The governor had lost control.

Vexed, Governor Sandys, followed by the burgesses, made for the arsenal, themselves. Jesse, John, and Moose Hunter went along with the crowd. Outside on the hot dusty street, all manner of chaos had broken loose. The sudden rumor terrified the town. Women pulled screaming children to-and-fro. Shutters and doors slammed shut with bangs and clangs, up and down the crowded street. Meanwhile, the moving mass of men gathered strength, from farmers to shopkeepers, as it approached the arsenal.

At the arsenal, one mean man shot Moose Hunter a menacingly dirty look.

"Who's the savage amongst us?" the man yelled, loudly.

"Hands off, mister. 'Tis a son of Wahunsunakok," Jesse warned him, threateningly.

"There's no friendly savages. He's likely a killer. Lock 'em up, I say," the man yelled, louder.

Jesse became enraged, pulled out his musket, and pointed it squarely at the belligerent man's face.

"Back off or die, mister," Jesse yelled back.

Startled, the man huffed and ran off.

"Moose Hunter take cover," Moose Hunter, himself, decided quickly.

"Wee'll go with ye," Jesse and John, at once, agreed.

Hurriedly, the three made for safety at the inn. Once in the room, a better thought came to their minds.

"If Opekankano attacks the town, then wee're sittin' ducks in 'ere," Jesse remarked.

"He'll 'ave to breach the barricades, then get through that determined crowd," John reasoned.

"Call that unruly bunch determined, if you will, John," Jesse retorted.

"I say wee make far away. No delay," Moose Hunter demanded.

Jesse and John saw the determination in Moose Hunter's face. They sensed he felt inhibited inside the inn. They searched each other's faces for courage.

"Very well, wee take our chances in the forest," Jesse decided.

"Agreed," John confirmed the decision.

Moose Hunter led the escape. The three horsemen entered the forest at the town's border. Within half an hour, the swampy forest became too thick to move through. The riders had to dismount and walk the horses under low-lying branches. In mid-afternoon, Moose Hunter broke silence.

"Do not believe Powhatan will harm Powhatan," he said.

"They might not know wee are, all three, Powhatan," Jesse feared.

"Not worry. Wee keep going," Moose Hunter said, fortitudinously.

At nightfall, the three men made camp, without fire, at the edge of a stream. Just as sleep began to creep over them, a faint but growing sound of war cries wafted eerily through the night sky. Suddenly, even before they could rouse, shrill female screams blended into the frightening sound. They got up to better determine the direction from whence the sounds came. What they caught filled them with foreboding. At a far distance, a fire shone brightly, like a tiny match light, through the trees thither.

"Plantation burning," Moose Hunter stated as he pointed toward the far-off fire.

"Wee must get away from 'ere," John said, softly.

"Wee stay and sleep. Safe in forest," Moose Hunter ordered.

Calmed by the native's wisdom, somewhat, but filled with horror and piteous dread, Jesse and John slept uneasily. The men moved on at dawn. Cautiously, they kept to the backwoods. At times, Moose Hunter lost his way. He did not let it show. The savvy native had been lost in the forest, on more than one occasion. He simply made his way by nature. The sun and the moss on trees marked his course. Finally, after a few days of slow-moving, the group came upon the river trail.

"Wee are far from Jamestowne. Safe now to ride on trail," Moose Hunter determined.

Once upon the trail, the riders moved swiftly upriver. Toward the end of the day, they slowed their horses to a walk before making camp. Relieved now, the riders conversed for the first time.

"Seems Opekankano caught thy new governor unawares," John began.

"No one knows Opekankano like Captain Smith," Jesse believed.

"Aye, he'd 'ave made the best governor," John agreed.

"If Jamestowne survives the massacre, then the king will want to send troops to Virginia, no doubt," Jesse guessed.

"Sandys will not allow it. He's not of the king's party. He'd train a Virginia militia, instead," John guessed.

"Ye are on thy mark, John. Sandy's gave the colony self-government. He has the liberty of Virginians at heart," Jesse boldly summed up.

Finally, the relieved riders reached the Muddy Creek Plantation. Surprised, the women exited the house and greeted them, in a rush. Their happy faces betrayed their innocence. None of them had any inkling of the massacre at Jamestowne.

"Why 'ave ye returned, so soon?" Anne asked Jesse.

Jesse hesitated on his mount. He looked down at Annie with concern. Then, he dismounted and grabbed her in a tight embrace.

"Oh dear, Jesse, ye 'ave only been gone a short time," Anne said with some embarrassment.

Jesse looked over at John and Moose Hunter knowingly.

"I get the natives," Moose Hunter offered, as he strode off.

"Whatever is on your minds?" Bessie wondered aloud.

"Let's get out of the sun," Jesse said, with heaviness.

Jesse and John allowed several comfortable minutes to pass on the porch, with mugs of cool river water in their hands, while they waited for everyone to gather around. Then, when all were present, Jesse began to speak.

"Opekankano is on the warpath," he said, seriously.

Moose Hunter interpreted the words for the natives. They shook their heads, discerningly.

"He burned plantations and moved toward Jamestowne as wee escaped," Jesse continued.

Moose Hunter continued to interpret to solemn responses.

"Wee need to be ready for 'im," John added.

"Opekankano not come upriver. No worry," Moose Hunter stated firmly, as he began giving sentry instructions to the natives, nonetheless.

That night, and every night for many years, thereafter, the plantation lived on guard. However, Opekankano's wrath paid no heed to the Muddy Creek Plantation. It lived on, under the iron cloak of the magic spell.

CHAPTER VII

DOUBLE-FIRST COUSINS

The memory of the eerie night in the forest haunted Jesse and John. For two decades, Opekankano lived on. Yet, Wahunsunakok's legacy remained strong. They would have peace of mind for years at a time. Then, without warning, a sweaty nightmare would come along.

A longtime later, in Summer 1645, the two olde pioneers sat on the front porch taking in the peaceful sight, of a throng of birds swooping for food, along the river. Junior and Bonnie, sat nearby taking turns reading aloud, in Middle English, the Prologue of Chaucer's *Canterbury Tales*. Suddenly, a flock of birds feeding on the lawn fluttered their wings and flew off. Unexpectedly, Freebird burst out of the river trail. Junior and Bonnie shot up excitedly, bounded eagerly down the steps, and greeted him.

"Give us news from Jamestowne, Freebird," Bonnie exclaimed.

"Opekankano dead," he stated, without expression.

The young cousins looked up at him, their mouths hanging open in astonishment. He thought that his language might have been too blunt for their innocence, and felt awkward for it. He looked down uncertainly at his horse, dismounted, but smiled broadly at Junior. Then, the three went to the porch where the household began to come together.

"Welcome back Freebird," Jesse greeted him.

"Glad to be back," Freebird responded.

"Have some cool river water," Anne offered.

The thirsty brave accepted it and drank eagerly from the proffered mug. Satiated, he put the mug down firmly.

Jesse leaned forward with intense interest.

"Well, tell us the news, then. How'd he die?" he asked.

"First, there is more to tell. Opekankano and his braves burn many plantations. Many die. Militia retaliate. Burn down Werowocomoco. A blaze to behold. Many die there. Militia capture Opekankano. Put him in gaol in Jamestowne. Then, stealthy assassin sneak pass sheriff and put knife in feared one's chest, while he sleep. No one knows whom," Freebird related.

Jesse, John, and Moose Hunter, at once, sat back in their chairs with an inaudible sigh.

"It took another massacre to prompt action," John said, in a tone that betrayed sarcasm.

"Indeed so, sir. Ever since King James rescinded the Virginia Companie Charter, back in '24, thy crown has been appointing governors instead of thy companie. If thy companie had continued to appoint them, then Sandys would have taken action, before now. King Charles patronizes Governor Berkeley like Roman emperors patronized imperial governors. The Staurts are creating an English empire," Jesse complained.

"Dear, thy burgesses have equal representation with parliament," Anne attempted to appease him.

"Nonetheless, one cannot say that wee 'ave self-governance, because thy crown appoints thy governors," John reasoned.

At that, Jesse pounded his fists, forcefully, on the arms of his chair and shouted out loudly, "Equality is no substitute for liberty."

Jesse's statement rang off the porch and through time. The massacre of '44 strengthened the issue of self-government in Virginia. In fact, the colony would turn into a proverbial powder keg, one day, over the dichotomy between equality and liberty. At that time, the liberty of Virginians would become paramount.

Meanwhile, safe from the terror of tomahacks in the night, the colony expanded. Up on the remote Muddy Creek Plantation, the pioneer family measured time nature's way. They measured their maturity by the repetition of planting and harvesting seasons.

As the seasons progressed, the olde grew wiser and the young more restless. Junior and Bonnie began kissing as teenagers. The time came when they had wont to do much more. One Spring day found them alone in the hayloft. They feared that restraint had slipped beyond their power. On that day, hand in hand, they told their parents they wanted to marry, for the legacy.

Jesse, John, Anne, and Bess felt so goode about it that they gave a tremendous wedding to their children. Dozens of natives, along with a few house guests from far-off Jamestowne, attended the event. More than fifty persons gathered at the plantation for over a week. The merry crowd consumed great amounts of meat, cheese, biscuits, pies, whiskey, tobacco, and smoking weeds. On wedding night, the revelers sang and danced, to native music, until shadows lengthened under the thick treetops. Only then, did the couple go to the wigwam in the woods, high up above the onrushing river, by the light of a full moon.

Ten months later, Bonnie gave birth to a baby boy. The cousins named him, John, after his maternal grandfather. The boy filled his four grandparents with the greatest pleasure of their bounteous lives. They knew, so deep in the thick of their hearts, that all the risk and hard work, of their combined lifetimes, would profit this boy someday. The plantation would devolve to him. Thus, they began to live largely for this grandson. As he grew, so too did the life they knew.

The men managed all the planting, harvesting, shipping, purchasing, and maintenance. The women managed the household, animal husbanding, and gardening. They spent their evenings reading, playing games and music, singing, talking, and writing. The bonds among them became ever stronger. Their love for family and lande so overwhelmed them that all four grew into olde age more happily than, perhaps, any American generation since. During the next decade, all four would slide into death peacefully.

Eventually, Jesse and John grew infirm. Incrementally, Junior assumed responsibilities around the plantation. As a young man, he had learned the skills of plantation management. His father and uncle taught him well. With help from Bonnie and the natives the place continued to prosper. One sultry Summer morning, Junior laboured at the desk over the plantation account book. Bonnie entered the room in high spirits.

"This heat has me beat down before the day is done darlin'. Let's refresh ourselves in the creek," she swooned in on him.

Junior did not look up.

"Not today dear. I must prepare for a trip to Jamestowne," he explained.

"You intend to see the agent?" she queried him.

"Yes, I'm goin' to secure the plantation's boundaries before another year passes," he answered.

"Can your preparations not wait another day darlin'?" she begged him.

"No, I think not. The impetuous new King Charles II riles me. He is no different than his father, the first Charles. He creates patronage to the crown, as a habit. 'Ere in America no less. His latest grant is for several hundred thousand acres, can you believe, to pay a political supporter," he complained.

"That's truly hard to believe, allright. Certainly, such enormous size taxes my mind," she coyly said.

"Truly, I don't know how one man can settle such a vast place," he wondered aloud.

"Dear, you need not bother yourself with politics. The king's grants are all far downriver," she attempted to assure him.

"Nay mam, with grants of that size, we'll 'ave English neighbors one day," he exclaimed.

The approaching politics of patronage, prompted Junior to ensure his independence. Thereby, Freebird and he made the long round trip to Jamestowne for that purpose. Jesse had given him the documents from Wahunsunakok as proof of lande ownership. Junior had a Jamestowne solicitor draw up a lande title to the plantation that included surrounding forestlandes. Then, he had it duly filed with the colonial government. The colonial government's lande title described the borders of the Muddy Creek Plantation clearly. However, the borders needed surveying to be beyond dispute.

Thus, back at the plantation, Junior, Freebird, and the rest of the natives quarried large stone slabs, with axes and picks, from the big flat rocks in the creek. They used the axes and picks to remove large chunks. Then, with hammers and chisels, they worked them down, for weeks, to smooth surfaces. They marked these huge heavy slabs of stone with the deeply chiseled initials MCP. Thereafter, they varnished the slabs with brushes, hauled the cumbersome markers to the corners of the plantation on a wagon, and set them into deeply dug slats in the ground. The boundary stones added accurate definition to the description laid down in the title.

Besides securing his property rights, hopefully, Junior had to manage the years-long fall in the price of tobacco. The English Civil War, that had ended back in '49, provided the first cause. The Protestants in parliament, led by the Puritans under Cromwell, had taken the government back from the Catholics at court. During the fighting, when the Puritans took English harbors, dozens of ships burned. The resulting shortage of ships gave Dutch shippers a temporary advantage over English ones. In this monopolistic shipper's market, shipping prices rose accordingly.

The new Puritan government responded by prohibiting imports in any ships other than English ones. Worse, that government placed price controls on several imports into England, including tobacco. Thus, the agent in Jamestowne could pay only little for tobacco and wait long for shipment. During the Puritan years, in the 1650's, colonial planters planted crops and simply hoped that the sale price would cover costs, and provide reasonable profit. However, the case turned out otherwise for the politically powerless.

Therefore, Junior learned foresight and frugality in one hard lesson. He let the tobacco fields lay in fallow for several years. As a result, he lacked tobacco with which to exchange for supplies. Thus, he innovated. He had no choice but to make the plantation less dependent on supplies from England, and thus more self-sufficient. He thought to travel, once again, to Jamestowne to obtain information.

At Jamestowne, he intently watched blacksmiths forge horseshoes and various tools; tanners tan leather; chemists mix chemical concoctions; and other craftsmen at their trades. He annoyed some craftsmen, because he stood about making meticulous notes and drawings. They did not understand his economic thinking. Notwithstanding the embarrassment, he went back to the plantation and brought the natives to Jamestowne to view craftsmen in action. Upon their return to the plantation, they built a long row of craft shops. After a few years, the plantation began producing numerous iron items; besides leather; medicine; glass; candles; soap; gunpowder; and even ice.

Junior and Bonnie lived their whole lives on the plantation. Except for a few trips to Jamestowne and Powhatan, they knew of no other world. Secluded in the wilderness with the natives, their parents, and their son, John, they could only imagine the world beyond. They read about it in books, and heard about it from their parents and those they met. Yet, it existed in imagination only.

As adults, the cousins lived during the Civil War, the Puritan decade, the Restoration, and on into the Glorious Revolution of '89. During these turbulent times, they developed strong political beliefs. They came to believe that the colonists labored primarily for the benefit of the English government as opposed to that of themselves. Parliament, they came to believe, saw their colony as a source of tobacco and little more.

Nor did the cousins care for parliament using the king to grant lande to its own political cronies. The Jamestowne colonists had paid for the lande on which they settled.

Jesse Senior and John had paid an even higher price to Wahunsunakok.

Like most Virginians, they adhered to the political legacy that Governor Sir Edwin Sandys had established. Like the colonial government he organized, it set forth a standard of independence. The incipient political philosophy that formed, thereof, would one day devolve into the patriots of colonial Virginia. They would carry the cause of liberty to the utmost.

Meanwhile, with the Restoration, the Staurts had regained the throne in '60, and thus the olde ways in Virginia ended forever. Political patronage became entrenched. The English government continued to grant huge tracts of virgin wilderness to supporters of the imperial faction. Indeed, the patronage system in the colonies was beginning to rival that in England, itself.

The pioneers knew these grantees as "Cavaliers." The name originated with the court poets who usurped olde Queen Bess' beloved Shakespeare, after she died. Later, the name came to denote those who fought against the Puritans.

The Civil War had ended in a draw, for the country party, in parliament, tempered the imperialistic impulses of the court party, though the difference would not last long. And, nonetheless, mercantilists remained in majority power. Therefore, enterprise grew in Virginia, but it did not grow freely.

Back in 1607, the original Jamestowne colonists had a strong vision of their future in the virgin lande. They saw themselves planting down and becoming self-sufficient farmers in the tradition of true liberty. During their lifetimes, however, they witnessed the slow erosion of liberty. Parliament prohibited trade with the Dutch. Worse, it went so far as to regulate trade with the English, themselves. Moreover, it turned the colony into a vast political patronage system.

Jesse outlived them all. In his olde age he had wont to rock away his days upon the porch. The memory of John, Annie, and Bessie sat beside him. High up on the porch, he could look out, over the river, into the wild vastness beyond, and dream. He dreamed of the virgin forestlande. He dreamed that he could smell it. The taste of the smell swelled his tongue and made him swallow the green aura. Then, a sudden whiff of lande brought him out of his delusion and into another dream. And, so too went the last to remember Tudor England, the goode Queen Bess, the landing at Jamestowne, and the virgin wilderness.

CHAPTER VIII

PIONEERS AND CAVALIERS

Virginian villagers and planters reached the end of the first generation, after restoration of the Staurts to the English throne. The second generation displaced the first one in leadership positions of all kinds. Tobacco planting spread throughout the Chesapeake Bay area. And, plantations now stood amidst virgin wilderness far up tidewater rivers. Staurt kings enlarged the peerage by about half in their attempt to enhance their political power. They granted away a great deal of lande, in the colonies, to their Cavalier supporters. The allotments of these new titles sometimes came in hundreds of thousands of acres. Thus, in villages and on plantations alike, the way of life headed in an alltogether new direction.

Out on the once, ominously, remote Muddy Creek Plantation, on a warm Spring day, after a heavy rain, with Jesse's grandson, John, bestride his back, Henry Tudor ran around and around the oblong paddock. The black stallion bestrew mud, with spatters and thuds, against the fence boards. At the seventy-sixth stretch, the stallion took a gulp and a double breath, and then gained speed.

"Hoe back Henry," John Boy yelled, as the agile animal reared back against the reins.

"Henry Tudor's the best horse, by far, that we've ever bred," he burst out.

"You're sure right. He's a swift stallion, John Boy," wise olde Freebird replied, as he slowly turned his gaze up at the sun, while shading his eyes with the palm of his hand.

"He's smart and strong," John boasted.

"The sun last long enough these days. It's gods' breeding time. Wee breed Henry Tudor now, agreed?" Freebird already decided.

"Agreed," John Boy answered.

A week later, John Boy and Freebird rode off the plantation and down the river trail. Up and down thickly wooded hills they went, until they came to a surprising sight.

"There 'tis, Freebird, sittin' right there yonder," John Boy squinted his eyes against the sun's glare.

"Many years our neighbors, now. You get used to it, John Boy," Freebird demanded.

After having said this to the boy, he pulled his horse forward and led the way to the large cabin in the distance. Purposefully, the pair of riders came to a halt at the porch steps.

"Bonjour, bonjour John Boy and Freebird," the Frenchman hailed them from his porch.

"My father asked me to bring Henry Tudor to you, sir," John boy said in greeting.

"Yes, and I thank him for the favor. This magnificent stud and my mare will make a great pair. But first, dismount, come inside, and have a drink, s'il vous plait," the Frenchman said, with a heavy accent.

"Wee come in," Freebird responded.

After sitting at the table for a few minutes, John Boy looked around the place, curiously.

"Where's your fine daughter, sir?" he wondered aloud.

With a momentary glint in his eye, the Frenchman shrugged. "Oh, she is around somewhere." Then he added abruptly, "Wee shall introduce the two now."

At that, the three walked out into the warm day. Freebird untied Henry Tudor and led him to the barn. As soon as Henry Tudor saw the mare, he began whinnying and snorting like a wild animal. Freebird found it difficult to pull him through the gate and remove the bridle. Once loose, the horse bucked and reared, over and over, in a great show of virility. The threesome watched, interestedly, until the two horses would no longer allow their gazing.

"Wee return in fortnight," Freebird said, as he began walking toward his mount at the porch.

"Very well then, au revoir," the Frenchman bid them as John Boy mounted his own horse and meandered, with a short glance back, behind Freebird into the forest.

Upon returning to the Muddy Creek Plantation, John Boy eagerly sought some answers from his father. While his mother and the squaws laid dinner out on the sideboard, he sat down intently at the table and began his queries.

"Why did the Frenchman settle 'ere father?" he began.

"He's Protestant like us, son," Junior answered.

"He's not English, father," John Boy countered.

"Well, you see son, Mr. David escaped from King Louie's Army in a rowboat. Alone, he bravely rowed across the treacherous channel, through the dark of night, to escape from France. Once in England, he gained safety because the English welcome French Huguenots," Junior began explaining.

"Huguenots, what's an Huguenot father?" John Boy asked.

"An Huguenot is a French Protestant. They protest against paying taxes to support the king's army and government. They prefer to keep their tax money for their own towns and villages," Junior explained.

"You'd rather 'ave the Frenchman as a neighbor than a Cavalier?" John Boy asked.

"Indeed, I would son. The Cavaliers buy Africans to work their fields instead of English indentures," Junior continued.

"Why do Cavaliers buy Africans?" John Boy asked.

Junior laughed at his son's innocence, but his outward demeanor hid his inner emotion. For, the importation of African slaves, whether to become indentures or remain slaves, created yet another point of contention between pioneers and Cavaliers. Generally, pioneers opposed Africans, in Virginia, because their culture was not, at all, like that of the English.

Some complaints one heard, among pioneers, were that Africans could not speak English. In addition, many resented the English. For, they resented having been sold away from their African masters and taken to a strange culture. Add, that voodoo religion made them so superstitious that, sometimes, they locked themselves in their cabins for days at a time.

Junior explained, "'Tis a matter of monopolism, son."

Bewilderment overcame John Boy, "How's that father?"

Junior continued, "An Englishman who wants to try the opportunities that one finds in thy colonies, but is unable to pay for his passage, indentures him or herself to a planter or tradesman for, usually, seven years. The planter or tradesman then pays for the indenture's passage, and livelihood. Sometimes, the indenture learns a new skill. Add, that the indenture gets paid for his labour, in someway.

Largely, indentures provide high quality labour during the seven years of their contract. Then, they usually become self-sufficient members of society. 'Tis a goode system. However, parliament granted a shipping monopoly in the Africa trade to the British Africa Company. Ever since, the company's trade in, first, African indentures, and now just plain slaves, has been displacing English indentures on the quays at the coast. In other words, son, the supply of English indentures is low because the British Africa Company monopolizes the labour trade."

"What do Cavaliers have to do with monopolism?" John Boy asked perplexedly.

"Cavaliers, unlike pioneers, are patronized by the government. By patronized, I mean that government grants them large tracts of lande, as political favors, in exchange for their support of the Staurt government. Thus, they have need for large amounts of labour.

"Could they not choose to employ how ever many English indentures free shipping would allow, and grow less tobacco, until the Africa Company monopoly would end?" John Boy figured.

"Indeed so, son, you are quite right. If the Cavaliers refused to purchase Africans from the monopoly, as we pioneers do, largely, then the monopoly could not continue. However, they choose quick fortunes over ethical business practice. They pay the high monopoly price for Africans because they are all that is available in large numbers. You're a smart boy to think, that the ethical thing to do is pay a fair price for indentures, while limiting the size of planting so as to make it proportionate to available labourers," Junior summed up.

As Virginia grew, so too did tensions between pioneers and Cavaliers. In truth, the original Virginians abhorred the establishment of Staurt patronage in the colony. For a generation, the pioneers had been experiencing ever-greater usurpations of their liberty. First, the English government began giving out political patronage in the form of colonial governorships. Second, it began regulating the tobacco trade and shipping. Finally, tremendous lande grants intensified frustration. The last action sorely tested colonial fortitude. Thus, in the year, 1676, tension broke out into open revolt.

On an uncomfortably hot and dense Spring day, in that noteworthy year, at a Jamestowne tavern frequented by travelers, traders, planters, and rouges, a rollicksome group held a meeting. Meantime, across the way, at another tavern, frequented by townsmen, officials, and the resolute, patrons conversed quietly. Outside, one found riders and strollers making their ways along the tree-lined dusty dirt street, or milling about the grassy town green. John Boy walked, purposefully, amongst the small crowds, all the while, taking in the excitement of town life with all his being.

As he neared the taverns, he heard the rollicking rouse and stepped inside. He made his way through the crowd of boisterous men to the bar, bought a mug of ale, and began surveying the scene. He heard men shout bitter words, that drowned out toasts and cheers here and there. Suddenly, a deep-voiced man shouted from the back of the place. Everyone became quiet, and then turned their sights toward the burly man who began speaking.

"Hail goode fellows, countrymen, neighbors, Virginians!" the speaker exclaimed.

At this greeting, a tremendous roar ensued, along with ear-piercing yells and the pounding, of a hundred clenched fists, on heavy wooden tables. Many moments passed before the deafening roar subsided. Thence, the confident speaker began again.

"All ye 'ere who support thy governor say ie," he shouted out.

"Nay, nay," the boisterous agitated men yelled, repeatedly, for a full half-minute.

"Then, let us vote in one of our own fellows, eh," he shouted.

At this statement the crowd went absolutely wild. The whole place shook from the pounding of fists on tables and stomping of boots on floor planks. More toasts and boasts went up until it seemed the speech would not continue. Yet, once the uproar began to subside, it died down quickly.

"If wee are unable to govern ourselves, then wee should fight for the right," he shouted.

Again, all hell broke loose and refused to subside.

"Wee should elect a new governor," he shouted above a rising uproar.

From all corners of the wild tavern, men began shouting out bravos.

"Bring us glory, Nathaniel," yelled one man from the crowd.

"Self-government," yelled another.

"What a hero of a man that Nathaniel Bacon!" one boisterous fellow yelled right into John Boy's face.

At that, John Boy pulled back, slightly, and began to respond. Yet, the fellow stopped him before he could get a word out.

"Say, thy looks to be a man who knows liberty, what say ye?" he queried.

"I say a governor should be a man that comes from among us. A Virginian, who knows our own country," John Boy nearly yelled back.

The fellow smiled broadly, threw himself back on his legs, raised his mug up high, and toasted John. So, John Boy raised his mug just as high. The two mugs met, in mid-air, with a loud clank, and splashes.

"Cheers for us then goode fellow," the boisterous man yelled, as another fellow grabbed him, by the outstretched arm, and pulled him away from John Boy.

John Boy's arm fell to the bar. His hand released the mug and felt his belt for reassurance. He packed his most reliable musket. He had left the plantation seeking to become involved in the political resistance. Eagerly, he had been following the building momentum of ferment by any means through which he could get news.

Opekankano's death, a few decades earlier, had marked a respite in savage attacks. However, the rapid growth of planters down, in the frontier forest, irked the warrior chief's followers. Eventually, bloody tomahacks returned in the night. Governor Berkeley was failing to provide a remedy. The government had become interested, mainly, in its own growing wealth from the lande's tobacco. It was not interested in the growth of lande wealth among pioneers.

Nathaniel Bacon, a young planter, at the head of planters' private forces, led two decisive onslaughts against the fierce savages. Heroism brought him acclaim and fame. Thereby, Virginians voted him into the House of Burgesses. Governor Berkeley convened it, unwillingly. Then, he arrested Bacon to prevent his taking a seat. Soon released, Bacon marched on Jamestowne and forced the governor to grant him a commission to fight savages. The circumspect burgesses then passed several reform measures. Berkeley fled to the Eastern Shore.

Subsequently, the rebellion that throve thrilled John Boy. Political passion prompted his trip to Jamestowne. He checked into an inn anticipating his own role in the cause. He spent his days at capitol hall and the conspirator's tavern in hopes of getting closer to the rebels. Tacitly, Bacon and his fellow conspirators held their tactical secrets close among themselves, however. Thus, John Boy remained outside the conspirator's circle, notwithstanding his strong-felt belief in the cause of liberty.

On an hot day, the rebellion reached a summit. Hundreds of colonists converged on capitol hall to witness the burgesses vote in a Virginian governor. The throng of spectators spilled out onto the lawn. John Boy edged up close to an open window where he heard the loud orations. One burgess rose up from his chair and began to speak.

"For a quarter-century, since 1651, wee 'ave lived under the onerous *Acts of Trade*," the speaker began.

"'Ere, 'ere!" an excited crowd burst out.

"The Acts prohibit us from developing colonial manufactures," he continued.

An agitated planter shouted back from the gallery. "Wee cannot even manufacture pipes in which to smoke our tobacca, sir."

His complaint touched a nerve in the crowd. A ruffle of shouting shook the hall.

The speaker continued, "Further, wee are prohibited from selling tobacca to and purchasing supplies from any lande but England. The lack of competitive markets keeps the price of tobacca low and the price of supplies high."

Another agitated planter yelled from the gallery. "Thy price of tobacca goes nowhere but lower, sir."

Again, the crowd went into a roar.

The speaker continued, "Further, the shipping monopoly floods Virginia with Africans."

At that statement, the sensitive crowd burst into its greatest roar, yet.

"Furthermore, the onerous Acts are n'er enough. The government adds tobacca taxes, to fund the bureaucracy that enforces the monopolistic laws, themselves. Therefore, wee pay to enslave ourselves!"

At these statements, the crowd went out of control.

While furious stomping, pounding, and yelling continued unabated inside the hall, a wild-eyed man came galloping across the lawn yelling at the top of his lungs.

"Berkeley's comin', Berkeley's comin'."

He stopped his wide-eyed snorting horse just short of the steps. Two sturdy men grabbed the reins firmly.

"Berkeley's sailin' into thy harbor with troops this minute," the rider yelled from atop his snarling and sweating mount.

Without hesitation, a torrent of angry spectators rolled through the doors and headed for the arsenal. The news caught the burgesses unawares. One stood up and called for a barricade. The rest, including Bacon, ignored him.

"The hall's not worth its defense, unless Berkeley's turned back!" Bacon boomed bellicosely.

Governor Berkeley's return, from his brief exile, threw the town into a siege mentality. Empowered by English troops, Berkeley declared Bacon and his private militiamen rebels and traitors. He then proceeded to retake control of the government. However, he underestimated the liberty of Virginians. A plurality of them threw their support behind self-government. A belligerent skirmish ensued.

John Boy, himself, manned the barricades, with his trusty musket strapped on his waist, and heavy sword hanging hard against his leg. That ancient weapon came in handy, at the meanest hour of the melee, when brutal soldiers hurtled over the barricades, swords drawn, and lunged forward at the defenders. With all the strength he could muster, John Boy threw up that sword to stop certain death. Glistening in the shining sun, hard metal hit like with a loud clang and slid off. Tense, sure-footed, he pulled back for position, braced his back, and swung the sword, again. Another ringing clang and slide filled his ears. The clanging volley continued until arm muscles ached. Worn out, but intent and yet nimble enough, he gained advantage and took a quick lunge.

Suddenly, shocked and breathless, the soldier broke away. But, John Boy did not let him get away. He reached in the holster for his musket and took aim. For an instant, the bang numbed and the smoke blinded him. Then, the breeze blew off the smoke and he licked the splattered blood off his lips.

At the end of that rough day, bravery brought success. The stalwart colonials held those barricades. Bacon regained the town and drove Berkeley out, once again.

A few weeks later, the rebellion seemed won. However, word spread, with chagrin, throughout town, that Berkeley planned to return, from nearby Middle Plantation, with an ominously larger force. Bacon envisioned doom. He determined that only the boldest action could save the cause. Dauntless, he spread word to vacate the town.

Without a town, he reasoned, Berkeley would have no government to regain.

Thereby, one still Summer night, stealthy rebels lit fires that burned Jamestowne to the very ground. Bacon obviated Berkeley's ability to regain Virginia. Bacon the hero, the valiant rebel, did not live to experience the fruits of his heroism. For, he died suddenly in October. Leaderless, the rebellion died too. In the bitter end, Berkeley hanged several rebels. The colonists gained some satisfaction however, when the burgesses finally forced Berkeley to return to England.

The fates favored John Boy. For, he might have hung with the rest of the conspirators, had he broken into the close-knit circle of Bacon's planters. Military heroism was not to be a part of John Boy's destiny. Remorseful, he made the long journey back home.

Once there, he spared no time for regrets. He knew Virginians. Another rebellion would come some day. He had arrived before news of the rebellion's demise reached upriver. Late one wet afternoon, with the wind pushing powerfully at a hard downpour, the bad news caught up.

From his second-floor bedroom window, Junior heard the rider coming before anyone else in the busy household. He ambled down the stairs and out the front door just as the horseman approached the porch with the printed news. He read it with intense interest to fill in the sad story that his son had recently brought him. He looked up at the horseman angrily.

"All my life I've waited for the spirit of *Magna Charta* to find its way into the hearts and minds of Virginians, and it comes to a failed end," Junior scowled.

"The Cavaliers are too powerful for the pioneers father," John Boy retorted as he stared into the pouring rain. "Neither they nor the English will stand for self-government," he added knowingly.

"The year, 1676, will go down in infamy. It will be remembered as the first, but not the only, rebellion. The spirit of '76 shall live on!" Junior exclaimed, with agitated yet profound vigour. "The liberty of Virginians can no longer thrive without independent government, just as Bacon believed."

"Cavaliers shall not allow independence from a government that gives them patronage, father," John Boy reasoned.

Junior became reminiscent. He stared through the pouring rain, refractively.

"If only goode olde Queen Bess had had an heir. Thy Tudor family could regain thy government, and thy Staurts could no longer patronize Cavaliers. Those who would 'ave lande, would owe no favors for it," he pined.

"Such an event, in England, would be a glorious revolution, indeed!" John Boy remarked sarcastically.

CHAPTER IX

A PIONEER WEDDING

As Junior and John Boy stood on the porch studying the fresh newspaper, the Frenchman rounded the last bend on the river trail. His horse briskly made its way through the narrow pathway, under pelting rain. It approached the trail opening. Bare-branched trees afforded the rider momentary glimpses, here and there, of the plantation house in the clearing.

When he pulled out of the trail and onto the open lawn, the rider spotted father and son. He hesitated on his mount, to get a feel for the mood of the place. He sensed the seriousness of the conversation, from his vantage point, and considered caution so as not to intrude.

With just a slight tightening of the reins and an adjustment of his seat, he slowed his mount. Junior caught the movements of body and hands out of the corner of his eye. At that moment, each man's eyes caught the other ones. Then, both pairs of eyes glanced, instinctively, at John Boy, and twinkled, for just a fleeting instant, with the memory of their own youth. The front door opened, and the sudden appearance of Deerslayer's two sons, Brave Eagle and Smart As Fox, broke their daze.

"Greetings David," both Junior and John Boy threw up their arms to hail the Frenchman, in unison.

"Dismount and come inside," Junior demanded.

"Be glad to, Junior," the Frenchman responded and then splashed onto the ground with both boots.

Once the three sat comfortably in the front room, Deerslayer's wife, Wisp Of Willow and her daughter-in-law, Birdsong, returned with a bottle of brandy and three glasses on a tray. Junior reached into a drawer in the chair-side table and retrieved a pipe, tobacco pouch, and matches.

"Your favorite, David, brandy and a pipe. Compliments of the Muddy Creek," Junior offered.

"Would not mind if I do, Junior, not at'll," David said. "And how are you ladies today?" he greeted the squaws.

"Just fine ourselves, Mr. David," Wisp Of Willow and Birdsong shyly responded.

"You caught John Boy and I discussing the news of Bacon's failed rebellion, David. What brings ye to the Muddy Creek?" Junior began.

"Oh, just the want for thy goode family to take the Christmas holiday at my plantation is all, Junior," David responded hopefully. "Last year 'twas your honour and this year 'tis mine," he added.

"Aye, and so it shall be," Junior roared out jocularly.

With the formalities covered, the men sat about peacefully enjoying homemade brandy and tobacco for a few minutes.

"Now, tell us, what think ye about the rebellion?" Junior queried him.

"Put my mind betwixt two stones," David answered with consternation. "I cannot think how wee are to be free men of destiny without self-government. 'Tis better, thy English system, than the French one, though. The government in London, is not so powerful as the one in Paris you know," he thoughtfully added.

"'Tis growing and becoming more powerful all the time," Junior retorted. "Regulating labour and tobacca markets, and adding taxation to tobacca, for the benefit of political cronies," he sat up and nearly shouted.

"Wee must not allow the injustice to continue," David impugned.

"'Ere, 'ere, long live the spirit of '76," Junior shot up and shouted out.

"Father's mad with the spirit of '76," John Boy spoke up.

"Now boy, listen 'ere. Give ye a close ear to some of the greatest knowledge in history. Its future depends on its knowing," Junior insisted.

"Do tell us, Junior," David pleaded.

Junior sat back down.

"Well, the number 76 is related to liberty in history. The mystery is held in numerology. A science of genius. Allow me a few examples. The ancient Greeks held their first Olympics in 876 B.C. The Olympics brought the various poleis together, in strength, against the slave-mongering threat of Persian emperors. 476 B.C. marked the strategic turning point in the Persian Wars against Greece. Add, in that year, the Greek colonists, in Sicily, began their revolution against the tyrants at Himera. In 276 B.C., Philip of Epirus, Alexander's son-in-law, valiantly led the Greeks of southern Italy, in their last stand, against the growing imperialism of Rome, at the fateful battle of Boneventum. In 476 A.D., the German, Odacer, removed the last Latin ruler of Rome, Romulus Agustulus. In 876 A.D., the death of Charlemagne's grandson, Louis the German, marked the Carolingian's end and the beginning of Medieval time. Several more examples could be added," Junior explained.

"Indeed sir, including this year, 1676. The year in which the imperial government of England denied the liberty of Virginians," David exclaimed.

"One day, passion will rekindle the spirit of liberty in the hearts and minds of Virginians. The liberty of Virginians is strong and growing stronger, I tell you. Liberty must survive. For, if wee forget the traditions of our Greek ancestors, then European civilization, itself, will end," Junior warned.

"Aye, and North America will, indeed, become the Northwest Passage to Asia. The Asians will enslave us all. They'll take the products of our labour and leave us a miserable existence," David added.

John Boy's brow furrowed, as he raised his eyebrows, in concern.

"My generation will take the lesson o' liberty from Bacon's Rebellion. Hereafter, wee'll hold it, for an hundred years if need be, until 1776, among any of us whom will live so long," his youth yelled from deep within him.

A few weeks later, on Christmas morning, with the wind wheezing through the rattling windowpanes, and snow swirling outside, John Boy awoke. He woke up, before anyone, to the sound of stillness. Mesmerized by the wind and cold, he remained in a sleepy trance. The Frenchman's son, Robert, slept snugly beside him. Junior and David slept the deep sleep of Winter in an adjacent bed. John Boy's mind easily wondered off into memories of Christmases past. The stories of Christmases in England that his grandfather, Jesse Senior, used to tell him on this day of the year occupied his mind.

"After light came over the horizon, church bells rang the holiday message across the meadowes and through the woods," olde Jesse's story began.

His imaginary picture of the English countryside impressed him, vividly. It reflected a scene portrayed in a book that his parents gave him, one Christmas past. The wooden cabin roof above him began to disappear. In its place he could see the thick dark-green of England that his grandfather knew. "Do not forget from whence ye came," he demanded that Christmas day.

In his daydream, he could hear the Sunday sound, of bells ringing in Jamestowne, that he, himself, knew so well. He lay there in such a trance seemingly forever. Then, suddenly, with the screeching shrill scream of Robert's baby, from the next room, the cabin stirred.

The two families had grown close during the years since the Frenchman broke the decades of solitude on the upper James River. The previous year, the house guests stayed on at the Muddy Creek, through holiday week, for New Year. The families relished the memory of Christmas week throughout the year, for they valued highly the company of neighbors in the lonely wilderness.

Both families left natives on their plantations while they stayed away. The natives left behind celebrated too. They ate, drank, smoked, read verse, told stories, sang, danced, and performed magical tricks to one another's delight. Natives who had left the plantations to become tradesmen or shopkeepers in villages, in pursuit of their own fortunes, often returned to celebrate Christmas with little regard for the Winter weather.

This Christmas would be special. John Boy had been keeping a secret for many weeks. On this day, he planned to ask the Frenchman for his daughter in marriage. Genevieve felt no surprise. The two of them had been pondering the event, since childhood. Not only did the Muddy Creek Plantation sit alone on this stretch of the upper James River for several decades, but since the Frenchman planted himself down, the two plantations comprised the whole neighborhood for several subsequent years. Although John Boy and Robert played together throughout their boyhoods, Genevieve and he grew close, only lately. Family loyalty was the rock foundation of their mutual attraction.

After having escaped France, in a rowboat, David learned the English language in England. Then, he set out for Virginia. He became one of the first French Huguenots to do so. Upon arrival in Jamestowne, he acquired lande upriver so as to settle away from English colonists.

Thence, he purchased farm animals, tools, and equipment with which to establish a plantation. Once prepared, he hired a few natives to take him to his lande. Jesse welcomed him with a gift of several hemp sacks filled with tobacco seeds. By these long and arduous means, the Frenchman had planted himself down on the banks of the James River back in 1647.

Thereafter, the Muddy Creek Plantation gave aid to its new neighbor whensoever he needed it. David first needed native labour. In particular, he had need for an interpreter because he had little success communicating with the natives in English.

In time, the two families began sharing native labour, breeding their horses and work stock, and shipping their tobacco downriver together. The association benefited the interests of both plantations. For, the combined crops commanded a higher price, at market, than each would have singly.

Thus, the two families already sensed the propitious news in the proverbial air, as they sat around the large wooden table. A French-style feast lay before them. The smells of marinated red beef in brown gravy; scalloped potatoes covered with cheese sauce and parsley; peas with onions in butter; dark biscuits dipped in thick green olive oil; and dry dark-red wine mingled in the air with the aromas of wood fire, tobacco, and smoking weed. John Boy sensed the group's anticipation and rascally withheld the news through the pre-meal toasts. Then, at meal's end he shoved his chair back, with a loud screech on the wooden floor, shot up, and raised his glass.

"If anyone present objects to the union in marriage of lovely Genevieve and me, then speak your piece now or forever hold your tongue!" he blurted out.

Everyone burst out laughing at his boyish awkwardness. Genevieve blushed at the sudden attention in her direction.

"Qu' est-qu'il ce tu dis, Genevieve?" her mother quietly asked.

"It would be my greatest pleasure to wed John Boy," she answered honestly.

"Hurrah," Robert shouted, as the rest of the table broke into applause.

John Boy and Genevieve's announcement thrilled the prospective in-laws. Heartfelt blessings gushed forth, in unison. The union of John Boy and Genevieve brought their hopes to fruition. The bond of matrimony added legal strength to the, heretofore, informal partnership between the plantations. Everyone sensed that both families would benefit greatly.

The ensuing courtship strengthened the legal formality of marriage, forasmuch as desire transforms itself into deed. The two had grown close gradually during their childhood years. Now, they fell in love. The slow ebb of Winter wind and cold took their childhood away with it, just as the flow of tepid Spring air brought their maturity. The warm hearths before which they sat in simple conversation, the fresh meadowlandes they traversed on long idyllic walks, the budding trees under which they held each other longingly, and the ever-brightening blue sky, above them, set the very stage of their life's play.

On Easter Sunday morning, under a brightly shining sun, to the loud chirping of an hundred birds, and with the olde river flowing onward, down under its banks, the two took their vows.

"Do you, John Hughes take Genevieve Hughes to be your lawfully wedded wife, in sickness and health, in poverty and wealth, in misery and happiness, till death you part?" the priest asked him.

"I do," John Boy answered.

"And, do you, Genevieve Hughes, take John Hughes to be your lawfully wedded husband, in sickness and health, in poverty and wealth, in misery and happiness, till death you part?" he asked her.

"I do," Genevieve answered.

"Very well then. By the power vested in me, by the Church of England, in the colony of Virginia, I pronounce you man and wife," he concluded.

So it came to be, that these two families, with the same surnames, albeit one English and the other French, became one. A year after the wedding, John Boy and Genevieve had a baby. They named him, John. Hereafter, the "boy" in John Boy's name devolved onto the baby boy. The following year, Genevieve's brother, Robert, and his wife, had a girl. They named her, Mary.

When Genevieve gave birth to John, Jesse Junior felt inward relief. One lived uncertainly, at best, in the wilderness.

A new chief might undo the tenuous relationship with the Powhatans that Jesse Senior had established back in 1608, the magic spell notwithstanding. Diseases of various sorts came and went in waves. About half of the babies born in Virginia did not reach adulthood.

Jesse Senior had felt lucky that Junior survived the dangers of childhood and married his Tarleton double-first cousin, Bonnie. Junior, himself, felt lucky that John Boy survived those same dangers and also married to the benefit of the plantation. The tremendous risks and hard work of two generations would benefit future ones.

The relief Junior felt for the family's future had a profound effect upon him. Now that he had a grandson, in his baby boy, he sensed success by fulfillment of his life's responsibilities. A profound feeling enlarged his outlook. He turned his attentions away from business and toward the lande, more and more.

During weekday mornings, at the desk, he proudly oversaw John's growing expertise in plantation management. Just the smell of the olde leather-bound record books pleased him deeply. On many afternoons, he found himself in his armchair looking back metaphorically at the home of his boyhood. While reading, he would pause at the end of some paragraph or other, look out the window, and become distracted by the sound of squaws talking or babies crying from somewhere in the house. Then, the view outside transformed itself into the very one that took place, there, a half-century earlier.

Boom! How he loved the sound of that musket.

"Ah, ye must stand firm, as I tell ye boy, otherwise ye 'ill miss thy mark. Now there, try it again," his father said.

Boom, the sound of the shot echoed off of every tree.

"'Tis the way, now. See what ye hit thither," his father exclaimed.

"Am I goode enough to hunt with the braves now, ye think?" he urgently hoped.

"Perhaps, perhaps methinks," his father answered, with a wink of his eye toward Moose Hunter.

Then, both men began laughing heartily, and continued to do so, while their laughter slowly faded into a mere echo from the past.

"Father, father, wake up," John yelled into Jesse Junior's face, as he began shaking him.

John could hardly stir him. Once roused, Jesse began coughing, roughly. Birdsong placed her open palm on his forehead.

"He sure burnin'," she said with concern.

"Father, let's put ye in thy bed," John said.

"Do that, boy," Jesse said weakly.

John and Birdsong lifted Jesse, by the arms and legs, and carried him upstairs to bed. Thereafter, Birdsong nursed him through her native methods. Daily, she applied a hot muddy poltice mixture to his chest and filled him with herbal brews. She kept the fire hot and the window ajar so that he would shiver off the evil spell. The native approach to medical science worked. By springtime, Jesse came back around. He became able to take his meals downstairs, at the table, and walk the grounds.

Jesse's long illness threw management responsibilities onto John and the natives. Freebird, the oldest native on the plantation, had long turned his responsibilities over to Moose Hunter's son, Deerslayer. Jesse Junior's childhood playmate knew the job well. Deerslayer took John into his confidence. He taught him more than just the routine tasks of management. He spoke more candidly to the young man than he would speak to the father. Walking, one day, through a tobacco field, while inspecting the leaves, Deerslayer betrayed his long-held concern.

"Since Lord Culpepper became governor, natives trek west and south. Mostly olde people in Powhatan, anymore. Young ones there keep busy hunting, farming, cooking, and taking care of olde ones," Deerslayer began.

"Freebird talks about those who move west to the Great Valley. There's goode farmlande there," John remarked.

"Freebird wise olde man. He sees Powhatan tribe removing to Great Valley beyond hills," Deerslayer responded.

"Freebird says that he knows the future," John told Deerslayer.

"Freebird has way of reading gods' messages," Deerslayer responded.

"He really does know, then?" John asked him.

"Freebird knows what you must learn, John Boy. He sees young going west. He sees forests all along river filled with plantations. No natives anywhere, anymore," Deerslayer explained.

In the following days, Deerslayer's words bothered John. He sought to distract himself from them in work. They haunted him, nonetheless. Thus, when Deerslayer suggested he accompany him on a wagon ride to the coast, he readily agreed to go.

They entered the bustling town on a busy weekday afternoon and headed for the quay, straightaway. Just then, a slave auction got underway. John shifted on the seat, slightly, and swallowed his pride. He could not prevent himself from looking aside. Deerslayer caught him in the eye. John caught the look reluctantly, and turned back, with a sigh, to espy the future.

Proud Africans crowded the quay. Their own leaders led the way. Englishmen milled among them, without concern. The auctioneer called out a price for one. The African stood his ground, staring down. His sinuous muscles bulged, from his body, in a show of profound virility. Another African came to the fore and flexed his own muscles, presumptively.

"Twenty-five going once, going twice, going three times, sold for twenty-five," the stout captain shouted.

"These people are not chained," John observed.

"Why you think they should be chained, John Boy?" Deerslayer asked him.

"Slaves might escape unless they are chained," John answered.

"And, where will they go, thence?" Deerslayer asked.

John could think of no answer. His face went askew and his mouth opened in stuttered confusion. Deerslayer tied the horses, and walked onto the quay. John stiffly followed him. The wily native walked among the Africans, without reproach. Quickly, he caught their attention. Whence they approached a handsome family, that kept to themselves, they stopped. Deerslayer raised his arm, in native greeting, and spoke to them. They responded, but not without condescension. Undeterred, Deerslayer persisted.

"How," he insisted.

The family matron grinned at his simplicity, looked down, and laughed under her breath.

"You come," he demanded, as he motioned to them all to follow him.

John interjected, "Father will not allow slaves on the plantation."

Deerslayer paid no attention to him. Instead, he caught the auctioneer by the arm, shoved a leather bag into his chest, and gave him a menacing look. John stood by, awkwardly.

Deerslayer left John in charge as he went for the wagon. When he returned, he ushered the African family into it, and ordered John to unhitch the horses. John refused. Deerslayer unhitched the horses, shoved John onto the seat, climbed over him, and sat down on the driver's side.

"Wee were supposed to bring back indentures, Deerslayer," John insisted.

"See any indentures 'round this place, boy?" Deerslayer shot back, with one raised eyebrow.

"That ain't the point, Deerslayer," John shouted. "And don't call me boy," he added, as the wagon abruptly jolted, turned, and bolted out onto the dusty street.

CHAPTER X

THE FIRST FRENCH AND INDIAN WAR

John's son, John, Junior, sat in the simmering swampy wetness that follows a late Spring shower, with his luggage packed, awaiting the arrival of Deerslayer's son, Brave Eagle, from home. With his friends already gone, the boy remained alone, in anticipation. He gazed over, and out the window, at the muddy street below.

He looked back at the opposite wall, bare now of his school souvenirs. A sense of solitude quickly overwhelmed him within the once bustling building. Alone for the first time in ten months, he thought of home. All the knowledge he had accumulated since September rushed in on him. His deep contemplation continued, while the sun marked time in its slow descent down the barren wall. When it reached his lap, he caught Brave Eagle's gaze from the doorway, thither.

"Mister Junior," Brave Eagle startled him.

The young man suddenly broke out of his trance, shot up onto his sturdy legs, turned, and faced the native.

"Brave Eagle, what held you up?" he asked.

"We talk on road. No time now, sun high in sky," Brave Eagle retorted.

The two rode out of Williamsburg and well down the road, expediently.

Junior wondered aloud, "Well, what did make you late, anyway?"

"Brave Eagle travels with many eyes these days," the native explained.

"You mean the war between England and France?" Junior asked, perplexedly.

"I mean the war between England and France. It cause trouble for many of my people. Some side with French. Cannot make difference between friends and enemies. Now, no talking on trip, we keep sharp lookout. Any crazy brave tries to rob us, we shoot him," Brave Eagle commanded the young man.

Nonetheless, the long lonely journey upcountry, through thick forest, turned out to be uneventful. When the pair entered the neighborhood, Junior began to sit up more energetically in his saddle. Once upon the Muddy Creek Plantation, he felt a strange sensation. Nothing had changed in his ten-month absence. Yet, he did not see the place the same way. John and Genevieve greeted him gladly, in the midst of their daily routines. They noticed a change about him. His face betrayed a new awareness of his surroundings.

"Thy scholar returns," his father jested.

"Look at the young man before me. What a joy, Junior," his mother exclaimed as she embraced him.

The following morning, at the family's first breakfast together since September, they talked a great deal. Junior described the events of the school year, at William and Mary College, in enthusiastic detail. He ended his discourse with the hope that the weather would permit him to come home next Christmas rather than take the rector's meal with the boys who had to stay over.

"I hope we shan't get snow like that again, son," John apologized.

Junior changed the topic. "Brave Eagle would not say a word all the way home," he began.

"'Twas a tough task too, talking Brave Eagle into bringing you back, son. I nearly had to come for you meself," John told him.

"We encountered nothing but fellow travelers on the road, father. I had no fear," his boy boasted.

"Brave Eagle has ample reason for caution, son. War has natives unsettled. Some are trekking about looking for new land. Some trek west, across the mountains, to join up with the French. There's discord and distrust between natives and English, and even among natives themselves, these days. He could not have been too cautious," John explained.

John's concern proved to be precursory. A few weeks later, under cover of darkness, in the dead of a moonless night, two natives approached the kitchen door, apprehensively. One put his rough weathered hand on the latch and stealthily pushed the creaking door open. The door, however, creaked open with a squeaking sound. Upstairs, in his bed, John opened one and then the other eye. Was I dreaming, he wondered?

Meanwhile, the hungry natives silently transgressed through the open door looking about themselves, all the while, for any sign of detection. Once inside the kitchen, they began loading their sacks with cornmeal from the barrel. Upon loading the bags to their limits, they began making their hasty retreat. The two minds of one thought.

Without warning, Brave Eagle appeared, truculently, in the foreground of their sight. A scowl covered his face. Uncertainty overwhelmed the two natives, for one unfortunate instant. In the shadowy darkness, Brave Eagle could ascertain their tense movements against the white boards of the house. Precipitously, he anticipated the direction their escape would take. Mechanically, he raised the musket from his side and fired directly into a moving chest. The gun's explosion brought a wild commotion to the scene.

The wounded native lurched back, fell onto his knees, then slumped face forward to the ground. The fleeing one took a giant stride, as if to fly, and ran as fast as his legs would comply. With the awkward cornmeal sack throwing him off balance, he lurched headlong into the darkness ahead of him.

Brave Eagle spared not a moment. Leaving the wounded one for the others to find, he sprinted toward the stable, threw a halter on his horse, and flung himself on its bare back before the steed could gain its bearings. The startled horse threw his head up into the air, shook his thick neck back and forth, as if to say, no, while he whinnied. Then, in a flick, he bolted out of the stable with Brave Eagle reeling back from the thrust.

At the kitchen door, the wounded native struggled up onto his hands and knees, and then stood up onto his wobbly legs. He tried as hard as he could, just to take a step, but stumbled and fell forward. Warm blood filled his tightening throat and gagged him. He rolled onto his arm to push himself up. In a panic, so locked within him that on-lookers saw only delirium, he reached out his right hand, to the amazed persons that gathered around him, and let out a blood-spurting choke. Would anyone ever understand, he wondered, as the blood under his back seemed to begin sticking him to the damp earth.

Birdsong approached the scene last. She let out a shrill scream when she saw the last gasping spurt, of blood, burst forth from the dying man's quivering mouth. The scream echoed through the forest far beyond the house.

Her penetrating scream intensified growing panic in the heart of the one who fled. He rushed more fervently, through thick trees in darkness of night, all the while groping toward the riverbank for direction. As he ran, blindly, he held his head back so as not to bash his face into a tree. The heavy sack of cornmeal bobbing off his strong back became heavier and more awkward.

Birdsong's scream had struck him with surprise and distracted his intense eyes. In his wild desire to escape, he failed to hear the sound of hooves stomping through the underbrush, behind him. Worse for him, Brave Eagle had the tactical advantage in this forest. For, he knew well the path through the place. He had ridden it hundreds of times.

Brave Eagle appeared on the snorting stallion just behind him. He slowed his mount, with caution, for the high riverbank lay just to the right. The running brave had no time for a quick look back. Smelling the closeness, he took a wild glance to his right, studied the cliff for a moment, and jumped into the unknown with wild abandon.

Brave Eagle almost lost his mount, when he brought the horse about. Even before he regained his seat, he saw the reeling brave fall, with a blood-curdling call, onto a sheath of rock at river's edge. With a thud, the crushed head spun and splattered in an hundred directions.

Brave Eagle sat his mount with satisfaction. He gazed down at the spatter and contemplated the lifeless body below for a few long minutes. Satisfied with success, he turned away and rode back, triumphantly.

In the kitchen, he found everyone sitting at the table and standing about.

"Did you catch him, Brave Eagle?" Birdsong asked.

"No, he caught himself. No good comes to evil men," Brave Eagle stated wisely.

"The war brought this tragedy to us," John said with dismay.

"The war comes close to us, Master John," Brave Eagle stated flatly.

"I wonder just how close it comes. If need be, if the French Army marches across the mountains, then we must take security precautions," John said with trepidation.

"I take trip west to learn what I can," Brave Eagle offered.

"Good idea, Brave Eagle," John agreed.

"Start out in morning, John," Brave Eagle added.

"Yes, take your brother, Smart As Fox, and all the supplies you can carry," John said.

"No, travel alone into danger, be stealthy," Brave Eagle determined.

"Very well then. But, if you don't return in a few weeks time, then Smart As Fox will come after you, with backup," John demanded.

"Done then, I leave with sun," Brave Eagle answered.

These stalwart statements displaced concern with calm around the room. A few family members continued to sit around the table, recounting the night's events, until fatigue overcame them. A few hours before dawn, tranquility returned.

When dawn came, Brave Eagle readied his horse, while Birdsong packed his saddlebags with needed supplies. Alone together, husband and wife took breakfast reminiscently without a word. Then, with the hot sun on their backs, Birdsong watched forlornly as Brave Eagle rode off into the uncertain wild west.

Brave Eagle rode, day after long day, ever gradually up into the high country. During the night, he slept snugly rolled within a thick heavy wool blanket, on another thick wool blanket, on the cold ground, close to a cadencing fire. Upon reaching the high country, he meandered his winding way to the Great Valley beyond the most western boundary of the Powhatan Confederacy. From there, he rode on, with caution and trepidation, into a land in which he felt uneasy. Always, his eyes and ears keenly saw and heard everything around him.

He had heard how far he needed to travel.

"Five nights on ground, five days on horse, and I came to many wigwams," he remembered his father, Deerslayer's, story.

"They stood in a cluster at the edge of a rushing river. Smoke poured forth from their tops and moved with the downwind," his father had continued.

Yes, Brave Eagle remembered well. Thus, on the fifth day, now in the Great Valley, he entered the Valley Road. At the end of that day, he spotted them. A cluster of wigwams pitched at the edge of a rushing river. These were the same wigwams of his father's time. They comprised the same supply and trading post for natives, and explorers, who traversed the Great Valley Road.

Brave Eagle rode into the post warily, for the place seemed strangely quiet, without even children playing about. He came upon the first wigwam. It sat somewhat apart from the rest. An odd feeling overcame him. Suddenly, the deerskin-flap door smacked open, with a hard push from within. Out came a belligerent brave, bare-chested, with tomahack in hand.

"State your name and tribe, traveler!" the truculent brave demanded in his Monacan language.

"I am Brave Eagle of the Werowocomoco Powhatans," he stated proudly.

"State your business here," the brave demanded.

"Come to 'ave look for meself at French soldiers. Never know French soldiers, only English ones," he answered.

"Why French soldiers interest Powhatan?" the brave asked, suspiciously.

"Many come to join with French. See for meself," he explained.

"You will see then, traveling one," the brave told him.

The brave proffered an invitation into the wigwam. Brave Eagle accepted the offer. Inside, many natives sat about. The brave offered him a seat on a blanket and a pipe to smoke.

"Cannot be too cautious these days, Powhatan," the brave began.

"War makes for dangerous times," Brave Eagle agreed.

"Times not what they used to be. Many moving through without place to go," the brave complained.

"Your people been 'ere longtime," Brave Eagle stated bluntly.

"This trading post came to us as gift to my great-grandfather from his tribal chief. In his time, traders and explorers stop here. He knew them all. Now, our own kind mostly," the brave said with concern.

"The war puts many on road, yes?" Brave Eagle asked.

"People pass through here, all the time, begging for food and shelter. My family and I move elsewhere, ourselves, if this keeps up. We cannot make livelihood giving all away," the brave complained again.

"You are generous," Brave Eagle complimented him.

"My ancestors have done well here. We have learned the way of trade. We can use the skill elsewhere. Farther down the Great Valley Road perhaps. Now, let us smoke pipe and have the pleasure of life," the brave said, hopefully.

And so, Brave Eagle had reached his destination. With the majestic mountain sun setting over the peaks beyond the valley, the pipe going around and around, squaws chanting poetry of the ages, and children playing about, the natives remembered their past and pined for their future.

When the bright rays of early-morning sun lightened the wigwam within, everyone began to stir. The children giggled as they awoke their parents, playfully, with feathers under their noses. The squaws hauled cold mountain water, in wooden buckets, from a nearby stream and prepared cornbread covered with berry jam. The natives washed themselves briskly and ate heartily. Then, the brave and his cousins readied themselves for the ride.

"We take you to see for yourself, Brave Eagle," the brave said.

"How far will we ride?" Brave Eagle asked.

"Until sun is high in sky," the brave answered.

Thence, they rode for one-half day out of the valley and up into the mountains. Finally, the small band of natives arrived at their destination high on the side of a steep slope.

"From here we walk. Horses can be heard," the brave ordered.

Quietly, the riders dismounted, tied the reins to small trees in a close group, and made their way down and around a steep incline, behind the sure-footed leader. At a clearing, he stopped and pointed into the distant valley beyond.

"There, Brave Eagle," the brave directed him.

Sure enough, over the trees, Brave Eagle witnessed an awesome sight. In the far distance, he saw an encampment of French soldiers. He made out many horses tied in a row, several wagons, men milling among tan cotton tents, and the French flag rippling in the breeze. At the edge of the camp, several brown-skinned wigwams formed a cluster.

"French never so far east, before. Some of our people join up with them for gifts. English lose trust in us. Those few cause many innocent to suffer," the brave explained.

"Yes, I see for meself now what brings trouble to our people," Brave Eagle said.

"We will lose, for choosing two sides in war, no matter the winner," the native added.

"Many have lost their land already," Brave Eagle said.

"Iroquois, up North, side with French. We do better with English. These traitors should be killed. Some are trying. But French protect them," the brave added.

"I have seen enough. Now we go back," Brave Eagle said.

With hardness in their hearts, the band of natives retraced their route back to the Great Valley. In spite of the tiresome journey, on winding paths and steep slopes, they slept less soundly that night than on the previous one. An evil spirit discomforted them. The next morning, Brave Eagle bade farewell to his Monacan hosts and began his long ride back home.

Two weeks in the saddle exhausted him. Fatigue showed in his face and slow stride. He swaggered into the house, through the back door, and greeted an elated Birdsong. The two embraced long and hard. Before they wanted to release each other, the kitchen filled with family members eager for news.

"Well, what did you learn, Brave Eagle?" John began.

"I spied French soldiers encamped just beyond Great Valley," he began to recount.

"That's close to home," John worried.

"Yes, and war making big trouble for tribes. Many pitch wigwams at camp. They aid French. English Army retaliate," Brave Eagle related.

"At the get-go, the colonial front was meant merely to gain a bargaining chip over King Louie, in Europe. Yet, if parliament is allowed to continue with this imperialistic venture, then the French might invade the seaboard settlements themselves," John surmised.

"If French forces become stronger, then colonial front will no longer be imperialistic venture. It will become a matter of defense," Brave Eagle surmised.

"We cannot rely on the English Army in that event. We must prepare to protect the plantation, ourselves," John determined pragmatically.

The conflict between France and England, over North America, truly began with King William's War at the end of the seventeenth century. For, not until that time did English settlements meet French aspirations. In addition, not until that time did the French align natives with themselves against the English. Generally, the natives aligned themselves with the French in keeping with their own self-interests. For, on one hand, the natives witnessed the tremendous expansion of English settlements into their ancestral lands. While, on the other hand, the French hardly populated their few scattered settlements. England's governmental system, itself, encouraged colonization while that of France inhibited it. The former tended toward colonialism, while the latter tended toward feudalism. Eventually, England would gain the eastern half of the continent from France. However, that event remained for the next generation to see.

CHAPTER XI

THE FOURTH GENERATION

The Summer after the trespassing incident, John played host to his neighbors, in keeping with a habit developing all along the upper James River. The tradition spread upriver from the tidewater. One weekend a month, one neighborhood planter played host to the rest. This month, the social obligation fell on the Muddy Creek Plantation.

The place held the scene of a gleeful gathering. Neighbors swarmed through the house, onto the lawn, and beyond. In the dining room, sagacious men gambled intently at cards. In the front room, intuitive women talked about goings on in the neighborhood. Upstairs, girls chatted excitedly about boys, books, and clothes.

Behind the barns, serious boys boxed in leather gloves, showed off their marksmanship with muskets, and threw horseshoes. On the expansive front lawn, leisurely persons sat about the thick green grass talking, laughing, and flirting. Meanwhile, unruly children ran about the whole scene playing as hard as kids can play.

One end of the porch held tables, covered in white hemp cloths, on which lay silver service filled with mounds of food. Stacks of plates, bowls, crystal, and silver utensils lay in a pile at one side of the table. Guests used them for walk-around eating throughout the day.

Mammy and Missy stood merrily behind the tables serving food. Both wore exquisite clothing of shiny white silk, cotton aprons, and red sashes. At the other end of the porch, Moses served drinks over a marble-topped bar. He too wore white, but cotton, with a red silk vest that accented his manhood.

Horse racing led activities during the preponderance of the afternoon. The natives and coloreds set up a racecourse, of sorts, over a fallow field that lay beyond the stable and paddocks. Bright ribbons hung around consecutive trees, at the sides of the field, to give form to the makeshift track.

Young men and boys drew piecemeal to the racecourse, during the early-afternoon hours. They groomed their horses, to the point of pampering them, with confident words of praise and inspiration. As they boosted their confidence, with words and pats of assurance, they eyed the other horses with calculated measure.

At two o'clock, several small boys scampered to spread word that the races would soon begin. Slowly, guests began gravitating toward the racecourse from throughout the house and across the lawn. Within an hour, a shady shelter under large spreading trees, along the long side of the course, became filled with spectators. The milling crowd let out a roar of yells and applause when the jockeys began parading their horses in front of it. An announcer, holding a speaking-trumpet, stood to the side, on a wagon parked for the purpose.

"Number one, Achilles, ridden by John Hughes," the announcer yelled through the trumpet as loud as he could.

"Hurrah, hurrah," issued from the crowd.

Achilles had a well-known reputation throughout the neighborhood. Thus, many members of the crowd quickly queued up to the bet-taker at the wagon.

"Number two," the announcer continued, as the jockeys paraded their horses, in turn, in front of the crowd, to greater or lesser applause and enthusiasm. Meanwhile, the bet-taker's work mounted up on the back of the wagon.

Finally, attendants led each horse and jockey to the starting line. Two strong men held up the ends of the rope, as eager horses pushed against it, here and there.

"Hold that there mount now, Mista Mason, or youse gonna be out da race," a white-eyed Joel Mason yelled at a sixteen year-old rider, straddling a rearing mount, as he, himself, held tightly to one end of the taut rope.

Joel's jumbled voice rang in Junior's ear when Achilles bolted. A moment later, he found himself in a rushing mad jam of unruly wildness. At the get-go, the horses on both sides hemmed him into a narrow path. He sat up on his thighs, as high as he could, to give Achilles all the forward thrust possible. The horse felt his rider's weight shift from his back to his writhing withers. Unconstrained, he freed himself from the pack.

Achilles charged forward like a mad monster. When a thick glob of saliva came streaming back, with a splat, on his face, from the snorting mouth, Junior momentarily lost his balance. Yet, horse and rider made the first turn heading toward the inside of the pack. As Achilles made the turn, around stacked bales of hay, he gained speed. Then, with the grunting horse galloping down the far side of the track, the rider threw control to the wind.

By the time Achilles approached the second turn, the other horses gained on him. He spent himself on the long stretch, Junior thought, as he held on for the ride. His unsteady seat made no difference, for the sight and sound of the crowd, now ahead of him, gave Achilles a second breath.

Junior regained the balance he had lost in the last turn. Confidence transmitted itself from rider to horse. Assured of their success, they came out of the turn and drove for the bright-red ribbon ahead. Junior felt time freeze, then and there. Yet, somehow it passed in a flash.

Achilles snapped the red ribbon in two, and Junior knew now was the time to make the horse know his master. He leaned back, as far as possible, and pulled tightly on the reins. At first, Achilles would have none of it. Junior leaned and pulled him to the left. Achilles threw back his huge head, buckled down his ears madly, and hissed violently. Then, stomping and shaking, he relented. The great beast bounced back toward the finish line, unforgivingly.

A thick throng of well-wishers converged, en masse, on horse and rider. Joel Mason grabbed the reins firmly under the horse's mouth and held down his head as best he could. Achilles displeasure grew, dangerously. The crowd hesitated, stood back reluctantly, and then surged forward again.

"Hoe down there now, hoe down," Joel attempted to soothe him.

"You won!" a thrilled Eddie Mason shouted.

"Hip hip hurrah, hip hip hurrah," the excited throng rang out in unison, as Junior sat smiling jubilantly from atop of the world.

Achilles began smiling, himself, as a strong teenage boy took hold of the reins from Joel.

"Come on down from there now, Mista John," Joel commanded as he grabbed his leg.

"Easy now Mista Achillus," Joel spoke soothingly into the horse's face.

"Come on Junior Boy, come on down now," Joel repeated.

Junior placed the weight of his left foot in the stirrup, and slung his right one up and over the sweating horse. Before he reached the ground, however, a mass of reaching arms pulled him in. They grabbed him firmly and held him up with shoves and bounces. Thence, they paraded him, boisterously, through the crowd, to cheers of "the winner, the winner" all around.

When he gained his feet, he shoved his way through the unrelenting throng of ecstatic neighbors getting slapped and shaken all the while. Just as he broke out of it, four young men grabbed him firmly and shoved him, once again, into the air with shouts of "hurrah." Again, he got roughed up.

Victory elated him. He filled with pride for Achilles. The great stallion stood at the top of the oldest bloodline in the neighborhood. He attracted admiration from everyone, and today he proved his worth.

Gladly free, Junior took a place among the enthusiastic crowd and watched the rest of the races, closely. Achilles' blood line ran through several neighborhood horses. These horses comprised the favorites in each race. Achilles' genes proved their worth. The breeding practices of the last several years produced the best compositions of disposition, durability, strength, and speed. The bloodline dominated the day.

After the final race, all of the mud-splattered sweaty jockeys swam and washed in the Muddy Creek. Fresh clothes awaited them at the stable. Clean-smelling and handsomely dressed, Junior found his first cousin, Mary, chatting with several girls on the front lawn. In his enthusiasm, he ignored Moses' admonition and poured out two glasses of sweet-smelling whiskey punch from the big silver bowl.

"Punch for my lady," John Boy said, with an air of jest, as he proffered the heavy glass into Mary's white-gloved hand.

"Oh, thank you brave sir," Mary returned the undertone of jest. She sensed his boosted confidence.

In his boldness, he continued the game. "Miss Mary Hughes, you know that our grandfathers possessed the same surname," he began.

"Of course, brave sir, but one was French and the other English," she reminded him.

"The one English and Welsh. Nonetheless, they must have been descended from the same man, long ago, because they had the same name," he reasoned.

"That might be true, John Boy, but their mutual ancestor would have lived very very long ago. Your paternal great-grandfather came from England and mine from France," she jibed him.

"'Tis true enough, my lady. Nonetheless, my original English ancestor harked from Normandie six hundred-fifty years ago. Captain Etienne Hughes, a valiant knight was he, rode in King William's Army, during the victorious invasion of Anglelande, in 1066. Thus, my dear lady, he too was French," he jibed back.

"A Norman, sir, is not a Frenchman," she retorted gleefully.

"The French and Normans are one today," he insisted.

"Ah yes, but France and Normandie were two countries then," she reasoned.

"Ugh, I give up. You are too savvy for me, dear lady," he responded with a mock bow to the giggles of the young women present. Shall we promenade on it, then?" he asked.

"It would be a pleasure and an honour, brave sir," she answered.

Junior led Mary through a spirited and admiring crowd to a secluded place, in the adjacent woods, overlooking the river. Mary broke free from his hand, sat down against a tree trunk, and rolled her eyes in unpretended exasperation.

"Honestly John Boy, what has your mind preoccupied today?" Mary queried him.

Junior bent over and looked slightly mockingly into her face.

"Us, my dear. I'm thinking that we are made for each other," he grinned again.

Junior's attempt at seriousness struck Mary humorously. She let out a loose long laugh.

"With all these boys in the neighborhood anymore, why do we belong together dear cousin?" she asked.

"We belong together because the Frenchman was our mutual grandfather," he answered proudly.

Mary bowed her head, imperceptibly.

"You know that we do not call grandfather the Frenchman, at our house," she whispered.

"I know, 'tis only in jest," he soothed her.

After a long pause, she spoke softly. "My father says the same."

"What is that, I cannot hear you?" he asked.

"My father says the same words as you," she answered.

"Do you agree with him?" he asked hesitantly.

"Yes, I love you both," she said.

Junior stood up, jubilantly.

"Great, then I shall ask him for his approval," he yelled.

It pleased Robert more than Mary knew to give the marriage his approval. First my sister, Genevieve, married

John, he thought. Now my daughter will marry John's son. Another union with the Muddy Creek Plantation bodes well for our shared future, he believed. John and he had been hoping for this end. Upon hearing the news, a sad reflection, nonetheless, interrupted John's happiness.

For, the news reminded him of his parent's last requests. Jesse Junior and Bonnie had demanded that their grandson marry his first cousin. When they died, a year apart, at the turn of the century, John promised to pursue the marriage. John Junior, however, knew his own fate. He pursued Mary, himself, with a single mind. John's blood swelled, at once, with sadness for his lost parents and pride for his suddenly grown son.

Notwithstanding that melancholy memory, he eventually became exuberant. Robert and John spared nothing for the wedding. In keeping with tradition, they chose the bride's plantation for the reception. It turned into the grandest one upriver planters had ever known.

Planter families, natives, and coloreds jammed the house and lawn. Merry talk and laughter filled the place with memories. The crowd grew so large that it became necessary to keep walkways open with porters and hemp ropes tied to stanchions.

Several guests sent gifts ahead of the reception. The gifts included charcoal; hogs; sauce; flour; butter; spices; cheese; potatoes; peas; whiskey; wine; and various flavors of fruit brandy. Yet others, sent their slaves, the day before, to aid in preparations. The two plantations combined could not supply enough ice to last out the day. More had to be hauled in from the closest neighbors.

That day, the humid Summer heat grew so intense that the river seemed to stop flowing. The air seemed to stop blowing and the trees to standstill. Yet, like the fleeting shadows glimmering off the flowing river, beyond the tree-lined bank, time moved on.

Far up the James River, plantations now stood, where seemingly impregnable wilderness once awed foresters. The olde pathway upriver from the coast, exhaustedly trodden for an hundred years, by courageous pioneers, now diverged off the river in places, as the shoreline became bordered with plantations.

Late-comers had to plant themselves down off the river. They built new roads leading to it. Natives in hut and wigwam settlements took down their dwellings and removed to the West. Those natives who lived neither on plantations nor in colonial villages saw the end of their simple way of life. The merry crowd on the lawn that wedding day, above the river, in front of a big house, in the midst of the once solid wilderness, marked a new beginning both for the young couple and the land they loved.

Horseback riders had become commonplace in the neighborhood. Many of them rode to and from a trading settlement getting established, just below the falls, nearby olde Powhatan village. The town of Richmond would grow from that landing. The presence of a landing eased life, somewhat, for planters upriver from it. Thereby, they no longer needed to go all the way downriver to the new capitol, Williamsburg, for supplies.

Moreover, the construction of tobacco warehouses, at the docks of the landing, enabled planters to store their tobacco and then transship their combined crops to the coast on large barges. Thereby, planters divided their transportation costs, among themselves, many times over. As a result, they took a higher price at the coast for the larger amount of crop. Subsequently, tobacco profits rose to a level closer to tidewater planters.

These new methods, of transportation and marketing, required collusion among neighborhood planters. The methods required collusion to ensure uniformity in the quality of crop for a single sale. Planters compared seeds and fertilizer for constancy. Also, they compared suckering, topping, harvesting, curing, and fallowing methods. In addition, planting and harvesting needed to take place in unison.

Thus, plantations throughout the neighborhood joined in a loose confederation, or corporation, of sorts. In such a gentlemans' agreement, no legal authority enforced production and marketing rules. Nevertheless, trust held sway. A man's honor assured that trust. The various planters' self-interests ensured uniformity of the neighborhood crop. Therefore, neither loneliness in the fresh countryside, nor the desire to combine plantations through marriage, sufficed in themselves as reasons to create a neighborhood of interdependent families.

As both his father, John, and his father-in-law, Robert, grew old, Junior's responsibilities grew accordingly. Mary and he inherited their parent's lives even while the former yet lived. In a country, such as Virginia, experiencing burgeoning prosperity, it is little wonder that he turned from carefree young man to plantation manager, eagerly. Prosperity begets enthusiasm. Moreover, the Muddy Creek Plantation led neighboring ones in prestige and success. It held the position as the oldest and most prosperous plantation on the upper James River.

Early most weekday mornings, John Junior passed from the dining room to the plantation office. In so doing, he traced the footsteps of his forebears. He worked at the same olde wooden desk, containing numerous drawers and compartments meant for order and safekeeping, at which Jesse Senior had managed his own humble homestead. During the first few years of Junior's newfound interest, his father advised him continually. John gave him expert advice about the plantation that he had taken charge of from his own father. John advised his son as to how he had enlarged crop production, herds, crafts, labour, and facilities.

Indeed, John multiplied output during his lifetime. The garden itself produced more, annually, than the tobacco crops Jesse Senior had grown a century earlier. Cropland now sat on innumerable acres once filled with dense forest. Old tobacco and grain fields became pasturage for a proliferating herd of livestock and horses. The barn and stable, that appeared capacious to Jesse Junior after he enlarged them in the forties, proved too small, a few times, and thus stood at multiples of their original sizes. More barns had gone up. At the bottom of the riverbank, the dock had grown large enough to accommodate large barges. Atop the Muddy Creek, adjacent to the natives' quarters, sat a row of two-story cabins that comprised new homes for the first generations of Africans on the plantation.

Junior became manager of a business that neared its production capacity. Cropland neared the limit of not only the plantation's capacity, but the land's ability to produce high quality crops. That is to say, fields pushed against the plantation's borders, and tobacco depleted the soil. To maintain the soil, fields had to lay fallow for more than one season. Plus, fallow fields took clover and alfalfa crops. Thereby, greater tobacco production resulted in larger herds of livestock.

Thus, Junior eventually turned the management expertise, that his father taught him, to efficiencies of production, as opposed to expansion of production. He studied and tested the latest techniques of crop production, animal husbandry, shipping, marketing, and labour management. Consequently, through his lifetime he raised profits considerably.

And, the plantation's largesse grew along with the growth of John Junior's family. Mary gave birth to a few children, through the course of many years. The couple gave them ancestral names. Two to survive were James and John.

CHAPTER XII

MOUNTAIN EXPLORERS

The year, 1715, marked a respite in hostilities between France and England. In France, King Louis XV succeeded Louis XIV. Like his great-grandfather, the boy was king at five years of age. Again, the Catholic Church and ministers managed the government in the king's name. In England, George I succeeded his second cousin, Queen Anne. Here, ministers and parliament managed the government in the king's name.

France had the foremost army in the world. England had a navy equal in name. Lately, in war, England had defeated both France and Scotland. After the latter victory, a new currency established the British Trade Union. Now, the government told the people to see themselves, not as English men and women any longer, but as Britons.

In North America, the British had pushed the French out of Acadia, and France all but gave up on taking the English seaboard colonies. French soldiers and their savage allies moved westward on the frontier. And, natives in those colonies, gradually began removing west into the mountains and beyond.

Frontier families slowly began sleeping soundly. These days, grandparents recounted gruesome stories about savages with bloody tomahawks in the night. Meanwhile, the western wilderness drew upriver men and boys beyond their homes. The allure of the unknown held inspiration for the old and adventure for the young. Exploration became all the rage.

Dirt trails that wound through woodlands were widened and packed higher with more dirt. Now, they allowed wagons to pass. More and more, pioneers traveled those hard dirt roads to the landing of Richmond. Although small, it sat at the center of upcountry life. There, on weekends, crowds filled the inn and tavern. Upcountry patrons drank, smoked, ate, and talked about politics, history, business, and sports. In this open frontier, equality of opportunity established itself firmly.

Largely, planters' sons became planters. By the tradition of primogeniture, the oldest brothers inherited their boyhood homes. Many younger brothers remained at home. So, large families lived in big but crowded houses. Others, bought parcels of wilderness land to the west. Or, they traded in lumber, hardware, supplies, and such at plantation stores or in villages. Some pursued professions.

Usually, fathers, grandfather's, uncles, and great-uncles underwrote mortgages that were paid back in tobacco. No central bank set interest rates, arbitrarily. Rather, they rose and fell, in accordance with natural supply and demand, for loans. Only land and slaves were taxed.

In fact, planters were more than willing to pay taxes. For, the man who paid the most tax wielded the preponderance of economic, political, and social influence. A planter's neighborhood brought together everyone who owed someone else a favor. Everyone was beholden to someone and everyone had someone beholden to them.

The neighborhood placed high standards on leading planters. Utmost, neighbors held them to their honor. A man's honor held more value than his land. His word was his contract. They expected him to serve as justice of the peace to enforce laws, with or without the assistance of sheriffs. Neighbors expected his sons to do the same. Usually, a planter's peers offered him the title, vestryman. Anglican Church vestries, spread into upcountry neighborhoods. Originally, back in England, vestrymen maintained vestries. Virginian planters, however, took on larger responsibilities.

These responsibilities included not only vestries but making your front room the local government office, or building a courthouse at a nearby crossroads; besides building and maintaining roads, docks, and post offices. Neighbors from near and far knocked on the front door and asked for loans. The best sort of planters would actually hire tradesmen more during a recession, just to create employment among neighbors having hard times.

Prosperous planters paid not only the preponderance of taxes. In addition, they had to pay for votes. During election week, voters ate, drank, and smoked at churches or polling places. They consumed wagons full of farm products including beef; pork; fowl; flour; oil; butter; cheese; milk; vegetables; fruits; whiskey; tobacco; and smoking weed. Much went home with many.

During Virginia's first few decades, vestrymen were elected popularly. After restoration of the Staurts, with the accession of King Charles II, back in 1660, they began choosing themselves from among themselves. Virginia had become too populated, with disinterested men, for democratic election to assure that the best man would win.

Paradoxically, at that time, the oligarchy of local planters lost control of parish management functions. Thereafter, decisions tended to get made, not among themselves at the various parishes, but in the capitol, Williamsburg. Power thus tended toward one man, George Hamilton Douglas, the Earl of Orkney, who followed Lord Howard as governor of the Virginia Colony in 1697. He remained governor until 1737. Not once did he ever step foot on Virginia soil.

From the seventeen-twenties to fifties, the Great Valley within the western mountains witnessed the movement of wagon trains down its broad path. The Treaty of 1713, that ended the First French and Indian War, removed large numbers of Scotsmen from the southern Scottish borderlandes. Under terms of the treaty, England made new baronies on the land for those who had supported the wars with Scotland. These displaced colonists landed at Philadelphia and Baltimore, mainly.

The original settlers comprised those Scotsmen who had left Scotland, for Ireland, back when the wars began a generation earlier. Since they first tried to settle in Ireland, and then moved on to America, they became known as the Scots-Irish. However, they were Scotsmen.

Those who came directly from Scotland, later, became known as Scots-Irish too. The misnomer notwithstanding, Scots-Irish land agents, sold Scotsmen homesteads and farms in the wilderness. Thus, they settled the foothills and mountains, from their northern to southern limits. That is to say, from Pennsylvania to Alabama.

In the seventeen-thirties, the western side of the Great Valley remained wholly unsettled. Surveying parties did not always return without death to report. Savages yet attacked camps, unprovoked. Bears and rivers got others. A few, adventurous, frontier planters' sons rode horses into the mountains, during Summer, to prove their mettle. Native guides led them through the fearsome forests. They canoed on rough cold rivers. However, no boy in the class of 1730 had yet ventured as far as the Great Valley and the high slopes beyond.

The fifth generation on the Muddy Creek Plantation never waited for a native from home to come fetch them from school in May. They sent their trunks on a supply wagon and rode their horses back. There had not been a savage attack east of the mountains in over a generation.

Happily out of school, seven upcountry boys started out from college on June first that year. They reached Richmond on just the second day of hard riding. There, they rested the horses and drank ale for three days. By the third day, they had built up enough courage to plan a mountain exploration. Thereby, they agreed to meet at the Muddy Creek in two weeks.

At the plantation, rolling fields of freshly turned dark-brown soil stood out, in contrast, under thousands of light-green tobacco plants, shades of clover, alfalfa, and golden grain. The natives and slaves took a break after planting and slowed down in June. They were not to be seen this steamy morning.

John Junior's first-born, James, awoke and thought to seek out Brave Eagle at his cabin. Instead, he found him downstairs, on the front porch, surrounded by kids, telling a story. They sat tightly listening to his vivid recollection of the time, many years ago, that he rode to the trading post, in the valley over the mountains, and espied the French Army camp with wigwams.

When Brave Eagle finished the story, the kids fled the scary scene, and James took the empty chair next to him.

"Brave Eagle, my friends and I are thinkin' 'bout an exploration," he cautiously began.

"Dangerous place, western Virginia," Brave Eagle flatly stated.

"We'll tame the place," he assured him.

Moses walked out the door and laid a tray on the table. "Youse goin' to get killed messin' 'round out there, boy," he warned loudly.

Junior, reading in the front room, heard the word western through the window. He put down his book, walked out the door, and saw an empty seat. The screen door slammed shut behind him. A short breeze blew. Brave Eagle's tan chest shivered, slightly. Moses' red tie tangled in the air. Rain clouds covered the sun.

Over at the stable, twelve plantation boys played. They saw the men on the porch, and came running back in a rush, shouting. They climbed the steps and packed onto the big brick porch.

Junior sat there thinking about the hurricane scene in Daniel Defoe's *Robinson Crusoe*.

"Y'all talkin' 'bout the West?" he asked.

James threw his right ankle over his left knee, to show his confidence.

"West dangerous place," Brave Eagle flatly stated.

"Expeditions go into the mountains to make maps for land agents," James had heard.

"Aye, the wanderlust has got hold of all Englishmen, like Robinson Crusoe," Junior joked, with a grin.

"What do you think of an exploration, dad?" James asked squarely.

"Well, son, it would be an exciting adventure allright," Junior thought out loud, as he cautiously turned his sight upriver.

Moses banged down the big silver coffee pot, on purpose.

"Besides horses and canoes, an exploration needs a few natives. They know their way around," Junior added.

"My sons, Powhatan Ted and brother, Ed, go," Brave Eagle suggested flatly.

Junior continued, "Let's ride to Richmond tomorrow. There's a cartographer you should meet and talk with. He has unfinished maps o' the mountains. He'd likely lend them to you as guides. You'd be doin' a deed for your country by fillin' in the maps."

"I'll do it, sir," James stated with certainty.

"Now hold your horses, son. There's more to it than glory. There's also honor. There's a deed for the plantation you could do, too. I'll draw copies o' the maps before you leave. Whilst explorin', fill in both sets o' maps. One set for the cartographer, the other for the plantation," Junior explained.

"Why not make the plantation set from the filled-in copy when we get back?" James wondered.

"The plantation maps need to include more detail. I've been thinkin' long 'bout the high price o' salt in the colonies," Junior began to answer his son.

"Natives say, so much salt in mountains they take bath in it," Brave Eagle stated knowingly.

"Whensoever you think you've come across main deposits o' salt in the earth, mark an S at that point on our maps," Junior explained further.

"I'll do that too, dad," James was glad to answer.

The boys who were to make up the exploration party lived all over the upcountry. Within two weeks, they all gathered at the plantation. The place hosted a rowdy group. During the days, they prepared their gear, sat around the dining room table making plans, and swam, for hours, in the creek. In the evenings, they drank whiskey or wine, smoked tobacco and weeds, played at cards, and ended the nights singing their school songs.

They roistered about, without reserve. Their enthusiasm spread. On the morning of departure, the whole plantation rose at dawn to bade the boys off. The back lawn overflowed. Those who could not get near enough to say something cheered loud as the horses pulled out. All of the kids kept standing there, on the back lawn, waving until the line of horses got out of shouting distance.

As the horsemen shrank into smaller figures, a theretofore restrained sense fell over all. In the quiet left behind, chirping birds seemed to sing in an unreal world. Only the sound of nature remained. No one knew of anyone, with the exception of natives, who had gone so far into the mountains. A hard premonition sneaked in.

The boys' jocularity diminished through long days and seemingly short nights of alternate riding and camping. Whenafter they crossed the broad valley and entered the rugged mountains, on their western slopes, they came face to face with the seriousness of their exploit. Narrow mountain trails proved tedious and tiresome paths for horses. The going slowed down to a near standstill, at times. Worse, they lost their way on occasion. The maps veered off scale more and less, here and there.

After days of tedious traveling, the group came upon a native village on the banks of a rapidly flowing mountain river.

"Me, Cherokee Charles. State your name," a stern native stopped them.

Powhatan Ted knew that French soldiers had made these natives deeply suspicious of English persons.

"Powhatan Ted and English boys. We explore," the native guide sternly shot back.

The Powhatan got respect from the local native. He invited the party into his village. Powhatan Ted offered the village chief a big bag of cornmeal flour.

The rest of that day, the boys joined braves, who sat on the ground around a big wigwam, smoking weeds and drinking whiskey. After a few hours of pleasant talk, with everyone getting along well, the natives offered the boys boiled mushroom juice. Just a quarter mug-full of this potent drink is all it took to immobilize them with awe.

Notwithstanding their inability to get up, they did not want to stand. They were enjoying acute sensations of spirit, smell, and sight. They sensed themselves and surroundings more perceptively than ever before. They smelled the thinness of the high mountain air. They saw the boldness of nature there.

Powhatan Ted and his brother, Powhatan Ed, had drunk boiled mushroom juice on more than one occasion. Thus, they wisely abstained, so as to keep an eye on the boys.

"Drinking whiskey, mushroom juice, and smoking weeds, better you boys stay in wigwam. Might walk off cliff. Who know what," Powhatan Ted said as he plopped down in front of the wigwam door.

"But, I have to pee," Wood objected.

"You pee next to wigwam, where I keep eye on you," he demanded.

At that, everyone laughed. They knew the wise native was right. The boys never went out that night.

Powhatan Ted awoke with the first light of dawn. After eating, he gained good advice from village natives. Besides giving advice, they agreed to keep the horses while the explorers went on in canoes. Bravely confident, the explorers shoved off in the cold river.

The sturdy dugouts took hard smashes and pounds in rough water. Yet, the eager young rowers did not envision what lay downriver. This uncharted and unnamed body of water was wild in comparison to the rivers they knew. As forbidding as the rapids in the James could be, they did not compare to this rush-and-tumble flow. Powhatan Ted's circumspectness continued to humor the party. Nonetheless, the caution of ages lurked underneath prudence.

At first, the ride thrilled them. Gradually, the dugouts became difficult. Then, for a long stretch, the current took them easily, before big rocks forced them to portage. They hiked, through thick brush, with the heavy gear-laden canoes held up over their heads. Their arms became stiff and tired before their legs felt the pain of fatigue. They made slow progress, at best, but they trekked on with tendentious purpose.

James kept a vigilant lookout for any sign of salt. At several intervals, he thought that he saw telltale signs of the mineral. He could not be sure where they were on the maps. At sundown, the explorers made camp. James removed the maps from the satchel and filled in both sets as well as possible. He had seen evidence of salt that day. He marked S's, to denote them, thus attesting to his discoveries on an atlas.

In the morning, the explorers trekked on through the winding maze of mountain trails. The early sun added to the directional aid of the compasses. After only a few hours of hiking, they were able to take to the water again.

As the easy-flowing river slid by beneath the canoes, the party became relaxed and jocund. Often, the swift current enabled them to pull their oars, sit back, and notice the slick steep canyon walls, on both sides, come closer, then farther away, as the swirling flow took them where it would.

They welcomed respites. Then, unexpectedly, at a whirlpool, water began pulling the canoes down. The boys rowed back-handed. The rocking and dipping, bow to stern, port to starboard, kept tossing them off balance. Then, they heard a heavy roar.

The canyon walls stood so high that the explorers saw no way out but downstream. They rushed faster, with the river dragging them closer to the roar. The canoes lunged and plunged even deeper. The boys fought furiously back with oars. A flat hard canyon wall loomed straightaway. The canoes rushed up to it. Then, just before crashing, the canyon turned slightly, but abruptly, toward yet another direction, and they lurched away.

Wood yelled from the front boat, "That's nothin' boys, look out ahead."

A bit farther on, the canyon turned crooked and the water looked really rough.

"'Ere we go again," Meriwether shouted out.

"Keep your eyes wide-open," Rogers added, as loud as he could.

"Looks good and rough ahead," the front rower shouted again, as the canoes came abruptly upon rapids. But, no one could hear him against the deafening roar.

The boys held tightly to their oars. They put all their might into steering the canoes down the middle of the awesome rush. Water roiled, over and over, inside the canoes. Blankets of spray blinded them. In no time, the canoes reached the steepest point in the falls. Each bow plunged hard, smacked the rock bed below with a dangerous thud, and shook the canoe. Then, the stern shot up into the air, behind, with a wrenching twist.

Suddenly, James felt free in the air, when flung from his seat, into the foam and glare. Clear cold blue water muted the roaring and shouting above him. He kicked, shot up quickly, and swam vigorously for the capsized canoe. His efforts mattered not, for the boat reeled away from his reach, like a mere reed, in the rough water. Dauntless, he swam even more rigorously for the nearest shore.

The shoreline constantly passed him by. Alarmed, he kicked as hard as he could. Yet, he made no progress, no matter how hard he tried. The mighty current just kept pulling him along. He decided to give in and drift with it, when the massive water yanked him into an unexpected rush of blue cold.

He felt a shiver to his very bones. No one has ever out swam me, he thought. Nonetheless, he struggled just to keep his head above water. Quickly, his breaths became gasps for air. Water rushed everywhere. Then, he could not stop thinking about sinking, until he simply stopped thinking.

Two hours later, the others got struck sick by the sight of James' bloody body lodged betwixt two immutable rocks. Wood and Merriwether grabbed each of his legs and dragged him out of the water. Powhatan Ted bent over him. A lone tear dropped down from his eye. He looked up, at the sky, and let out a terrifying cry.

"No," Wood shouted.

"James is dead," Merriwether moaned in disbelief.

Everyone felt stiff, like the night they drank mushroom juice. Shock drowned out the river's roar and fixated them on the stunning sight, lying there in the shining rocks. Mason busted out crying. He made everyone feel worse.

"Damn, shut up!" Rogers yelled. "We don't need ya ballin' 'bout it," he yelled again.

Powhatan Ed stepped up.

"We 'ave his body," he said, as he knelt down and took the bloody bruised head in his hands.

"It'll not be the same without Jim," Merriwether mumbled.

"We go back now, evil spirit up 'ere," Powhatan Ed demanded.

And so, the exploration ended on that sorry note. Jim's friends actually enjoyed carrying his body back. That Summer, the young explorer became famous in his country. When news of the fateful exploration reached the map maker in Richmond, he bent over the unnamed river and etched in James' surname after the hero it claimed. The Hughes River would forever proclaim his fame.

CHAPTER XIII

BOUNTY HUNTERS

Back on the Muddy Creek Plantation life went on, though it would never be the same life that once lived there. For, when an old person dies, everyone becomes sad, but not often surprised. However, when a young person dies, they deny it. John Senior, and Genevieve, took the news of their grandson's death hard, but courageously. They each lived on, yet. With John Junior and Mary, they placed their hopes on the next son.

For several months, Junior and the men, both native and colored, lost direction. They had been grooming Jim to be master one day. They had imparted the best parts of themselves to him. When he went away, he took a piece of them with him.

The native and colored women tended to Genevieve and Mary, loyally. The strength of their bonds grew stronger as the women grew older. For, loyalty grows stronger with age. The native women wore their lucky feathers and the coloreds turbans, of various colors, during births and deaths. The mistress, along with her niece and daughter-in-law, both, had heavy wooden double beds in their rooms that accommodated two women at such times. Sometimes three shared sleep in them. Hardwood bonds of emotion kept them close. The women followed directions from no one except Genevieve and Mary. Deep in their hearts, each one felt loyal, in her own way.

As a habit, at each birth and death, the natives and coloreds, throughout the plantation, sang and clapped, with some intermittent breaking into dance. The singing would go on for days. With Jim's sudden death, however, the place stayed unusually quiet.

Jim's younger brother, John, felt the loss most intensely. That Summer, unlike any other, fun ended before the hot days, themselves. Sullenness lasted until Spring.

During Winter, like most neighborhood boys, he sat fidgetingly on hard seats, at wooden school desks, in the book-filled library, for several weekdays at a time, whenever men could be found to tutor the kids, that is. Eventually, the time for college came. As a rule, England had the best schools. England's schools, however, set strict standards and took several weeks sailing. Thus, the sons of the great, and not so great, from both tidewater and upcountry, went to college in Williamsburg.

John Boy, on his first trip to college, rode a horse named Henry Tudor II. No one, of course, called him that. Everyone called him, Henry. The boy sat happily in the saddle for one, two, three, and then six days, slowly taking in a view of a Virginia he never knew. He spent six sleepy nights at as many inns.

As he approached the town, a sixth sense struck him. The rolling hills of the upcountry had given way to marshland. Yet, the sensitive teenager sensed a more profound difference than that in geography. Once he got into town, he walked wonderingly around the college, all afternoon, taking in the whole campus. He encountered many older boys and sensed their scorn for fourth-class boys. He felt as if he were in another country.

He felt such strong satisfaction to have finally gotten where he wanted to be, after having waited for so long, that autism overwhelmed him. Everywhere, he saw what the college must have been in his father's time. Whilst he walked about campus, he looked at buildings as, in his imagination; his dad would have seen them a few decades earlier. His trance-like state seemed to last for a whole long hot afternoon. Whence, in front of the statue of King William, at college center, a rude jolt bolted him back into his own generation.

"Hey, country boy, get a move on," some first-year boys prodded him.

All fourth-year boys resented fowl treatment. Many upperclassmen, however, seemed to really enjoy bullying them. After upperclassmen made them drill hard all through September, the fourth-year boys got bold about it.

"Damn, how did they like it when they were us?" John Boy asked one of his fellow plebes.

"Huh, I'd sure like to know, meself. The Bonnie Prince Charlies think this is their empire," he answered.

"Aye, and we're the slaves," shouted another.

At this, uproar ensued among the plebes. The bullying thus turned into a joke, of sorts. Nonetheless, serious politics lay hidden underneath that joke.

It took John Boy some getting used to. In effect, the tidewater stood as a country apart from his own. Bacon's Rebellion, back in 1676, no longer meant much here, even though his grandfather referred to it as the greatest event in Virginia's history. Moreover, the term "Cavalier" commanded respect, not contempt, in this country.

Paradoxically, Cavalier's sons and grandsons had taken up the cause, itself. But, where Bacon rebelled against slavery, mainly, Cavaliers condemned taxation. Bacon, and his fellow planters, rebelled against the British Africa Company's monopoly in shipping that crowded out indentured labourers and brought slaves, instead. Cavaliers condemned the British Parliament for excessive taxes. Notwithstanding that difference, like Bacon, they demanded self-government so as to legislate against monopolies, in slavery and taxes respectively. Cavalier boys went so far as to hang colonial flags in their dorm room windows, as opposed to British flags, to show allegiance to the cause of liberty.

In fact, the cause of '76 had returned, back in 1712, when the Virginia House of Burgesses had dared to fight the postage tax with efficacious arguments. The Whig Party majority in parliament, and the king, laid a tax on the colonies to help fund the, largely, European wars against France and Spain, that in North America, however, were fought for wilderness land. The burgesses gloriously forced Governor Spotswood to exempt merchant's letters from the postage tax. Later, in 1732, the burgesses stopped parliament from raising the import tariff on tobacco smokers in England. Indeed, Cavalier boys acted as if they had begun the cause themselves, notwithstanding, that their forefathers, back in England, had been the king's men once.

Actually, the death of England's last Cavalier has a date. In 1746, during a British war with France and Spain, over colonial trade, the fourth generation Charles Stuart; a Scottish duke and great-great-grandson of the first Cavalier, King James I, after whom olde burned-down Jamestowne was named; led an army into Edinburgh, Scotland. He seemed to have seized Scotland from England with popular support. Then, he marched into England where his support sank.

King George II's son, the Duke of Cumberland, would not allow an independent Scotland. Ferociously, he assaulted the Staurt Army with the force of English industry at arms. So barbarous was he that the duke became known as the "Butcher." Thereafter, the word "Cavalier" fell from use, in England.

In North America, during the 1740's, King George's War took up where Queen Anne and King William's Wars had left off. That is, trying to wrest land from France. Britain's population was booming out of proportion to land and houses. Concurrently, large land holders were fencing out tenants, from their estates, to pay for a growing government. Thereby, cities were becoming congested. Many Britons became colonists. In New England, textile millers issued subscriptions that paid their passage and employed them as apprentices and, or indentures, once there. Otherwise, everywhere else, a black market in illegal indentures established itself.

With neither land nor trades, young colonials enlisted in the British Army and Navy in large numbers. War presented an opportunity, for young men and older boys, to gain glory, honor, and perhaps fame, plus possibly land. The fighting with France and Spain, though, on the North American front, stayed mainly on remote seas. Nonetheless, newspapermen and pamphleteers wrote about it with flair. Enlistments rose.

In Summer '45, landless New Englanders, with a bit of assistance from the British Navy, captured Fort Louisbourg in eastern Quebec. All commerce between France and Canada sailed under its commanding guns. Under British control, during the war, the massive stone walls held the Saint Lawrence River shipping lane hostage.

For a few years, it seemed Canada would become British. The end of the war, however, did not go well for Britain and her German allies on the European front. There, the French Army occupied Nederland, including the harbor, Amsterdam. Britain had mastered sea and France land. Thus, the *Treaty of Aix-la-Chapelle*, in '48, returned Fort Louisbourg to France. The treaty dashed the hopes and dreams of war veterans and many would-be pioneers.

In a North Carolina cabin, one young pioneer, Daniel Boone, dreamed of the West, nonetheless. He would lead the way one day. Needless to say, the rolling bluegrass wilderness, in the Shawnee Confederation west of the mountains, held a lure. With the French Army yet secure in the wilderness however, they held their horses.

By the outbreak of the Second French and Indian War, in '54, colonial towns and villages would be more crowded than ever with dissatisfied colonists. Unable to attain self-sufficiency on wilderness farmland, they labored for barter, swarmed into trades in villages and towns, or purchased small parcels of land from large holders, at high prices. Therefore, any talk of renewed hostilities with France met with wide approval, for France held the preponderance of the vast and largely unsettled continent.

Among Virginians, antipathy for France displaced the old antagonism between pioneers and Cavaliers. For sure, newcomers continued to focus their hopes on the unsettled wilderness. However, that wilderness was moving farther west. Equality of opportunity lessens when opportunity lessens. And, in the West, the French, not Cavaliers, inhibited opportunity. The "West" thus tended to equalize opportunity.

Meanwhile, the mountains meant adventure. Explorations attracted the bravest boys. John Boy wanted to go up into the mountains as much as his older brother once had yearned for that adventure. Yet, explorations were risky. Luckily, at the end of his second school year, a classmate's older brother, an upperclassman, turned friendly and gave him an opportunity.

A couple slaves, from their plantation, he said, had left the place. His father wanted him to go after them. He instructed him to take his younger brother, one of John Boy's buddies, along for the job. He thought some of his brother's friends might want to ride up into the mountains, too. Eagerly, John Boy and Luke Lewis, took the offer.

After school let out, the group of boys met at an inn in Richmond. After a night at the tavern, they rode to the courthouse. They planned a rendez-vous with the Carter brothers' father for instructions.

In an hot bright morning sun, the boys dismounted, tied their horses, and headed for the courthouse door. Inside, the sheriff, solicitor, judge, and others stood about arguing politics, friendly like. The sheriff sat back in his leather chair, folded his hands behind his head, and propped his legs upon a table.

"You boys plannin' on goin' after those Carter slaves?" he grinned.

"Yes sir, we sure are," Mister Carter answered.

Master Carter stood by waiting to relay instructions.

"I stand obliged by your checkin' on these 'ere boys, sheriff," the father thanked him with an even eye.

"You're welcome," the sheriff said, in a friendly enough way.

"I'll deputize 'em," his deputy shot up, eagerly.

"We're men enough for the task, sir," Mister Carter countered.

"Now looky 'ere," the sheriff began again. "Most free coloreds dwell in town. So, runaways come to town seekin' shelter from the free ones, and try blendin' in among 'em. Folks say there's lack 'nough o' opportunity, in towns, without free coloreds and runaways runnin' all the trades. We'll catch 'em, 'ere in town," he assured Master Carter and the boys.

"We know where they are. And, it ain't 'ere. They're in the mountains with natives," young Carter shot back.

His father backed him up, "My boy 'ere 'ill give each runaway a bag o' coins as a reward for comin' back. You can't 'ave a problem with that, sheriff. There ain't no place 'round these 'ere parts to spend 'em, anyway. They'll save 'em is all."

"Well allright," the sheriff backed down, somewhat. "The boys need to be deputized, anyhow" he demanded.

"'Ere's the badges, right 'ere," the deputy added. "Bounty men shouldn't be catchin' runaways. Slave catchin's the sheriff's job," he said. Then, with a second thought, he took a quick, discerning, look around, to see whom agreed.

The sheriff agreed, "These 'ere boys couldn't catch a rogue walkin' down the road," he mocked with a licentious grin.

Agitated, the solicitor could sit by silent no longer. He stood up and busted into the disagreement.

"Sheriff, I'd like to remind ya, that planters been catchin' their own slaves since foreva. It's their own problem. Consider the premise, that all slave catchers should be deputies, because only deputies are capable of cathin' rouges. Then, it doesn't follow that all roads 'ill be clear of rouges. Rather, it follows that only deputies 'ill be chasin' slaves," he humorously reasoned, as his logic elicited bursts of laughter.

"Aye, aye, we'll catch 'em ourselves," the boys yelled out, in unison.

"What's worse, the low type o' man who catches slaves today for bounties, 'ill be wantin' to catch 'em tomorrow for sheriff's pay!" the solicitor finished, to a blast of boasts and applause.

The judge got right riled at the thought of the sheriff deputizing bounty hunters to catch slaves. He moved to the center of the room and entered the exchange.

"Let me remind y'all that William the Conqueror, Duke of Normandie, established the original sheriffs, back in England, in the 1070's. He meant, for 'em to enforce Norman law on the Angles, Saxons, and Jutes, besides the original Celts."

Everyone followed intently.

Then, he yelled, "I say, do we want to form gangs o' bounty hunters at the sheriff's office?"

Everyone began shouting in agreement.

The solicitor then changed his tack. He began in an academic tone.

"Gentlemen, where does the private system o' bounties err, that we should make slave catchin' a public one? What cause is there to make tax funds out o' bounties? To patronize slave catchers?"

Everyone began shouting again, as if on queue.

"'Tis against the liberty of Virginians," came a brute shout.

"And Englishmen," came another.

Everyone began yelling and shouting even louder.

Mister Carter yelled loudly for attention.

"Now, the sheriff says, he reasons for public safety, to rid the roads of rouges, that is. Yet, the judge believes, that the sheriff's reasoning would be a detriment to public safety, because it would make deputies of greedy bounty hunters.

"Aye, Aye," rang out again, and again.

"I put forth, that the latter argument holds. For, if bounties become taxes, then the sheriff relaxes. He gets all the bounties and shares none. Politics 'ill pursue crimes, instead of the sheriff pursuin' 'em. Then, political crimes 'ill go unsolved, while poor men go to gaol. I say, 'tis patronage, and Virginia needs none of it," he shouted.

"I say we go," John Boy yelled out.

"'Ere, 'ere," the whole room, except the sheriff and deputy, yelled back.

Master Carter waved his arm toward the door, and yelled, "To the mountains, boys."

Boldly, and fast, before the sheriff could stop them, the boys made their way out the double doors to the horses. They cantered, straightaway, down the dusty street and onto the road.

At the end of that first hard day's ride, they drank and ate at a crossroads tavern.

"Thy governor 'ill outlaw slave chasin' one day. Then sheriff's 'ill 'ave their monopoly in slave catchin'," Carter predicted.

"Aye, Virginia's gettin' just like England, where a man casts his vote for his patron and not the best man," Lewis added.

"Aye, and if he's out o' work, then he can always apply to be a slave catcher," Turner joked.

At that, everyone busted out laughing, and kept laughing.

"We'll 'ave Tories and Whigs right 'ere in Virginia one day, and all the sheriffs 'ill be Whigs seekin' monopolies in enforcin' law," Carter predicted again.

"Aye, and all the rebels 'ill be Tories," Turner joked again.

At the idea of Tory rebels, everyone stopped to ponder. They wondered whether or not it were possible. Everyone waited for someone to say something. Goode got up. He lifted his mug and made a joke that rhymed.

"The Tories 'ill be wantin' to free the slaves an' pay 'em a wage."

At that, everyone laughed harder and longer, because he didn't say it the way everybody would have expected him to. That is, the Whigs 'ill be wantin' to free the slaves an' pay 'em a wage.

As the boys drank on however, they had no way of knowing, they had predicted the future. The culture in which they lived had traditions that were more effective than laws. Planters maintained their own lives like they maintained their own roads. They not only policed their plantations, but they put out their own fires, nursed the injured and sick, and educated their children. Their offspring took care of them in their old age. Plantations were governments, in themselves.

Carter knew, through the proverbial grapevine, where the runaway slaves had gone. They harboured deep in the mountains among natives. Three weeks later, when the boys rode into the native village, that lay on the winding road west, the slaves espied them and hid in a wigwam.

The village chief greeted the boys. Carter offered him a bag of coins but he refused them, on principle. The chief nodded toward the wigwam. He betrayed a knowing expression on his wise and weathered old face.

The chief told Carter, "Go look in wigwam, but they no want to go."

Carter walked right into the deerskin wigwam, without a second thought. The two big colored men, within, shot looks of amazement at his confidence. Carter sat down. And, at first, the slaves refused to go back.

"Youse tell your daddy, wese done gone an' that's it, Mista Carter," one of the slaves stated, adamantly.

Carter walked back out to the horses and fetched the coin bags. He returned to the wigwam and bartered with the coins. The slaves argued between themselves for a while. Then, they set forth a condition.

"Allrights, wese go on back, this time, but under one condition. Wese all gets to change jobs," he bartered with the coins in hand.

"'Tis a deal," Carter stated triumphantly. "You'll do what you like to do best."

The natives outside heard the agreement. The chief pulled the wigwam flap open and peered inside.

"We smoke now," he stated.

And on that, the natives, coloreds, and boys smoked weed and tobacco, and drank whiskey and wine, the rest of the night away. The natives played tom-toms and sang the poetry of ages. In the morning, after good sleeping, they all bathed and swam in the cold river.

The boys never forgot the ride into the mountains that Summer. They neither had so much fun before, nor since, at least, not that kind. Once the slaves joined them, they had determined to have more. With Elisha and Daniel they rode farther west. They led the horses through narrow steep native trails along the Hughes River.

They approached the spot where Jim drowned, and looked far down, from high atop a rocky ridge. The hard-rushing water, in the craggy canyon below, awed them. They never imagined anything so awesome. Speechless, John Boy stared down at the roaring river roiling against rough rocks.

Lewis spoke out boldly, "Ain't nobody could stay alive in that, no how, John Boy."

Nobody said a word. Their bodies felt stuck on the spots where they stood. The roar and echo of river drowned out their silence.

Elisha sensed the awkwardness of compassion in boys.

"Spirits are memories. They forget," the slave insisted.

And so, the boys rode. A west wind at their backs, warm, sun-burned and worn-out, but older, with the knowledge of freedom and death.

CHAPTER XIV

FREE ENTERPRISE

One June afternoon, the leading edge of an eastward-moving storm front bore downstream, toward the river home. It threw a heavy torrent of rain down hard on the water. Here and there, the sky hurled out lightening bolts that banged brightly on the trapped earth. Westward-facing windows rattled relentlessly.

Dogs whimpered and hid. Some put their paws over their eyes to protect themselves. In this wild weather, a whoosh of wind found its way in and fluttered the edge of a map for just a rippling moment, or maybe more. Whence, John Boy sat back, feeling oddly struck by the sixth sense of fate.

"Shut the winda boy, you'll catch your death," his mammy demanded, as she thrust the window closed.

Jolted, John Boy tried to think. "But its Spring Mammy, there's no death in the air," he protested.

"I don't care, it's there, you jus' don't sees it," Mammy exclaimed.

John Boy could not think of anything to say to this mystery.

"Jus' what in tarnation are you doin' anyways, boy? A mess ah your brotha' James' maps, all ah scatter, is what I sees," Mammy exclaimed again as she forced her fists onto her hips, thrust back her powerful chest, and turned up the pink of her bottom lip, sternly. The large whites of her eyes gave away her disapproval.

John Boy looked perplexedly into her face, as if there might be a chance.

"Well, I'm studyin' the maps is all," he answered.

"Now, what you wannna mess wid that for, boy?" she raised her voice in protest, and her left eyebrow in suspicion.

"Well Mammy, I'm thinkin' 'bout goin' out there an' finishin' what got started," John Boy announced boldly.

"Uh huh, that's what I thought," Mammy retorted.

She shook her head in dismay. "You always was one to study geography books an' talk 'bout the adventures of Robinson Crusoe, Gulliver, or some such fantastical character. Now, youse wantin' to go up there an' explore that there riva. Why, I do declare boy, the spirits done got a hole a you!" Mammy boomed out laughing, half apprehensively, half knowing he would follow his brother's trail one day.

John Boy gazed down at the maps on the table. He studied the wriggly lines that represented rivers.

"I'd sure like to go up into those mountains farther than James got," John Boy said, quietly and courageously.

Mammy put her fists on her hips and threw herself back again, but this time with more conviction.

"See there. Jus' like I said. Now, boy, youse listen 'ere. Deys some mean natives in them mountains. I hears 'bout 'em myself," Mammy warned.

"No dey ain't Mammy. They've all gone out West to join up with the French Army," John Boy countered.

"Well, the ones that's left ain't friendly to English boys neither," Mammy scoffed him.

"We can take native guides," John Boy tried to reason.

"Uh huh, so you been thinkin' 'bout this plenty, already. An', who's the "we" in your talkin', Mista Morton?" Mammy guessed.

At that very moment, fate delivered William Morton on queue. He sprinted up the porch steps and pounded on the door.

"Lordy, lordy, who's it be a poundin' so hard?" Mammy wondered aloud.

Moses opened the door.

"Youse drippin' wata all ova the floe, boy. Now, you go right back out an' round to da back doe," Mammy ordered him.

"Oh now, nonsense Mammy, the boys already 'ere, jus' get a rug, if you will, mam," a wide-eyed old Moses appeased his wife.

Hardly aware of his wetness, Will Morton rushed in, anyway. He removed his coat and muddy wet boots. He walked into the front room and plopped the mail down on a table.

"The new maps are 'ere," he greeted John Boy.

Will then spread them out on a large rectangular wooden table. John Boy and he poured over them, intently.

Mammy and Moses followed Will into the front room.

"Moses! These boys are studyin' maps an' schemin' up anotha one a those explorin' trips," she nearly yelled.

"I knows all 'bout it, mam," Moses waved her off.

"Yes mam, when we go, Abe is goin' too," John Boy shot out.

"Oh no he ain't," Mammy exploded.

"Now mam, who's goin' to look afta these 'ere young men," Moses appealed to her, with a congenial smile.

"The twins can look after 'em. They looked after y'all brotha Jim, allright," Mammy countered Moses.

John Boy furrowed his brow. She would mention Jim again, he thought.

"The boys need a colored man, besides the natives, now" Moses said earnestly.

"Why?" Mammy asked with sarcastic doubt.

"They need to take some home with 'em. They needs lookin' afta, mam," Moses answered.

These 'ere boys been gettin' in plenny a trouble since they was naked. They don't need Abe helpin' 'em get in more," Mammy demanded bellicosely.

"Miss Mammy, you sure 'nough are da boss, but they is goin'," Moses contended.

Mammy threw her head back, as was her way, and scowled. Then, the pink of her bottom lip came out.

"Well go on then, risk y'all fool necks," she huffed off.

Indeed, the risks themselves lured explorers. Risks made the adventure of exploration worth more. The adventure consumed the risks in John Boy, Will, and Abe's minds. In the following weeks, their optimism attracted the whole plantation to the plan.

The braves sensed Junior's approval beforehand. They knew he had been waiting years for John Boy to take up where Jim had left off. Expectantly, they began studying the new maps for any conflicts with native knowledge. Meticulously, they began preparing another wilderness trek.

The exploration pulled out from the Muddy Creek on a clear day in May. There, outside the stable, as Junior watched John Boy ride off, regret suddenly seized him like a choke hold. His throat muscles contracted. For a few moments, he gasped, inaudibly, for breath.

Nonetheless, he conjured up enough will to throw regret aside. Reminiscently, he stood long watching the wagon train disappear in the distance. The rest of the farewell party sensed his remorse. The ones who remembered also sensed a difference that day. Seriousness replaced the jocundity attendant at Jim's departure. This exploration meant business.

Notwithstanding the thrill of exploration, business enticed John and Will even more than adventure. They carried a square leather satchel in which Jim's folded maps rested. This time they would not only locate, but mine salt. Wheresoever substantial deposits were uncovered, they would insert details on the maps. They planned to mine the most propitious sights. The group anticipated hard work.

The exploration party encountered more foresters and pioneers and fewer natives than Jim had several years earlier. In fact, the natives had deserted the first settlement the boys came to. The twins, Powhatan Ed and Powhatan Ted, heard several times, from those natives they did encounter, that many braves had gone west to join up with the French Army. This troublesome topic came up one night in campfire conversation.

"Why do you think so many natives trek west, Powhatan Ed," John and Will queried him.

"French make strong alliance with natives. One squaw say she hear war tom-toms sometimes now," Powhatan Ed responded.

"That means there's war comin'," Will said.

"It mean war not over, just long break between battles," Powhatan Ted interjected.

"Gosh, I sure hope we don't get caught up 'ere when another French war breaks out," Will worried aloud.

"Not happen, French camps west of mountains. They claim that land. Mountains no man's land, now," Powhatan Ed assured them.

Several days later, the exploration party got as far as Jim had. It seemed a forlorn and forgotten spot in the massive wilderness. A slight breeze blew through the thick trees and the sun glared blindingly off the tricky water. Nothing seemed amiss with nature. Yet, the rocky rapid, that had claimed life, stole the majestic scene.

The boys walked far downstream, and found a place where they were able to climb down a steep embankment. Down at water level, they made their way back upstream where they found the blood-stained boulder. John Boy took a step forward. He wanted to wade out toward the very spot where, he sensed, his brother had drowned, as if he could somehow replace Jim's death by being alive there. Powhatan Ed read his mind. He threw out his arm and held him back.

"Let the spirits keep him, you stay," he stated flatly in his monotone way.

John Boy froze cold in his tracks. Will turned to stone. The wind died down and the leaves went dead.

The explorers trekked on. Many weeks later, they rounded back to the best mining sight they had found. There, a token crew encamped. The rest of the party went back to the plantation.

John Boy, Will, Abe, and the twins rode on to Williamsburg. More tired than they could remember ever having been, they checked into an inn. They slept soundly that night. Clean and confident, they sought out the plantation's solicitors at the small harbor capitol. By the end of the day, the solicitors were drawing up a business charter.

The five men walked back to the inn and up to their room. They felt more ambitious than ever because events, so far, had gone according to plan.

"'Ere's my half of the start-up costs," Will said, as he laid out his tobacco credit slips on the table.

"'Ere's my half," John Boy repeated, as he did the same.

Powhatan Ed interceded, "What name business?"

"Yes, what name it?" Powhatan Ted wondered aloud.

"The Virginia Salt Mining Company," Powhatan Ed suggested.

"'Tis good name. Yet, if we don't name it after ourselves, then we might not own it for long," John Boy believed.

"The Western Mining Company!" Powhatan Ted suggested, enthusiastically.

"'Tis true, John Boy. Folks don't name their plantations after themselves, and seems like there's land disputes regular," Will figured out loud.

"That's cause a folks dyin', bein' born, and gettin' married, Will," John Boy half jested.

"Allright, I have one," Will shot out.

"We hear it," Powhatan Ted demanded.

"We'll name it the Hughes Morton Mining Company," Will suggested evenly.

"No, we'll name it the Morton Hughes Mining Company, in honor of your idea," John Boy said just as evenly.

"No sir, we name it the Hughes Morton Mining Company, in alphabetical order," Will insisted.

Powhatan Ted threw out his arms and put his open hands on their chests to separate them.

"It fair name," he interjected.

The native settled the question. Everyone grinned broadly, got bear-hugged, and congratulated themselves. They felt good about having their name on their business.

Once Will and John Boy finished their business in capitol town, the fivesome rode home to start up the mine. They built a wagon train consisting of horses; mules; oxen; wagons; camping gear; huge amounts of food; building lumber and carpentry tools; mining tools, including wheel barrels, picks, axes, shovels, and candle lanterns. They would need yet more wagons to transport the mined salt back out of the mountains to the river and barges.

Thus, carpenters and wheelwrights went to work on more wagons. Meanwhile, Powhatan Ed and Powhatan Ted put out word in Richmond for miners and crew. Men needed to apply at the Muddy Creek with a horse and camping gear. The natives offered salt and, or tobacco as payment for labor.

Once the long train got off, it became difficult to keep all of the wagons together. The food wagons held up the rest of the train. They trudged along slowly, making the wagons ahead of them travel at unsteady rates of speed.

The crew used foresight in packing many mules lightly, as opposed to a lesser number heavily, so as not to tire out the few before reaching the work site. However, they did not foresee the cumbersome length of the wagon train. The awkward ride notwithstanding, the train reached the mines with due diligence.

After many slow-moving miles, the men set up camp nearby the sight. The mine sight lay off a narrow river embankment. The embankment led to a cavern. Deep inside, the high huge cavern contained a tremendous hard shiny salt deposit.

The deposit stretched for miles along an escarpment. As vast as it seemed, the men had no way of knowing that they worked at the center of the continent's biggest near-surface salt deposit. Nor did they know that the mine they worked meandered so deep into the mountain.

Soon, the hardy miners found mining salt a greater endeavor than they had anticipated. The group, of necessity, had to rely on the natives' tried and proved techniques. The natives, however, had mined only very small amounts with small simple tools.

John Boy and Will enlarged on native techniques. John Junior had taught the two what knowledge he had meticulously gathered from English manuals. The young partners themselves had studied English salt mining techniques extensively.

Nevertheless, the self-taught engineers encountered unanticipated problems on the Virginia frontier. Thus, they applied customary mining methods, along with a trial-and-error approach to problem solving. The trial-and-error method played a difficult instruction master.

Mistakes cost a great deal of time and energy. Yet, no lenders stood by demanding payments. Nor did miners and crew stand by waiting for pay. Thus, the firm could afford delays. Therefore, the work progressed, but at an unpredictable pace.

Once the removal procedure became well established using division of labor in mining tasks, the men turned their attention to storage and transportation. They utilized the forest to solve the storage problem. A separate crew broke off, of the miners, to work on barrels.

They cut down trees, chopped off branches, and sawed down hundreds of slats. They set up a forge to smelt iron belts. By the time the stacked salt became a hindrance to mining, innumerable brand-new wooden hogshead barrels stood ready to roll the load.

On time, more wagons arrived, from the plantations, to haul several tons of salt back to Richmond. Once loaded, the cumbersome heavy wagon train moved laboriously out of the narrow mountain trails. Rough steep terrain caused the wagons to roll dangerously. The heavy loads went downhill, precariously. Sometimes they would hardly go uphill at all.

The only resolution possible meant less salt per wagon. Thereby, wagon trains needed enlargement. That meant more wagons, mules, and crew.

The crew pampered the mules, with breaks, at intervals. Nonetheless, the animals slowed, with fatigue, by the time the wagon train reached the Great Valley and trodden roads. The train made camp, in the valley, for a few days to rest the mules and horses. Thereafter, traveled roads made the haul easier. Finally, after a long slow trip, the wagon train came to a halt at the docks in there.

The train's arrival caused a big stir in Richmond. No one on the waterfront had ever seen anything like it. Folks had seen long wagon trains pull in, but their size did not compare to this one. Nor were any of them packed with salt.

Wagon after wagon pulled in until the waterfront filled with them. The people of the village marveled at this long train packed with nothing but fresh new barrels. The cobblestone quayage and wooden docks did not accommodate the wagons.

Thus, the drivers parked in a long row, to await their turns to unload. Excited villagers approached the waiting drivers with unending questions. Their excitement turned into awe, when they learned about the tremendous mining operation back up in the mountains.

The crew split the load at Richmond. They placed part of it in a warehouse for upcountry demand. The greater part went onto barges for downriver demand. Exhausted, the wagon crew took several days off there.

John Boy and Will, however, needed no rest. At daybreak, they shoved off with experienced boatmen. The trip downriver became tedious and dangerous. They were made to travel with extra caution to keep the salt dry. Finally, after a strenuous trip down the James River, the barges made port in Williamsburg.

There, John Boy and Will left the barge crew on board, while they sought out the agent in the commercial center of town. No tobacco agents had ever seen a barge full of salt. Some made a point to voice their skepticism about the undertaking. Those with keen business sense, however, sought to know more about the mining operation.

John Boy and Will took the various agents' comments with an open mind. Nonetheless, they dismissed pessimism. After all the work they had done, they firmly believed that a large mining enterprise, with high start-up costs, could succeed with a monopoly grant from neither parliament nor king, as the salt mining business in England operated.

Finally, John Boy, Will, and the crew secured the cargo in warehouses. The crew congratulated John Boy and Will. The first load had reached the marketplace with neither accidents nor deaths. No unsolvable problems had developed. The sale price meant that the partnership could meet the large start-up, plus operating costs, in reasonable time, and yet make a profit, according to the accounting method employed.

Back at the mine, when the partners finished the final details of the first haul, they felt too exhausted to enjoy the satisfaction of success. Yet, they certainly felt the relief of it. They had taken an expensive risk and lost nothing.

The risk declined with subsequent loads as start-up costs continually divided. Thereafter, loads reached the warehouses in continual streams, with seasonal interruptions, until long after the partners would die. The business thrived.

The market for salt in the colonies grew exponentially. The tremendous influx of colonists added to the growth of families. Every person and all livestock consumed salt. They utilized it to keep meat edible long after slaughter and for animal health. Indigo planters in South Carolina and Georgia used it in their dark dye mixtures. The vast deposits in the high mountains of western Virginia supplied that need.

The salt company mined more of the mineral as demand for and price of it warranted. The miners and crew became permanent. More horses, mules, oxen, wagons, barrels, and tools, plus equipment enlarged the wagon trains. Larger trains unloaded onto larger and more numerous barges. Bigger hauls lowered costs per mile. Eventually, the partners secured their own warehouses in Richmond and Williamsburg. Thereby, costs fell even more.

The tremendous amount of salt the firm produced raised the market supply so high that the price fell low, permanently. Indeed, the price fell so significantly that, thereafter, Americans would come to take salt for granted. Nevertheless, that would not become a problem for many generations, because the miners merely scratched the surface of North America's bounty. And so goes the story of the first salt mining industry in the colonies. The partner's firm became a household term.

CHAPTER XV

THE SECOND FRENCH AND INDIAN WAR

Success solidified the already strong amity between John Boy and Will for a lifetime. Subconsciously, they sensed that fate. For, their friendship drew them into each other's families. It drew them toward a blood-like bond. They spent their free time together, at one plantation or the other, where they became brothers-in-law. The bond served as the base of John Boy and Sarah Morton's marriage.

The two families' fates wound together even more tightly, at the Morton plantation, on a sweltering Summer weekend. A large crowd witnessed the wedding, outside, under the muggy shade of maple trees. Every wooden chair the families owned, besides many more from neighbors, formed neat rows. An array of purple, pink, and deep-red flowers decked the makeshift altar. Porters in white cotton and black ties, with scarlet silk vests seated the guests.

John Boy's grandparents, John and Genevieve, had places of honor in the front row, on the aisle. They had lived longer than anyone on the plantation that day. A century of hardy frontier life kept them alive. The good life would keep them alive longer, yet.

Their closest friends, Moses and Mammy, sat next to them. John Junior; Mary; Powhatan Ted and Ed; their wives, the sisters, Song of Sparrow and Sunflower; Moses and Mammy's nephew, Abraham; and their daughter, Missy; filled out the row. Sarah Morton's family sat happily on the opposite side of the aisle. Will stood, at attention, grinning with the bridegrooms.

After the ceremony, across the thick green lawn, a cool river breeze kept the crowd comfortably at ease. Piquant scents of Summer pervaded the air. Young men and women felt free to flirt. Married couples made their merry ways around. Children scurried about helter-skelter.

Here and there, on the lush lawn, through the leafy green shrubs, and under shady trees the children played wild. Nannies in white silk and light-grey cotton dresses, with ample aprons, lullabied babies in their wholesome brown bosoms. Now and then, piercing shrill screams of discomfort drowned the peace.

The Morton's stallion, Patroclus, ran faster than any horse that day. Robert Morton jubilantly led him around, by a lead line clipped to his leather halter, with wide red ribbons straddling his withers. Everyone cheered loudly and long. Muddy Creek's Achilles II, that everyone called Achilles, ran second that day. After the running, youngsters took naps and the race crowd dispersed.

In Morton's Creek, boys bantered about in good-humored raillery. They jested and jabbed one another in an ongoing game of phalanx warfare. Over and over, in mock assaults, one group pushed through the water like the wall of a wave. Then, it plunged into the other one and wrestled it down.

After numerous charges, breathless, and beaten, their attentions turned elsewhere. Each, in his turn, took to the creek bank and repeatedly climbed an ancient oak. They stood nimbly, on a heavy limb, and grabbed for a heavy hemp rope that hung from a high branch above. Then, they swung out over the water, like naked natives, yelled pau wau cries, and plunged into the creek.

In the dining room, around the copious cherry wood table, men of all ages gambled at serious cards. The pungent aromas of tobacco and smoking weed permeated the air. The clinking of coins, and snapping of shuffling cards, signaled the start of each hand. Sighs, grunts, groans, or an occasional hoot and howler, along with the pounding of fists, signaled the end. During hands, concentration grew so intense, around the table, that the only sound players heard were of lips puckering cigars.

The festivities lasted late that Saturday night. At noon Sunday, they began again with a bountiful breakfast. The plantation and its guests ate mounds of eggs, bacon, fried potatoes with tomatoes, toasted brown bread, butter, and berry jam. They drank chicory coffee with raw honey and cream. After the meal, guests smoked pipes, cigars, and native weed. The musically talented took up the fiddles where they had laid them the night before. Dancing music went reeling all afternoon.

The last guests left Wednesday. A fortnight later, John Boy brought Sarah to the Muddy Creek. The plantation welcomed her easily, because everyone knew her brother so well. A newly painted and plaid-papered room awaited the couple. Newly woven heavy hemp, over thin silk, drapes covered the windows. On Sarah's shiny mahogany dresser, in front of a large mirror, sat fresh red flowers, in a crystal vase, on a silver tray.

Sarah easily came to love life in that room, at that house, and on that plantation. She rode her chestnut mare almost everywhere, most every morning, and became acquainted with the whole plantation and everyone on it. She became a daughter to Mary. Will spent much of his time there. He stayed in the boys' big dorm room. Usually, when Will stayed over, John Boy would sleep in the dorm, too.

Life seemed brand-new and full of living to Sarah's young spirit. The old plantation, however, had seen five generations and almost one hundred fifty years pass across its forests, fields, and meadows. It had seen the tobacco crop spread from one acre to many hundreds. It had seen the little barn become several big ones plus stables. It had seen the cabin grow into an house and that into a mansion. It had seen the natives' cabins proliferate into tens of white-washed slaves' quarters extending far up the bank of the Muddy Creek. The river home had seen three generations placed under thick marble gravestones, that stood neatly in a row, overlooking the windy river, when John and Genevieve took places there.

The combined legacies of three generations' toil accumulated on Junior. Three generations had purposely built legacies for their heirs. The family's longevity thus served as the foundation of its fortune.

The fourth generation inherited not only his forebears' successes but their standards, too. That tradition of ethical standards separated him from greedy men. It guided him in his business life. His honor actually had economic value like his tobacco.

With the plantation producing at near capacity and its borders abutting the neighbors, he looked beyond the banks of the Muddy Creek for opportunity. Where most masters of mature plantations looked to buy another plantation, for a second-born son perhaps, Junior looked beyond planting. He had applied his business acumen to salt mining. Now, that business thrived.

Upcountry planters admired Junior's reputation for honor and ethical business practices. Thus, when two professional printers thought the time had come for an upcountry newspaper, and looked around for investment partners, they approached him. The printers planned a meeting for prospective partners at a tavern in Richmond.

John wanted John Boy to attend the initial meeting. He knew his son adhered to the family's honor besides that of Virginians. And, that honor gave him political conviction. He would support only the best type of men in editorials.

John Boy walked into a crowded riverfront tavern at dinner time. He took in the large crowd. A massive stone fireplace burst forth heat on kids sitting, on the floor, in front of it. The huge fire mesmerized them. The pine wood-paneled tavern had a slight smell of stale cream ale. The patrons did not seem to mind. At one side, ten men sat around a heavy long table, on flatback chairs and a bench, bordering the wall. He took a seat.

"Well, John Boy, glad ya came," one of the printers greeted him.

"Thanks, I'm glad to be 'ere," John Boy answered.

After the greeting, the printers introduced John Boy around the table. Every planter the printers invited to the meeting had shown up. For their own part, two years worth of preparations had brought them to the table that evening.

During those two years the printers learned about the newspaper business from professionals. They determined their start-up and operating costs, meticulously, and laid them out plainly. The costs included a big brick building in Richmond; a large cumbersome printing press imported from England; plus office equipment; many barrels of ink;

and rolls and rolls of paper. The printers described all of these preparations, with the aid of figures and drawings, while the assembled planters listened with skeptical interest.

When the printers finished their sales pitch, one of the men stood up.

"'Tis a great plan ya 'ave there allright, but methinks to expand my tobacco crop and my livestock during the next few years," he made an excuse.

At that bidding, more excuses went around the table. Several men voiced similar sentiments. They believed the planned newspaper business seemed a likelihood of success. Yet, since the market for tobacco and livestock continued to grow, they saw little reason to invest in a business about which they knew nothing.

After a short while only the printers, another young planter, and John Boy remained around the big table. They gathered closely at one end. The tone turned from skeptical to serious.

"My father thinks that the best time to start up a newspaper business is at the beginning of a war," John Boy began.

"Right, that's when everyone wants to read a newspaper," the other fellow added.

"He thinks there's sure enough a war comin', with France, for the West. British garrisons in all of the colonies grow larger every year," John Boy knew.

"What's 'ere in the South doesn't compare to what's up North. Rumor has it the British Navy is buildin' up slowly and stealthily like. Most of the ships are merchantmen, in disguise," the young man knew.

"You two could write all the articles about the next war that you want. Meanwhile, the factor, back in England, wants to get paid for the printing machine. If we don't buy this one, then we'll never get one so low-priced," one printer pressed them.

"You two just leave it to us. We can sell advertizing and print the paper. You two could contribute news articles and manage the enterprise as you like," the other printer came right out and suggested.

I'm not sure how much time I could devote to this enterprise," John Boy tried to counter their eagerness.

"An even partnership, eh. Twenty-five percent apiece," the young man raised one eyebrow.

"That's right," the printers said, at once.

John Boy sat forward. "It sure 'nough would be the first regular newspaper in the upcountry," he echoed everyone's thought.

"True, but the building and big iron machinery are expensive. It might take longer than ya think to recover the start-up costs," his fellow planter surmised realistically.

"We broke the plantation bank startin' the salt mining business. We just recently recovered our start-up costs. We're only just startin' to make worthwhile profits," John Boy hedged.

Several moments of awkward silence proved resilient.

The two of them did their own figuring, for a lengthy time, while all of the men drank and smoked.

"We 'ave to print four papers a year," they figured.

"At that rate, it'll still take ten years, or more, to recover our start-up costs," John Boy added.

The printers thought to direct the conversation toward the positive. They sat forward in their chairs and paused. Then, they stuck out their hands to insist on getting shook.

"Its not like either of you to pass up a good deal because of high risk," one printer said.

"My dad just sent me 'ere to hear your plan. He'll want to study the plan and those figures himself," John Boy said, as he shook their hands anyway.

"Mine too," his fellow planter admitted.

"If they think it's a good investment, then we're partners," John Boy smiled broadly, as he shook their hands.

"Yes sir, it's a possible deal. We 'ave a printer, an add salesman, a writer, and a manager. All we need is the tobacco and we'll have the building and the press," one printer added eagerly.

"That's a ship full o' tobacco," John Boy joked.

The amount of tobacco credit needed to start up a newspaper gave John Boy pause. Nonetheless, he raised his mug and made a toast.

"Eh, free enterprise, 'tis the way o' liberty," he toasted the others.

The other fellow raised his mug and made another.

"That every man be self-employed, as us," he boasted.

"'Ere, 'ere," the printers responded to the clank of mugs in mid-air.

One year later, the Richmond newspaper proudly published its first edition. That first printing sold out. Thereafter, every printing sold out. The newspaper became the most reliable source of news and advertizement in the upcountry.

During the newspaper's first years, the young partners experienced lean times. The price of ads had one precedent. That was in the Williamsburg paper. However, no one wanted to pay that rate in an upcountry publication. Thus, the partners agreed to charge twenty-five percent less than that established paper. Nonetheless, most merchants were not much interested in advertizing. They reasoned that their customers already knew about them.

In the meantime, the paper made a profit on numerous newer small pioneer businessmen who wanted to get their names in the paper. Thereby, the partners became acquainted with all of the businessmen in Richmond. Eventually, those who advertized realized gains. They came to rely on advertizing. Word spread.

The rest of the town, along with upcountry plantations and farms, awaited its publication with eager interest. Not only was it the sole source of news, but more than that, it recorded the culture of the upcountry. Indeed, one cannot say, for certain, whether the paper came to voice upcountry culture or form it. Whichever, the paper became a part of it. Pioneers took pride in it. They came, eventually, to hear it known as the "Voice of the Frontier."

The paper's popularity grew as war neared in the 1750's. One of its first important stories was about a newspaper editor named Ben Franklin, from the foremost town in the southern colonies, Philadelphia. He wrote political prose, during a convention in far-off Albany, up the Hudson River. He attended a colonial confederation convention. Franklin's poignant prose put forth, persuasively, that the colonies must unite. Common issues, such as negotiations with the natives, could get resolved that way.

The congress of colonial office holders agreed. They had traveled to Albany, New York, from all thirteen colonies, from New Hampshire to Georgia. Never had colonial office holders assembled together, theretofore. There were those, few, colonial governors who worked against such a confederation. They threatened to withhold patronage from those who attended the assembly. Thereby, the congress of colonial office holders lost the support of parliament and their own resolve.

The Richmond paper supported the Confederation. Colonial pride waxed in earnest. Upcountry readers sensed that the governors' patronage was corrupt. Yet especially, the upcountry sensed, that not just French but British, imperialism boosted the savageness of the Shawnee. For, in truth, not just the French, but the British government sought to monopolize the fur trade.

The French took fur from New France like the British took tobacco; timber; turpentine; cotton; rice; rum; whiskey; wool; and leather from its North American colonies. The French Army maintained the fur trade through brutal native alliances. The British, too, sought to make alliances with the natives, but under force of military might, rather than through gift negotiation.

Frontiersmen resented the British Army's failure to win allies among the western tribes. French Army guerrilla soldiers and their camouflaged savage allies often attacked and slaughtered British soldiers. Their bright-red coats, and habit of marching through forests in formation, made them easy targets, too.

In fact, the British Navy dominated the seas but the Army had yet to adjust to wilderness warfare. Soldiers got shot, in rows, while marching obediently into fire. Orders for the brutal discipline came down from England's German king, George II. In Europe, he knew, tight formation moved aside anything in its path. Frontal attack formation, however, does not work in the wilderness. Britain's native policy thus failed. Sagaciously, the savages sided with the French.

Meanwhile, frontiersman had begun to see farms built, not only on wilderness land, at the western edge of the frontier, but at borders of old plantations. Virginia was becoming crowded. Colonials, from Britain, were planting themselves down, on small parcels, wherever they could find them. A small number of planters freed their slaves and gave them shares, at plantation borders. Many possessed too few acres for a farm. They built homesteads, instead, where they consumed all their crop and livestock output. Many others, with neither land nor trade, and thus without liberty, lived in towns and waited for the West to open up.

The Shawnee Confederation held savagely to the bluegrass and surrounding country that lay west of Virginia. They meant to prevent more persons planting themselves down. Their alliance with the French ensured their intentions.

However, men considered practical, like Franklin, believed in a premise; that, since the British made up the preponderance of North America's population, they had a natural right to settle the wilderness, notwithstanding France's claim to it. Landless men needed land and the liberty it provides. Therefore, the various colonies needed to negotiate with native leaders for the lands that lay to the west of their frontiers.

Few Frenchmen, in comparison, populated North America. And more, many Frenchmen in maritime Acadia had just vacated their land. The British Army and Navy had removed them to the French West Indies and Louisiana, at the end of King George's War, in '48. Now, the manifest destiny of Britons seemed more viable than ever. Indeed, British colonials began to see North America as theirs by virtue of their vast numbers.

Where British colonials saw the West as farmland, however, the British Parliament saw it as a fur trapper's bounty. In parliament's view, a victory over France could bring the British government the fur trade monopoly. In that event, Britain must subdue the natives to operate the fur trade safely. Thus, the common ground between parliament and the colonials at the outbreak of the French and Indian War, in '54, existed in the land and therefore in the war itself.

During the few years before war, British ships quit adding to the burgeoning colonial population. Now, in those deep wooden hauls, lay canon, muskets, and powder. Unhappy horses, cows, and pigs made the voyage on the decks above them. British and French fleets, in the North Atlantic, sailed the narrow sea lanes tensely on alert. At times, they fired on each other. A few of those ships brought General Braddock and his army to North America. He came, full of intent, to show British arms in action.

One day in 1755, General Braddock sat his mount sternly looking about. He led a long train of troops and pioneers. Deep in the wild wilderness, he had since rode pass the last hardy homesteader cabin. He crossed the great river at the rapids, with the sun, at the Cherokee and Iroquois Confederations' border. He headed northwestwardly. He aimed straightaway toward the impregnable Fort Duquense, in the western Pennsylvania mountains.

The general's stern look did not betray his deeply hidden fear. His heart beat hard, nonetheless. Alertly, his officers rode behind him. All of his men listened and looked about, closely, for natives in the surrounding forest.

Foot soldiers walked warily behind the mounted men. They felt less apprehension for the protection. Farther back, behind the soldiers, stalwart Pennsylvania, Virginia, and Maryland pioneer women rode in wagons. Their men folk plodded along behind them. The general's army brought an entire village with it.

They heard, but could not see, the sweet sounds of several singing birds. Suddenly, the singing struck up. A quick glance at the general saw his stern look turn to dread. The officers' eyes took quick glances around the forbidding forest. Horses whinnied from the strain of reins. The soldiers paused and gave, momentary, thought to seeking cover. Horses slowed in confusion. The pioneer men sensed the commotion, from behind the wagons, and went for their muskets.

In the next confused moments, some spotted French cavalry officers. In the next instant, a hoard of whooping and hollering savages tore out of the trees and descended on the train. The fiercely yelling savages held their tomahacks high to gain good aim.

The terrifying sound and sight of colorful paint and feathers distracted many for that deadly instant. The officers shouted orders that no one heard in the rear. The soldiers took whatever cover lay near.

Quickly, they overturned the wagons and barricaded themselves behind them. Just in time, they began firing into the tan chests of the first wild savages to take a leaping jump over those barricades. They killed every one of them.

But then, the second wave came over the top. The English met their match and then some. Wearied, the soldiers and pioneers faced a third attack. A slaughter ensued. In the quiet, following that assault, those yet alive, panicked. Terrified, they fled into the forest as fast as they could fumble away.

The attack party left behind a bloody mess. The bodies of men, women, children, and animals lay strewn about the scene. Here and there, scalped heads hung loosely from broken necks and gushed forth warm blood. Lifeless eyes stared at the sky.

The merely injured and maimed gritted their teeth while they held their wounds and groaned. At the front, the general and most of his officers lay dead. Worse, the hardy pioneers took the brunt at the back.

The attack on General Braddock brought an end to his plan to strengthen Fort Duqeunse. The rugged mountains, themselves, remained the border between the colonies and New France. Yet, the old border, alike between the Cherokee and Shawnee as between the British and French, lasted just one more year. For, in '56, the British Army and Navy invaded New France with all the might they could muster.

For the first time in colonial history, English-speaking people, around the world, united. Whether in England; Wales; Scotland; Ireland; North America; Australia; Africa; or Asia, the British flag meant liberty. The initial British advance proved successful.

The French killed General Wolfe, on the plains of the Quebec farmer, Abraham, in the second year of the war. And, heroism notwithstanding, French guerrilla tactics continued to prove deadly to the British Army in the dense wilderness. After seven years of it, however, the French fight failed on the European front.

Both France and Britain had spent thousands of lives, and tons of equipment, by the end of the fighting in '63. The conflict had been the farthest reaching, and likely bloodiest, war for imperial spoils known to history. The price of war nearly bankrupted the belligerents' treasuries. And, that price gave Britain the major portion of France's coveted prize, the lucrative and expanding North American fur trade.

The British government anticipated prodigious profits from the monopoly trade, that had added so much wealth and power to France. That is, once she recovered the colossal costs of war. For now, Englishmen everywhere were made to drain their own wealth into the bitter bucket of taxes.

Many colonial men fought in the world war. Now, they expected land as payment. Resolute, militiamen had battled for that bountiful, beautiful, and big bluegrass that rolled out west of the Blue Ridge. Thousands of landless colonists prepared to trek west. Some planned to plant themselves down on plantations, farms, or homesteads. Others planned to set up a trade or shop at fort towns. Colonials knew that self-sufficiency is the precept of liberty.

Nonetheless, parliament prohibited settlement of the hard-won wilderness and thus the sacred liberty of Englishmen. Parliament's primary concern was that the natives accept the loss of French arms. The policy of the British Army was to protect fur traders only. Restive militiamen grew frustrated.

CHAPTER XVI

THE SONS OF LIBERTY

Back at the old plantation, life went on. The bloody war for wilderness never invaded the tranquility of nature there. The ancient river just kept flowing on year in and year out. It washed pass the peaceful plantation with neither pause nor cause. Nature gave no thought to the effects of war on humans. Annual crops got planted and harvested. Colts, calves, and piglets enlarged the stock. Chickens laid eggs. In both the big house and the quarter, babies took their first breaths of fresh frontier air and old folks took their last.

Powhatan Ed followed Powhatan Ted to the great afterlife of spirits. Their wives, Sunflower and Song of Sparrow, went with them. In the end, the war added a trace of confusion to their firm faces. They left the land of their forebears, with unsettling uncertainty about the past and future of their people. Ed's son, Powhatan Tom, inherited his father's talent for history. These days, the kids gathered around him to hear stories about the old days.

Moses and Mammy spent their last decades easily. They cherished each other and the new life they had come to love. The content couple thanked fate for having brought them to Virginia. They envisioned a better future for their progeny in this promising land, of liberty, than they would have had, as slaves, back in Africa. That progeny proliferated. Their nephew, Abraham, and their daughter, Missy, managed the big house now. Their grandchildren,

Jeremiah and Jemimah, were assuming more and more responsibility.

John and Mary waited a long time for grandchildren. More and more, Mary passed on her position as plantation mistress to Sarah, just as John passed on his position as manager of the family enterprises to his son. The circumspect couple taught the young generation well. These days, they enjoyed the proverbial fruits of life's labour. Mary took satisfaction from Sarah's loyalty and love. John spent the seasons reading, riding, and hunting mainly.

Daily, instinct drew him toward the place where his father, John, Senior, had rocked away his own age. Late in the afternoons, he often found himself on the front porch surrounded by the icons of his memories. Indeed, his memories yet lived on that lofty lawn, even though the river flowed on, into the unknown future. The rushing river flooded his mind with memories. As the water washed pass his eyes, so the years swept by.

One warm day in May, he wistfully rocked away watching wind whipping water into white tops. On his lap, the Richmond newspaper rippled in the wind. John Boy sat back, with a sigh, in a chair beside him.

"The stamp tax on thy newspaper, slows down business, eh son?" Junior pried John Boy.

"Sure has dad. It reduced profits to nearly nothing. First, it raised the price of paper, for we must purchase the stamped paper on which to print. Second, it raised the price of ads, for we must add the tax to each one. Even that is not enough. We had to raise the price of each copy to cover the tax on each one of them. Our paper cost rose, ad revenue fell, and fewer papers get purchased. So, we print fewer papers now. I say, if the stamp tax is not rescinded, then we'll cease to publish for lack of profits," John Boy complained.

Junior contemplated his son's explanation for several long moments.

"'Tis a triple tax on the newspaper business then, eh?" he opined.

"'Tis indeed," John Boy agreed.

"'Tis sound business practice to continue reducing the number o' papers printed. And, leave none unsold. If costs remain less than revenue, then you'll stay in business until the tax crises passes," Junior advised.

"True enough. But, we've already reduced the number to the minimum. If we print and sell any less, then we won't meet operating costs," John Boy explained.

"Perhaps demand has fallen as far as it will. Colonists are worked up about the stamp tax and want to keep abreast of the news," Junior concluded.

John Boy felt the injustice, intensely.

"'Tis the first direct tax on us colonist in history. The sugar tax is not a direct one. Rather, 'tis a customs tax on foreign sugar," John Boy made the distinction.

"'Tis worse in England. The Englanders pay more taxes than any of the king's subjects," Junior consoled him.

"'Tis not taxes, per se, that 'ave readers riled. After all, the war debt must get paid. Britain won all New France, and Florida too, in the bargain," John Boy surmised.

"What ye think riles readers, then?" Junior queried him.

John Boy pondered the question awhile.

"Riled colonists think the tax is unfair. They complain that parliament taxes, arbitrarily. Thus, they believe the power to tax lays, rightly, with colonial legislatures," John Boy opined.

"A fair tax is one assessed, equitably," Junior stated.

"And, not just paper. The Sons of Liberty demand an excise tax on all goods or non atall. What shall parliament tax next, tea?" John Boy joked.

"The Sons of Liberty remind me of grandpa's story 'bout Nathaniel Bacon's rebellion against the tobacca tax," Junior reminisced.

Thoughtfully, John Junior gazed up at the same sturdy trees that his father, John, Senior had known. All of a sudden, two high-bred boisterous horses broke out of the river trail in a near gallop. Will and Matt Morton's mounts rushed right up to the porch where the snorting stallions stopped. Several boys playing on the side lawn saw the horsemen and got excited. They ran toward the porch, as fast as they could, reached up and grabbed the reins, with wide eyes, and gently nudged the black beasts over toward the stable.

"How y'all?" Will and Matt asked, as they climbed up the big brick steps.

"Dad and I are talkin' bout the rebellion of 1676," John Boy returned the greeting.

"Oh, the whole country of Virginia's riled up," Will waived his hand broadly.

"Rightly so, too. Only equitable taxes are fair ones," John Boy insisted.

Will smacked his heels together, threw back his chest, and saluted in mock attention of a son of liberty.

"No taxation without representation," he jested.

"Most o' those liberty boys are militiamen. Methinks, perhaps their wantin' to fight savages for land, like the hero Bacon back in '76," Junior said sagely.

At that moment, the front door opened and Powhatan Tom withdrew from the house.

"Sons of Liberty want Virginia Militia to lead wagon trains into Shawnee lands," the native imparted in his monotone manner.

"Dey's sure 'nough o' us coloreds needs some o' that there land an' liberty," Matt Morton made known.

"Wise men both speak truths," Junior observed.

"Day will come when not be enough land for so many to have liberty. Too many already," Powhatan Tom predicted.

Matt Morton sat forward, placed his open palms on his knees, and concentrated hard. "One day, Shawnee lands gonna be covered wid folks plantin' down. A land o' liberty," he envisioned.

A distracting squeak and moan from the heavy wooden door hardly disturbed Matt's vision. Jerimiah walked out, followed by his father, Abe, carrying a tray of tea and cigars. As Abe placed the tray on a tall table, Jerimiah grabbed the back of an empty chair. He turned it around, and sat down, resting his folded arms on the top of the backrest. John stood up and ambled over to the table to serve himself. He knew there was no getting any work out of Jerimiah when the boys were all together. "Grandpa John used to say that liberty is not the same as freedom. The liberty of Greeks meant, simply, that all Greeks either farmed or traded. Aristotle, himself, had liberty because he farmed his own land. Yet, he did not have freedom, because he was a slave. King Philip owned him. He was obliged to tutor Prince Alexander. Philip compensated Aristotle with farmland of his own. Grandpa got it that way from great-grandpa. Methinks, great-grandpa got it from olde Jesse," John advised them all.

"Grandpa said that great-grandpa used to get worked up real good 'bout liberty. Grandpa's the one that shot British soldiers at Jamestowne in '76," John Boy added proudly.

"Grandpa used to say that a man at liberty toils for himself, right Masta John?" Jerimiah asked.

"That's right, boy," John encouraged him.

Will shot up and slapped John Boy on the back.

"Sure 'nough, liberty's in the air these days. Folks at the tavern in Richmond work themselves into shoutin' 'bout it," he said.

An animated vision of the alehouse put a smile on everyone's face for a few moments.

"How 'bout we all get to Williamsburg for the next house meetin' and hear their resolutions to the stamp tax," Will exclaimed.

"I'm for it," John Boy and Jerimiah shouted out, in unison.

"'Tis settled then. We'll leave tomorrow," Will shot out. Enthusiastically, he pulled his chair in close to the others, and thence they began to devise a trip plan.

After dawn, three days later, Will, John Boy, Matt, Jerimiah, and Powhatan Tom rode eagerly into the forest at the river trail, with the warm rising sun ahead of them. They rode fast and slow until near nightfall then pitched their bedrolls under a starry sky. In less than a week, sore but ardent for action, they walked the horses into the fervor of capitol town. The wide streets swarmed with pedestrians, riders, wagons, and coaches. Numbers of Virginians were gathering there to hear the resolutions to the stamp tax. The tired riders tried three inns before finding beds. Once there, they were made to wait long for hot baths. While they waited, they skillfully threw darts at the multi-colored cork board, with marked-off targets, that hung from a far wall. They washed down barbecued pork chops and hot buttered cornbread with cool ale.

The next morning, refreshed, they walked through the triple Roman-arched entrance of capitol hall and into the Georgian architectural masterpiece. Their promptness for the occasion gave them time to admire Wren's brick, slate, marble, concrete, and wood structure from the large veranda.

"I ain't neva seen such a mess o' people in this 'ere town," Will exclaimed.

"Good thing I gots y'all up early, or we'd a neva gotten seats in 'ere," Matt told them.

At that, the great clock chimed the time and the crowd began to move into the huge hall. Once seated, the sound of the crowd did not subdue. Then the gavel pounded.

"Here ye, here ye, this session of the Virginia Burgesses is now in session. Order, order, please, we will 'ave order," the speaker pounded and yelled.

Heads turned toward him. Suddenly, silence rolled over the rows of seats, like the wide wall of an unexpected wave. Tactfully, the speaker introduced business and called for the resolutions. His very mention of the tax elicited hoots and howls, all the way from the gallery to the crowds that spilled through the doorways, and without the wide-open windows. One man after another took the podium and gave his resolve. Some tried to defend the tax, albeit reluctantly. Heated argument spread from the burgesses, themselves, throughout the hall, and then outside after each speech. The crowd grew more intense. Finally, a young upcountry planter and lawyer, Patrick Henry, strode boldly to the podium and began speaking.

This eloquent outspoken orator stirred up political passions like a storm squall stirs up wind and water. He echoed the general sentiments of Virginians, when he claimed that the tax violated the constitution of English laws and traditions, because it countered the natural right to liberty. Thereby, he claimed, a people at liberty taxed themselves. Audaciously, he issued a grave warning against the government.

"Caesar had his Brutus, Charles I his Cromwell, and George III may profit from their example," he boomed with conviction.

At his warning, some stalwarts jumped out of their seats shouting, while pummeling the air violently with clenched fists.

"Treason, treason," they clamored.

The majority, however, drowned out the naysayers with cheers. Finally, the uproar reached a pitch at Henry's conclusion.

"No taxation without representation!" he ended.

The crowd became uncontrollable. A long low roar broke into pounding and applause.

"Resolves, resolves," yelled some.

"Liberty or death," echoed others.

The frustrated speaker shouted for recess. The crowd began moving in massive unison. Out the doorway and through the airy arches it pushed, thitherward, toward the tremendous square. There, on the cobblestone expanse and throughout the town green beyond it, crowds of persons exclaimed about the audaciously defiant rebel rouser.

In the midst of commotion, the five upcountry men made their way out of the hot hall to a shady spot under several tall trees. They lit up cigars and puffed away awhile in reflective concentration.

"Eh, that Henry's a tough guy, ain't he?" Will commented.

"He's smart too, self-government is a natural right. Liberty is the natural state of, not just society, but politics too," John Boy reasoned.

"Henry's a hero now. His speech 'ill move the burgesses to condemn the stamp tax. His name 'ill become known in all of the colonies," Will added.

"In England, too," Powhatan Tom warned, sternly.

The wise native's words hardly sank in. The four others puffed away, agitatedly, at the heady thought of revolt for a long while.

"Well, what think ye, Matt my boy?" Will uttered, uncertainly.

"From what I'se hearin', they's gonna' say, no sir Mista Henry, y'all gots to pay mow taxes. The guvment needs mow taxes to git richa," Matt felt sure.

Everyone laughed hard at Matt, plus their pent-up doubt.

At the end of the long recess, other house members responded to Henry's speech with strong orations and shouts of agreement. The majority thus condemned the stamp tax and supported the idea of self-government. By the end of the afternoon, the burgesses passed a set of Resolves declaring that it had "...the only and sole exclusive right and power to lay taxes...upon the inhabitants of this colony." Thereafter, the spectacle of a showdown with parliament hung ominously ahead. Yet, the emboldened crowds feared not the wrath of imperialism. They took to the taverns. Revelry rolled over the whole town.

At the town's most popular tavern, plenty of patrons stood for want of seats. Fiddlers fiddled from the side of the expansive room. Bartenders poured ale, whiskey, and wine from wide wooden barrels and bottles. Mugs clanged noisily, here and there, without care, as toasts went up and tips got made. The roisterous crowd sensed the momentousness of their times. Then and there, the tax resolution transformed itself into the cause of liberty.

The British government spent the sugar and paper taxes on troops to protect its fur trade, but not pioneers. Many folks resented it. They felt that the government served its own interests rather than those of the people for which it actually existed. Henry had spoken heroically for them. Those would-be pioneers hoped for a day when militiamen might blaze a trail through the vast wilderness. They sought equal opportunity through land and trades. They included the families of veterans who expected compensation for their hard-won war with France. In addition, they included sons of liberty who sought equal opportunity in the military.

At a big bulky table that bordered one wood-paneled wall, the five friends talked about the speech.

"The Sons of Liberty wrote those words for Henry, if ya ask me," Will began.

"They might 'ave. Their a secretive bunch o' guys, allright," Jerimiah commented.

"It ain't like we don't know they're names," John Boy said that which everyone knew.

"Aye, but most of these 'ere folks don't know the sons' identities," Will added.

"That's cause ya 'ave to fight unseen, like a painted native, French style," Jerimiah joked.

"If fightin' breaks out, then they'll come out in the open to defend the cause and one another, allright," John Boy predicted.

Suddenly, loud shouting erupted from across the tavern. Brutally, the door burst open and red-coated soldiers, in dark-blue breeches and black boots, stomped into the smoky tavern. Disciplined, they stood, at attention, blocking the doorway from anyone who would think to exit. The commanding officer swept the room, back and forth, with a rank gaze and sneerful scowl. Patrons moved back uncomfortably in their chairs and on their feet, from fear, as the commander ripped into a group of hardy revelers and grabbed one man, roughly.

"You'll be comin' with me, you," he yelled authoritatively.

"Wait just one minute, sir. What's the charge against this good fellow 'ere?" one of the men queried him, from the other end of the long table, by the door.

"'Tis treason, if need be. Now, back off, mister, or you'll go too," the commander threatened.

Thence, the commander reached out, firmly grabbed his intended prisoner by the arm, and yanked him toward the door. With quick steps, two soldiers rushed forward and aimed their shiny bright bayonets right at the man's back.

"Come along peaceful, now," the commander ordered him, with a threatening smirk.

On the far side of the silent place, Will leaned forward, conspiratorially. One eyebrow went up. "Methinks thy governor means to arrest all of the sons, one at a time," he whispered.

The dead silence holding the place hostage made Will feel suddenly self-conscious. He glanced to-and-fro, to determine whether or not anyone had overheard him. All eyes and ears remained riveted on the sensational scene.

Cautiously, the belligerent officer, and his stiff soldiers, backed the prisoner toward the wide-open door behind them. As they neared the outside, quiet grumbling grew menacingly from surrounding tables. Jerimiah leaned forward, just slightly.

"Any of 'em makes a move now runs a risk o' givin' the sons away," his hushed voice stated, almost inaudibly.

"If they arrest 'im, then they'll get secrets enough," John Boy added, ominously.

Just then, Will's chair screeched noisily back across the floorboards, as he jumped up, pointed to the fight, and spoke boldly out loud, "They'll not allow it."

In the melee, a rush of patrons had pushed a long table on its side, jolted over it, and attacked the arresting officers with furious fists.

Stunned, the soldiers missed the advantage. The wild attackers wrestled them to the whining floorboards. Thinking and moving swiftly, they struggled against the growing onslaught. Then, the rest of the crowd became unrestrained. Men rushed forward roughly into the ruckus. Fear confronted colonials from no quarter. On the contrary, no one wanted to get left out of the excitement.

Boldly, the crowd threw caution away, to the wind, and cheered for the fight. Belligerently, the sons tightened their fists and whacked the soldiers with all their might. They grabbed them around the shoulders, from in front and behind, and wrestled them down. Any man who wanted to fight grabbed a loose leg, and tried to pull them around.

At the forefront, a sheer wall of jeering crowd constantly pushed the commander back. Two rough men, at once, got hold of his arms and yanked him hard. Then, all of the soldiers got pushed back. The men in the crux of the fight did not see fit to stop until all of them had fled the front yard.

Needless to say, the prisoner got away. Tables and chairs were put up the right way. The crowd calmed down and toasts went around. The sons of liberty, however, gave ground. The stealthy sons slid slyly into the night. The confederates rode out of sight.

CHAPTER XVII

THE LIBERTY OF GREEKS

The *Virginia Resolves* lit a fire from New England to Georgia. In October, 1765, the colonies came together, for the first time of their own accord, to form a confederation. Everyone knew it as the Colonial Confederation. Confederates, from all thirteen colonies, drew up a document, that became known as the *Declaration of Rights and Grievances*.

The Declaration condemned the stamp tax. More, it demanded a greater degree of political liberty than practiced by the several colonies' assemblies. For, it boldly demanded that parliament give colonials the authority to tax themselves. It did not, however, go as far as to insist on the total political liberty, of self-government, independent of England.

Parliament countered that the Declaration lacked power of law because colonials had no legal authority to make laws. Pugnacious, parliament wouldn't back down. Opposition grew. It backed down. The following Spring, parliament voted to rescind the tax in face of vehement and widespread opposition.

Then, with a show of authority, parliament passed the *Declaratory Act*. This act subtly reaffirmed its authority to tax the colonies. Unfortunately, the legality got lost on a majority of the people. For, their loyalty to the British government strengthened as they celebrated rescission of the detested stamp tax.

The Richmond newspaper covered the confederation's actions and parliament's responses starting with the Declaration. Everyone, from big planters to homesteaders got riled up about taxes. On the frontier, folk's traditional guide, just plain common sense, told them that everyone should strive to pay less taxes.

So, in June, '67, when parliament proved the *Declaratory Act* by passing the *Townsend Act* for taxing America, the celebration of the stamp tax showdown victory ended. Political loyalty, the kind based on emotion anyway, is fleeting. Adamantly imperialistic, it laid import customs on paper, glass, paint, and tea payable in sterling no less! Like, as if anyone had many coins. Most people made purchases with credit in goods they produced.

To colonials, these import taxes, contrasted sharply with the internal taxes theretofore laid, on tobacco and such, under the century-old *Navigation Acts*. The confused distinction between import and internal taxes raised, already high, vexation. Confusion added to anti-tax sentiment.

In addition, parliament established the American Board of Commissioners of Customs, in Boston, to oversee tax collections. It mandated that tax proceeds would get spent for defense, plus judge and governors' salaries, to ensure their independence from colonial assemblies. After the first year of collections, colonial leaders discovered that a tremendous forty-percent went to administrative costs only, a mere fifteen-percent to defense, and forty-five percent to England!

Perturbed, colonials responded with boycotts, non-importation agreements, and destruction of tea cargoes. At the end of the economic cycle, the taxes brought on an economic recession, naturally. Governments tend to cause recessions, after wars, by regulating the economy, with taxes, to pay for the wars. This recession began in Autumn, '67.

In Richmond, at the tall one-story brick building on a thick stone foundation, the partners worked to record the news, objectively. Political news tested objectivity because readers tended to respond, subjectively. In Winter, '68, by the light of a southern sun, the partners began printing John Dickinson's *Letters of a Pennsylvania Farmer*.

These letters pried open the minds of readers and imbued them with an alltogether new philosophy. It became known as federalism. A concept, that held the proverbial seed of states' rights.

Through the months of '68, Dickinson expostulated on his inventive vision. He foresaw a confederation of colonies, sovereign in themselves, yet united for the purposes of commerce, defense, and justice. The idea of a central government whose authority derived from the colonies, as opposed to vice-versa, harked back to the days of strong dukes and weak kings. Those were the days of feudalism.

Dickinson reminded colonials of the liberty of Englishmen; that the dukes had secured from King John I, in 1215, and set forth in the *Magna Charta*. Thereby, thinking men, and women, began to question, not only the economic precepts of mercantilism, under which they lived and worked, and by which England regulated trade with her colonies through taxes; but they also began to question the political precepts of imperialism, that vested legal authority in the central government at London.

Not everyone who could vote read Dickinson, however. Thus, dishonest candidates confused many voters. The liberty of Englishmen always meant owning land, or at least, practicing a trade. Now, confusion between liberty and taxes became embedded.

One might say, that the Sons of Liberty emotionalized thought, itself. Newspapers reported on their grandiloquent liberty tree rallies, throughout the colonies. At these roisterous events, by great trees, in town centers, classically educated speakers appealed to emotion with symbols of Greek liberty. In Summer, some even wore togas, like Greeks.

In '70, Lord North became prime minister, with tremendous financial assistance from King George III. The king threw his support behind North's old faction, of the Whig Party, in hopes of boosting the monarchy's power over parliament, through the alliance. North's election victory thus enhanced the king's political influence.

The king and his new prime minister sensed, that negotiating with the colonials might further abet the old Whig faction's power in parliament. To that end, they rescinded the *Townsend Act*. Parliament just couldn't bring itself to give up the tea tax, however. To the less perceptive, it seemed the government kept the tea tax as a symbol of power over the people. Yet, on closer scrutiny, rigorous thinkers found a greater issue.

The British East India Company long had a parliamentary monopoly grant. Like any monopoly, it operated inefficiently, because it lacked the incentives for greater productivity that competition provides. Thereby, the monopoly needed the tea tax to cover its high operating costs. Monopolies don't exist, naturally, they must have government patronage.

Colonials took issue with the monopoly. Largely, they circumvented the tax. Smuggling is the natural result of any prohibition. It boomed. Meanwhile, rescission of the other Townsend taxes began to benefit the economy. Vindicated, colonials took aim at the tea tax.

The boycott of tea spread, from neighbor to neighbor, through subsequent seasons. More and more, colonials smuggled Spanish coffee as a substitute for tea. In fact, it became patriotic to drink coffee.

Newport, Rhode Island sat at the center of smuggling operations. The Royal Navy concentrated its patrols in Narragansett Bay. A showdown between the navy and smugglers only awaited opportunity.

It came one warm night in June '72. On that night, a bold plan took effect. A slick speedy smuggler lured *H.M.S. Gaspee* to shallow water where its foreign commander went aground, in the dark, on a sandbar. Boldly, patriots boarded her from sciffs, captured crew, beat them bloody, and burned the boat to the water line.

The British government responded with a threat of arrest and trial, in England, for the culprits of the crime. Unforeseen by imperial authorities, however, was that a jury trial abroad would spread so much outrage up and down the colonial coast. English justice required a jury of one's equals. The imperial government had overplayed its hand, this time. As with most newspapers, editorials in the Richmond paper resounded with rough indignation.

Forthwith, Virginia led the initiative to establish committees of correspondence, throughout the colonies, like one just set up in Massachusetts. Within two years, all of the colonies followed suit.

Before two years, the prime minister compromised to stop the committees forming. He allowed the East India Company to import tea, into the colonies directly, without stopping in England first. Thereby, he enabled it to undercut the Dutch price by doing away with middlemen.

But, tax reduction came too slow. His action actually fueled the fire of freedom. Now, lower-priced tea made the term "freedom of enterprise" meaningful to colonials. At the end of that year, '73, tea cargoes were raided and thrown into harbors from Boston to Charleston. Raids became known as "tea parties."

The following Spring, the prime minister responded with the *Coercive Acts*. Largely aimed at the center of sedition, Boston, these acts included a blockade and arbitrary British rule. The prime minister thus used the town as a scapegoat with which to set an example for the rest to fear.

One English philosopher, Edmund Burke, opined succinctly that, "The rendering the Means of Subsistence of a Whole City dependent upon the King's private pleasure, even after the payment of a fine and satisfaction made, was without Precedent, and of a most dangerous Example."

Indeed so, for patriots responded by setting up an independent government outside Boston. No, Britain's stern example there did not intimidate the other colonies. Rather, it alarmed them.

They sent money and food to the beleaguered place. Virginia sent hundreds of barrels of corn and wheat flour. Nor did the significance of the *Coercive Acts* escape colonial leaders. Now, the decade long battle over taxes transformed into one over liberty. It transformed into one over the power to have, nothing less, than a colonial parliament.

In retaliation for the aid, Governor Dunmore dissolved the burgesses in May, '74. During that seething Summer, Virginians chafed under the governor's tyranny. Again, the liberty of Virginians led the cause. The newspaper rallied the upcountry. Covertly, the tobacco colony organized the various committees of correspondence.

On September fifth, all of the committees, except that of the thirteenth colony, Georgia, came together to form a colonial parliament. It became known as the Continental Congress. Its delegates determined that Philadelphia was the de facto capitol of the colonies. So, there, leaders from the various colonies made strong speeches. To a man, they posited liberty against imperialism.

In addition, the treasonous congress formed a trade association. Through it, the colonies agreed to neither trade with nor consume products from Britain. A boycott. On October twenty-second, the congressmen went home to await parliament's response.

In Winter '75, parliament responded with the *Conciliatory Resolve*. Under its terms, any colony that raised a proper quota for defense and assumed the cost of its civil list, would get exempted from the decade old *Revenue Acts*. Ominously, the power to tax remained with parliament, however.

In addition, parliament passed the *New England Restraining Act*. Under its terms, it forbade New England from trading with any part of the world except Britain. Add, that it denied New England the bounty of Nova Scotia and Newfoundland fishing banks.

Therefore, by Spring '75, the tax issue reached an impasse. The divine hand of fate had cast the proverbial dice. Rebellion awaited only an inciting event. Colonials had become too conscious of liberty to accept arbitrary taxation.

At rallies, in papers, and pamphlets the Sons of Liberty had convinced a plurality of the people that they had, not just a right, but a natural right to tax themselves. And, to exercise that right, the colonies must have their own parliament. Otherwise, colonials must become politically independent, alltogether.

In Virginia, through the years of contention over taxes, political momentum moved upcountry from Williamsburg to Richmond. The Cavalier tidewater tended to remain more loyal to the British government than the pioneer upcountry. The Richmond newspaper reflected that transformation. The printed word rallied readers to the cause of liberty.

Slowly but surely, readers came to understand that governments tend to raise taxes, beyond that amount necessary for defense and justice, to pay politicians' patronage debts, primarily. That is, to maintain and enlarge their political power. Like the imperial Romans, who taxed high only to return a portion to the obedient voters in various forms of patronage, such as grain distributions and gladiator fights, the British government grew too large to govern, justly.

And, to a lesser degree, frontier intellects became rigorous enough to comprehend the long-term effect of excessive taxation. Economic theory taught thinkers that transfers of wealth from producers to government reduces savings. Importantly, saving is the proverbial key to wealth. Without savings, persons cannot afford real estate, livestock, lumber, equipment, tools, nor other costs to start a farm, trade, or profession.

Like slaves then, they give up the excess product of their labor to an employer instead of investing it in themselves.

And, in time, as excessive taxation continues, the number of employers lessens until only the ultimate one, government itself, remains. Therefore, government slowly enslaves people through taxes.

All ancient Greeks were self-employed. Only slaves worked for someone else. Therefore, the liberty of Greeks, like its heirs, the liberty of Romans, the liberty of Englishmen, and now, the liberty of Virginians, demanded self-government for self-taxation, self-employment, and savings. Not for two thousand years had liberty been so alive.

CHAPTER XVIII

EQUALITY OF OPPORTUNITY

Meanwhile, landless colonists, from New England to Georgia, looked west. In the former French wilderness, beyond the mountains, they envisioned equality of opportunity for liberty. However, through the *Quebec Act*, of '74, parliament gave French Catholic Canadians seigniorial rights south to the Ohio River, mainly to shore up its imperial fur monopoly. In effect, Britain denied the newly won West to New Englanders, New Yorkers, and Pennsylvanians. South of the Ohio, lay the Shawnee hunting grounds. Like the North, parliament had prohibited settlement of these lands, by the *Proclamation of 1763*. And thus, in effect, Britain denied the newly won West to Pennsylvanians, Virginians, Carolinians, and Georgians.

In defiance of the prohibition, Daniel Boone, and several other known "long knives", explored the awesomely thick Caintucky forests to the rolling bluegrass lands. Boone's laudable description of the wilderness spread quickly throughout Virginia. The sensational strength of popular opinion moved Governor Dunmore to acquiesce to the demands of the Vandalia and other land speculation companies. He granted Shawnee lands to World War veterans who possessed warrants that they had received in exchange for military service.

The Shawnee, however, remained steadfastly imperious to the governor's attempts at negotiations. Adamant, he sent two parties of Virginia volunteers to take possession of the grants. In July '74, as one of these parties trekked through the fearsome forbidding forest, along a wide bank of the Caintucky River, it succumbed to the horror of tomahacks. On word of the gruesome massacre, the other party made a hasty retreat.

Virginians responded to the news vigorously. Without hesitation, Colonel Andrew Lewis called to muster his fellow upcountry militiamen. His order reached upper James River men and boys in villages, on farms, and plantations in the dead heavy heat of Summer. The opportunity caught the sentimental ears of Powhatan Ed's son, Powhatan Tom, and his proud son, Tommy Junior. The young native yearned to fulfill his destiny with the brave experiences that his ancestors knew.

Father and son sat in shade spread by spruces, at the front of their two-story house, above the muddy creek. At a distance, a boisterous group of boys played hard in the water. On the porch, Tom's wife, Pocahontas sat, in earshot, reading the *Almanack*. On the lawn, Powhatan Tom read aloud, from the newspaper, about the Shawnee massacre. As he read the article, he insightfully read his son's restive face. At the article's end, he placed the paper on his lap and contemplated its impact on his people.

"White man get serious now, Junior. Send Colonel Lewis west to war with Chief Cornstalk," he began.

"The five nations come to aid of Shawnee," Tommy Junior wanted to believe.

"Perhaps not. Northern tribes profit from fur trade. Interest lay with British, foremost," Powhatan Tom advised his son.

"Five nations shall turn their backs on Shawnee then?" Tommy queried, incredulously.

"Worse has happened among natives," his father answered, heavily.

Momentarily, a short hot breeze blew through the trees and swept his answer away. The sensation of mid-summertime lingered behind. Whimsically, Tommy turned to his father. Powhatan Tom caught the capricious thought like a quick flash of lightening, and sudden panic grabbed him from behind.

"Shawnee lands on your mind, boy," he stated sternly.

"I am Powhatan brave. Shawnee lands are native lands," Tommy retorted.

His boy's sharp words cut clear through Powhatan Tom's chest. He betrayed nothing nonetheless. Fervently, he hoped for another breeze. None came.

"Englishmen know that land begets liberty. Many want it. Few have money to purchase it. Besides, British government owns all land. None for sale," he explained.

"Governor Dunmore gives land grants to veterans," Tommy blurted with wild hope.

"You are no veteran, boy," his father insisted firmly.

"If Colonel Lewis wins war against Chief Cornstalk, then his soldiers get land," Tommy asserted.

Powhatan Tom summoned all his confidence from deep within him. Bravely, with caution, he turned to read the boy's future in his innocent face. There, he saw that which he so dreaded and feared. His son must get land and English liberty or die trying.

"I ask John to write letter to Colonel Lewis. Recommend you for Virginia Militia. You go. Fight Shawnee. Learn life your ancestors knew. Then, you return to Muddy Creek," the desperate father demanded of his son.

Choked, Tommy could only nod his head affirmatively. Up on the porch, Pocahontas had long since ceased reading.

She turned slightly to the west. Her eyes blurred and one tear rolled down her auburn cheek.

At dawn, two days later, early risers on the plantation gathered at the stable to see Tommy off. The sinuous, black-haired, buckskin-clad boy leaned down from his tall brown mount and shook the proffered hands of well-wishers who blocked his way. He packed saddlebags and a backpack filled with food and clothes, along with sundry items, and most importantly, John's recommendation. At his sides lay a trusty new Pennsylvania rifle and knife. He looked the image of a quintessential forester.

Having so much attention focused on him, from the ground around his mount, made him feel uneasy. Doubt reached out from nowhere. He had been anticipating this scene for many days, yet, for a few moments, it all seemed unreal. He felt as far from his feet as from the ground. His dream overtook him. He became unable to focus on anything nearby. Woods in the distance kept his gaze.

Those several uncertain moments, however, got blocked from his memory forever. The bright glare of the sun brought him to his senses. Once again, he saw everyone smiling around him. He threw up his hand in a broad wave. The spirited stallion jolted out of the throng, and Tommy broke away.

The virile young horse and rider tore through the river trail with wild abandon. At mid-day, Tommy rode the sweaty stinking stallion into the cold river at a rocky rapid. The fast-flowing water refreshed them. Reinvigorated, they took off for the foothills ahead. Near sundown, Tommy began looking for the next big plantation that would come along. Within a few more miles, a long winding white wooden fence appeared. He followed it to an opening and rode onto the place.

Up a long narrow dirt road he rode. He traversed pass a large herd of menacingly mooing bulls. At the top of the hill, he spotted the big house, set in trees, on his right. The stable and barns sat off on his left. His mount did not need direction.

The horse stopped short of the wide-open stable doors where several barking dogs stood sentry. He whinnied loud and stomped once, shaking his big head all the while. The dogs backed off.

"Easy now, easy now," Tommy bent down to soothe him.

When he looked up, he caught the eyes of three colored men approaching him.

They greeted him with broad smiles that betrayed their gladness to see someone new, "How y'all? Come needin' somethin'? What's we do for ya, now?"

"I am Powhatan Tom, Junior," Tommy began.

"Yessum," the eldest stableman smiled more broadly.

"From the Muddy Creek Plantation. A day's ride back yonder," Tommy continued.

"YES-sum," the eldest repeated, more emphatically.

"I ride west to join up with militia and fight Shawnee," Tommy proudly added.

"YES-SUM, sure nuff," he agreed, with his broadest grin.

Tommy looked down and around. He swallowed his pride with a discernable gulp. Then, he reached into his bag and pulled out a silver coin.

"My horse needs feedin', if it ain't no bother," he asked, as he proffered the coin.

"Why, 'tain't no botha 'tall, boy. Now, come on down an' rest yourselves. An', youse can keep that there coin," the colored man demanded generously.

"Thanks much. Don't mind if I do. Jus' don't be callin' me boy. I ain't no boy. I'm a Powhatan brave. Son of Powhatan Tom and grandson of Powhatan Ed, from the Muddy Creek Plantation," Tommy retorted.

The colored man glanced, back and forth, across the ground in front of him, and shook his head in discernable dismay.

"Well, allrights, allrights. What's y'all like to be called then?" he asked in appeasement.

"Tommy," he answered.

"Tommy. Allrights. Now, lets us git that there hot saddle off o' this 'ere horse's backside an' git y'all washed up an' fed," the colored man said, as he began unbuckling the bridle.

That night, Tommy slept soundly on stable loft hay. The hot sunny day kept the loft warm that night. He slept so soundly that he fell into a deep dream. In the warm air, he swam with the boys, back home in the muddy creek. His mother was calling him from the distant house. It ain't dinnertime. What could she want, he wondered? That's when the morning sun broke over the blue horizon and aimed, straightaway, at his eyes.

Tommy sat up without hesitation. He ambled nimbly down the loft ladder, pulled a clean outfit out of his saddle bags, and put himself into his clothes. The stablemen brought breakfast out of the big house kitchen. He savored steaming hot coffee, biscuits, bacon, and eggs. Satiated, he thanked them, saddled his horse, and rode out with the colored man's warning behind him.

"Y'all keeps clear o' what ain't y'all business now, hear."

On the second day of hard riding up the river road, he reached the headwaters below the Blue Ridge. Before sundown, he reached a sight to behold, forever. A panoramic view of the great Shenandoah Valley spread far out beyond him. Awed, the boy took in the broad scene. Then, he turned back through the thick trees, meandered down the winding trail, and into the valley below.

Dusk brought him to the tiny native trading post to which his father had directed him. At that ancient crossroads, valley natives had been bartering with travelers for more time than any of them knew. Tommy took some hay for his horse and left him in the corral. Then, he made himself at home in the big wigwam meant for the road weary.

Tommy sat down and folded his legs on the ground, among members of the large family that made their home there. Their wise old patriarch greeted him in a parental manner. His face betrayed pride for the native brave's prowess. His look boosted Tommy's confidence.

The father spoke, "I remember Powhatan Tom from two days ride away. Many years pass now since he be traveler. How does he?"

"My father lives well. On plantation. My mother too," Tommy answered.

"And you. Why you travel?" he asked.

"Come into mountains to militia camp. Join up. Fight, under Captain Lewis, against Shawnee Chief, Cornstalk," Tommy explained.

Tommy's explanation threw the family's faces into expressions of doubt and concern.

"We know militia camp. Not much farther," the sagacious old man said.

Then he paused, sat back and smoked awhile. A granddaughter proffered a wooden bowl to Tommy, with a smile. He ate heartily of the deer meat, thick sauce, and cornbread held within it.

Her grandfather sat forward and spoke again. "Lately, men, and boys, come through here on way to camp. All white men. Some with coloreds.

"If Virginia militiamen win war, then they get Caintucky land," Tommy blurted out just as he had, in response to his own father.

The old man drew back stiff with doubt. "Englishmans' war, boy. Not our war. You not go. Stay here at village long as want. Teach grandson to ride and shoot gun," he offered.

"You are old and wise. I am young and not wise. But, I go west with Englishmen," Tommy insisted.

The next evening, anxious excitement unexpectantly swelled up, from somewhere unknown within him, as he rode into the bustling camp. He dismounted at the command post, tethered his mount, braced himself, walked in, deepened his voice, and made an introduction. Colonel Lewis and his officers greeted him forthrightly. Then they queried him. He handed over the recommendation. Master John's family name worked wonders for the native boy. Colonel Lewis placed his hand on his neck and led him to the commissary tent. From there, the colonel introduced him to his sergeant and quarters.

He bathed in a clear cold mountain creek with several soldiers. Afterward, they ate a meal of meat, potatoes, and peas that tasted like home. Afterward, he took a stool in front of his tent. He spent the twilight tinkering with his rifle and listening to soldiers' talk. That night, expectation prevented sound sleep.

Within a few weeks, Tommy made fast friends. Daily routine set in. The militiamen practiced drilling, shooting, and worked out difficult maneuvers for hours each day, excepting weekends. In mid-August, the camp broke up.

Alert and disciplined, the corps began trekking northwestwardly. They headed out of the Allegheny Mountains and onward toward the headwaters of the Kanawha River. Simultaneously, Governor Dunmore led a corps southwestwardly from near Fort Pitt. The strategic plan called for the two groups to meet at the Ohio River, gain tactical advantage, and lure Chief Cornstalk into a decisive battle.

On the Kanawha River trail, the going got rough. At times, the narrow trail grew so steep that the men had to pull the reluctant horses and stubborn mules by taut reins. On the down slopes, they sometimes slid on their hefty hindquarters. Gradually, the little river broadened. The flood-level trail opened up, somewhat, and the corps rolled on.

At nights, in the massive mountain woods, the corps, fifteen hundred strong, slept safely by the shimmering moonlit water. Five weeks out they reached the Ohio River. There, on a broad riverbank, the steadfast soldiers set up camp and prepared to live or die.

Diligently, the men prepared for battle against the brutal savages. Over and over, they formed ranks and charged the nearly impenetrable woodlands. Stealthily, they scattered into trees only to converge, out from behind their covers, onto small groups in clearings. For hours, they competed for marksmanship, by carefully aiming knives at tree targets painted up like natives. With more strength than skill, they wrestled their opponents to exhaustion. They tended to weapons and gear. Before dinner, they bathed in the big river. At night, they slept insecurely with one eye and ear open.

During those early Autumn days, Tommy grew in different directions, at once. He grew more confident. He grew more relaxed. He grew closer to other boys than he had ever thought possible. One starry Saturday night, he sat cross-legged in front of a flickering fire. The sounds of fiddles and flutes filled the air. Tobacco and whiskey made minds fair.

Soundlessly, a young soldier approached Tommy from behind, bent over, and whispered into his ear.

"Hey, Tommy, come into the tent yonder. The pipe's goin' round," he motioned toward the tent.

"Sure," Tommy responded eagerly.

Tommy followed him into the packed tent where several soldiers sat around a brass-and-glass globe candle light. He found a space and edged in between two friends.

The pipe came his way. He drew long but not hard. Closely, the other boys watched him smoke the native weed. When the pipe came their way, they imitated his way with it. Their imitations made him feel a sense of solitude. The pipe came around again and again. With each turn on it, his eyes became more fixated on the candle light. His mind mellowed and surrounded him with ease. His true nature broke free from his fears. His face betrayed the proud look of his long, and careful, royal lineage.

On the other side of the tent, one young soldier became overwhelmed by similar sensations. For a fleeting, yet certain moment, he caught the image of brave native genes in Tommy's tight face. Long-standing self-doubt got the best of him. Deep down within his sub-conscious, the blond boy panicked. For, he sensed his own flaccid face giving away his common ancestry.

"Powhatan Tom, what thinks ye to get out o' this 'ere war, land?" he asked, with a tone of tendentiousness.

"Adventure brought me 'ere," Tommy answered flatly.

"Why do ya fight your own kind?" the tenacious soldier taunted him.

At that question, the others shifted in their seats and frowned. A barely perceptible aura of discomfort rolled through the tent.

"Shawnee not my people," Tommy riposted menacingly.

Tommy's tone transformed discomfort into tension around the circle of young soldiers. Some of them thought to break it by standing up, with pretended ease, and heading for the music outside.

"You're drunk, quit askin' fool questions," one fellow shot at the sarcastic soldier.

"Oh ya, how'd we know he ain't no spy, no how? He's one of 'em, ain't he?" the soldier retorted.

Grumbling agreements, and otherwise, rolled around.

At that charge, Tommy lunged angrily onto the cynical soldier. Everyone began yelling. Rambunctious pummeling ensued. The boys twisted around each other while turning to-and-fro. From the get-go, Tommy had the best of him. Firmly, he held him down while punching passionately away. At one point, the entangled two rolled into the canvas tent wall. It bulged precariously. Stakes popped from the ground without. They rolled back in. Excitement grew riotously. The yelling became loud shouts and hurrahs that drowned out the sound of fiddles and flutes.

Colonel Lewis rushed into the tent.

He slowly roared, "At-ten-tion."

Abruptly, the music stopped. Sudden silence isolated the sound of Tommy's last smack. Knuckle hit bone with a whack. In the vacuum of their own sound, the shouted order caught the two boys unawares. Reluctantly, they stumbled upon their feet and stood at attention.

Bloodied, bruised, and emboldened, the colonel's stern expression had no effect on them. He stared harder, yet without result. He gave in. Experience with soldiers told him let it pass, because he saw justice writ large on Tommy's face. Thus, he ordered the two separated permanently and assigned extra duty to both of them. Satisfied, he turned deftly and walked out.

Several of the boys congratulated Tommy for a fight well fought, while they slapped him soundly on his butt. The soldier who invited him into the tent, in the first place, admired him more than did the rest.

With a slight choke, he said, "Anyone who defends his honour as you do, Tommy buddy, rightly deserves Caintucky land."

Tommy's red blood rushed, at once, with pride and satisfaction.

And so, Tommy became a Virginian. On the battlefield, where Chief Cornstalk surprised the Virginians, his confidence assured him of glory. On that fateful field, above the onrushing Ohio, he courageously shot down three savage Shawnee and lunged a knife into another. The victory at Point Pleasant, on October 10, '74, extended the Virginia Colony's western border clear across Caintucky to the mighty Mississippi River. At first, parliament obstructed emigration. However, it could not long deny the liberty inherent in land ownership. Eventually, Virginians went west. Tommy trekked too.

CHAPTER XIX

THE LIBERTY OF VIRGINIANS

During the post-war years, the liberty of Virginians poured over the first colony's borders. The ideal of the Jamestowne colonists took firm root from the rocky cold soil of New England to the sandy subaqueous swampland of Georgia. The tradition established by the ancient Greeks had weathered the storms of Roman and British imperialism. Once again, delicate blooms appeared.

The fifth generation pioneers, on the Muddy Creek Plantation, had long lived lives of liberty. Since 1608, when olde Jesse planted himself down on the virgin lande, the generations witnessed the determined growth of the ancient ideal in this wild new world. From up above the onrushing olde river, they had seen Opekankano attempt to deny pioneers of it. They had seen monopolism deny Africans of it. They had seen Bacon rebel for it. They had seen the Scotch-Irish come to partake of it. Now, they saw colonials, from near and far, rising up against imperialism to gain it.

Nowhere, on the plantation, did the cause live more certitudinously than in the book-filled library. There, in that warm sanctuary, on a wet windy Spring evening in '76, John read aloud from the worn copy of Herodotuse's *Persian Wars*. Beside him, his brother-in-law, Will, puffed pleasantly on a pipe. To the left, their wives, followed by Missy and Abe, sat in rapt attention. Jemimah and Jerimiah sat on each side of them. On Will's right, sat Powhatan

Tom and Pocahontas along with his brother, Powhatan Ted Junior and his wife, Pocacosin. Several other adults and children filled out the wholly absorbed audience.

As the storyteller approached the final sentences, the memory of his grandfather and father's reading, that very book, sneaked up from the corner of his mind. Heavily, he lifted his eyes from that last page, to the group of intense listeners, and slowly began to paraphrase with profound purpose. The timeless meaning, of those sagacious words of wisdom, struck him as for the first time.

"In the end, with the last Persian War won, there is nothing left to say. Except, to ask the question: When will the Persian Wars ever end?"

Mouths fell open and faces went blank.

Jeremiah asked the question that clouded all of their minds. "Mista John, why does Herodotus wonda when the wars 'ill end afta they done ended?"

John answered, "His question is a riddle that holds a warning for the ages. The answer to the riddle is: The wars will never end. That is to say, cultures lacking the tradition of liberty will always attempt to deny it."

The pertinence of the poet's foresight stirred uneasy passions in the room. Will allowed the smoke to roll between his teeth as he shifted in his seat. He enlarged on John's answer.

"We must heed the poet's warning, ourselves, otherwise we'll lose the liberty of Virginians!" he exclaimed.

The poet's adept intuition moved Sarah, too.

"Indeed. The British attack on the independent government at Concord, in Massachusetts, last Spring, denies self-government in all of the colonies. The loss at Breed's Hill needs to be remedied by General Washington and the United Army of the Colonies," she vigorously insisted.

Sarah's vociferous voice woke two of the little kids who had fallen asleep. They began screaming fretfully.

"Oh, that's it. Time for bed, chilen," Jemimah ordered.

At that, the kids rebelled.

"No, no, not yet," several of them cried out querulously.

Imperviously, Jemimah got up and clasped one hand around two tiny wrists, at once. Aiming for the stairs, she pulled without pity.

"Yessum, now. I knows y'all tired. I sees y'all yawnin'. Ain't nothin' Jemimah don't see," she said adamantly, as she yanked the suddenly obstinate youngsters toward the hall. That gave notice for the reading to break up.

In the aftermath of bedtime commotion, the adults sat alone. Quietly, they sipped whiskey, brandy, and smoked. Only the sounds of nature remained. Relentless rain rushed onto the rattling windowpanes. Howling wind sucked at the fire.

Slowly, the effects of spirits began to ease long-standing caution. Lurking fates lured lumberingly from deep history. Precociously aware, Sarah precognized destiny. Assertively, she licked her lips and laid down her brandy goblet.

"The time comes to reveal our secret, Babs," the two knew, instinctively, as she got up, walked to a bureau, and slid a brass key into the shallow bottom drawer.

The screeching obstinance of the old wooden drawer got swallowed by a furious bang of bright white lightning.

She stood up, turned around, and unfurled a large rectangular sheet of brightly colored cotton. Then Babs and she proudly displayed the brilliant red, white, and blue flag.

"We know that boys like to carry flags into battle," Sarah said, softly.

Will's pipe nearly dropped out of his mouth. He shot an incredulous look at John.

"What? Stars instead of a union jack in the canton. That's not the United Army of the Colonies' flag," he expressed in disbelief.

Sarah smiled firmly.

"It's the daughters' new flag of independence," she responded boldly.

"Looks like ole Tom Paine's *Common Sense* has moved you girls to radicalism," Will remarked.

"Tom Paine knows that independence must come even though the second congress hesitates. Especially, since parliament prohibited all trade with the colonies, to prevent self-government, complete independence is the only guarantee of liberty," Sarah insisted.

"Independent countries can trade with the whole world, and manufacture what suits them. And, that's the way to win a war," Babs added.

Jerimiah sat forward in his chair and clasped his hands, uncertainly.

"Yessum, eva since General Richard Montgomery invaded Canada an' started this 'ere war, I been wantin' to go inta battle, myself, Mista John. Then, last year, when the burgesses moved again' the East India's tradin' monopoly, I says to myself, 'why, Jerimiah, slavery be illegal but for that govament monopoly.' Yessur, I be proud to fight for liberty too, right sides y'all," he hoped.

"Why, glory be. Your goin' to get yourself killed jus' talkin' like that. You ain't neva even shot a gun ridin' a horse," Jemimah huffed.

"Now looky 'ere, mam. Maybe I 'ave and you jus' don't knows it," Jerimiah countered.

Again, the crackle and flicker of thunder and lightening brought pause. The focus of attention turned to John and Will. After several unsure seconds, John spoke realistically.

"War is risky business, in any case. In ours, the military odds favor the enemy, by far. If this war for colonial government turns into one for actual independence, then there would be no possibility for compromise," he reasoned.

"Win or lose, at that event," Will agreed.

"Yes, and if we lose, then it could cost us everything. Not just the seditious newspaper, but the salt mines, and even the plantations could be confiscated. We might even get arrested for treason. Before I put on a militia uniform, I'd like to travel to Philadelphia to see how much resolve the congress really has for independence," John opined.

The thought of traveling so far caused pause. Many ponderous moments passed.

"'Tis a good idea, John. We shall all go," Sarah said with assurance.

The couples caught one another's anticipative glances in mid-air.

"'Tis settled, then. We shall prepare to travel," Will agreed.

Early on a muggy warm morning the carriage sat waiting at the stable doors. Will, Babs, Sarah, Jerimiah, and Jemimah stood anxiously nearby. Several children scampered, thereabouts, in the excitement of travel. John kept them waiting. Sarah grabbed Abe's grandson.

"Jacob, go upstairs and see to Mr. John," she asked the bright-eyed boy.

"Yessum, miss Sarah. I gets 'em for y'all," Jacob responded quickly, as he rushed off to the house.

Jacob, however, did not find John. For, he stood far-off at the plantation graveyard. Isolated in space and time, he gazed fixedly over the marble slabs at the muddy creek. A slight breeze turned up timid ripples on the brown water below. The busy sound of birds, in a feeding frenzy, filled his ears. Mysteriously, he felt as if two centuries had compressed into the present moment. All of his forebears, at once, came to life.

The benignant aura of his ancestors assuaged his doubts. His great-great-grandparents had come to the wilderness to gain liberty through tobacco planting. His great-grandparents had enlarged that hard-earned liberty on these well-tilled fields. His grandparents had seen the spirit of '76 go down in defeat. His parents had waited eagerly for its resurrection. His brother, James, did not live long enough to see it. Now, without them, alone in space and time, he stood at the precipice of destiny.

For just a few fateful moments, the fickle breeze flew from a new direction. Clusters of blowing leaves bent back, belligerently. Momentarily, he got a racy whiff off of the young green tobacco fields.

The pungent smell reminded him, that tobacco had planted this English country in the virgin lande. The plant made the Virginia Company powerful enough to foment sedition against imperialism. It had been King Charles' desire to monopolize the tobacco trade that induced him to recognize the House of Burgesses and thus the beginnings of self-government. Discontent with tobacco regulations, under the *Navigation Acts*, had been potent among the causes of Bacon's Rebellion. Most recently, tobacco's controlled price, that is: tax, provided grounds for contention in Patrick Henry's *Parson's Cause*.

Suddenly, John saw the inseparability of tobacco and liberty. An attack on one is an attack on the other. The very culture of tobacco, and, indeed, smoking itself, is one of liberty. Virginians must protect that singular culture or loose liberty. It is the fate of Virginians to lead the cause. He would do his part for independence. Reaffirmed, he turned away.

The long journey to Philadelphia, through rolling plantation country, rolled by. Once there, the three couples encountered an excited throb of fellow travelers. A small crowd of colonials had gathered to partake in the politics of independence.

From the first day, the largest and wealthiest place in all of the colonies infatuated the frontier couples. The unsurpassed greatness of Georgian architecture, throughout the tree-lined cobblestone streets, awed them. They wandered the whole of one day through the library. They studied Franklin's printing operation in close detail.

Shortly after their arrival, excitement built up with news of events back in Virginia. Governor Dunmore had been overthrown. The burgesses readied to formally declare the colony a free and independent state. The rights of Virginians became the talk of the town. On the seventh day of the sixth month, in that year of '76, they witnessed a fellow Virginian, Richard Henry Lee, declare the Virginia delegation's resolve for independence in the Continental Congress.

"That these United Colonies are, and of right ought to be, Independent States, that they are absolved from all allegiance to the British Crown, and that all political connection between them and the State of Great Britain is, and ought to be, totally dissolved. That it is expedient forthwith to take the most effectual measures for forming foreign alliances. That a plan of confederation be prepared and transmitted to the respective Colonies for consideration and approbation."

Lee's eloquent and emotional speech brought down the huge hall. That evening, at their favorite inn, Virginians came together to celebrate. At the end of the meal, one young planter stood up and started a round of toasts.

"To the most radical of heroes, Richard Lee of Leesburg, in the former colony, now state, of Virginia," he roared.

"May his progeny live long and prosperous," added another.

"May the liberty of Virginians live long," added yet another.

"That it shall meet every test laid in its path and succeed," added a fourth.

"To the future General Lee," a fifth man shouted.

At that nomination, the crowd went tumultuous. When the uproar subsided, loud clanking toasts ensued. All of the honourable men and women, of the first colony, got at least one toast in, before the merriment ended in the wee morning hours. The crowd had forgotten the hour. However, no one present, that night, ever forgot the glory.

The next morning, Sarah, Babs, and Jemimah took off for a day in the shops. They entered a coffeehouse, once a teahouse, just a few minutes walk from the inn. A crowd had already filled the place.

"Sorry, mam, there are no tables," a steward informed them.

Sarah's eyes spotted an empty booth, in back.

The steward's eyes followed hers, reluctantly.

However, there's an empty booth, that the gentlemen have just vacated, in the back," he offered, hesitantly.

"We'll take it," Sarah said, boldly.

"Oh, Sarah, we can't sit back there with the men," Babs objected.

"Nonsense, the times excuse us," Sarah responded.

"Ohh," Jemimah moaned, uncertainly.

Once seated, the steward served the women. At first, they sat silently drinking the warm brew. Suddenly, the sound of a pounding fist, on marble tabletop, emanated from an adjacent booth. The unmistakable drawl of a Virginia frontiersman accompanied the pounding.

"I need neither book nor pamphlet to write this declaration. The principles and language of our cause are laid down right 'ere in Locke's *Second Treatise of Government*. In the tradition of Aristotle, liberty is the natural state of men. And, government must be accountable, by legal contract, to respect that natural state. Now, I'm off to work," the man insisted.

At that, the wiry red-haired man ejected himself so energetically, from his booth, that a cup and saucer flew to the floor in front of the women. The man bowed slightly.

"Excuse the commotion ladies. We gentlemen quite lose ourselves in philosophy," he apologized.

"That's allright, sir. No harm done," Sarah offered.

"And, to who do I 'ave the pleasure, mam," he asked.

"Sarah Hughes, Muddy Creek Plantation. My sister-in-law, Babs Morton, and my mammy, Jemimah. And, you, sir," Sarah asked with a smile.

"Tom Jefferson, mam, Monticello Plantation. Pleased to meet you," he replied.

"Thank you, Mr. Jefferson," Sarah said.

"Why, you'd be the wives of John Hughes and William Morton." Jefferson remembered. "And kin to George Mason, who will soon issue the Virginian's *Bill of Rights*, I might add. Strong patriot bloodlines, ladies," he added admiringly.

"Fearless, sir," Sarah replied.

Babs bowed her head, with a slight smile.

"Well, I'm off," Jefferson said.

"Good luck, sir," the ladies bid him.

"God be lookin' out for y'all, mista Jeffason," Jemimah added, with concern.

A few weeks later, the Continental Congress adopted Jefferson's *Declaration of Independence*. A few days afterward, a crowd heard him read it from the balcony of the statehouse, that most everyone had just started calling, Independence Hall. The preamble predicted a classical document. The *Magna Charta* paled in comparison.

"We hold these truths to be self-evident, that all men are created equal, that they are endowed by their Creator with certain unalienable Rights, that among these are Life, Liberty, and the Pursuit of Happiness."

Overwhelmed, the hushed crowd anticipated the historical significance of subsequent paragraphs. Ominously, they also sensed the danger. For, they felt that the strength of those poetic words must certainly bring all of the accumulated power, of centuries-old imperialism, down on their colonial necks. By the end of the Virginian's daring war prose, fear had gripped every patriot. Nonetheless, they stood intrepidly and applauded wildly with all their strength.

"We, therefore, the Representatives of the United States of America, solemnly publish and declare. . .that as Free and Independent States, they have full Power to levy War, conclude Peace, contract Alliances, establish Commerce, and to do all other acts and things which independent States may of right do. And for the support of this Declaration, with a firm reliance on the Protection of Divine Providence, we mutually pledge to each other our Lives, our Fortunes, and our sacred Honor."

CHAPTER XX

THE WAR FOR INDEPENDENCE

From the commencement of war, in '75, General Washington, Commander-in-Chief of the new-formed Continental Army, found it hard to maintain a formidable force of fighting men. Short enlistment terms caused his army to expand and contract with the farming seasons. The general's attempts to lengthen terms met opposition.

A long war, against their fellow Britons, seemed unlikely to most colonials. Worse, many did not think enlistment mandatory civic duty. Paradoxically, it seemed to conflict with the ideal of liberty.

Indeed, colonials were an interdependent and subservient society. Planters and merchants were dependent on farmers and tradesmen. Planters purchased neighborhood farmers' food crops, to feed the one-crop plantations. Merchants purchased tradesmens' products, to market. Likewise, farmers and tradesmen were dependent on planters and merchants. Farmers sold their own cash crops as a part of the planters' crop, to get a greater price per unit. Farmers depended on planters' slaves, for labor to plant and harvest. Tradesmen were dependent on merchants, to market their products. Both farmers and tradesmen gained credit from planters and merchants. The latter, thereby, became patriarchs of neighborhoods and villages.

Thus, soldiers expected to get paid regularly. In truth, political apathy hid a plurality of the people in its feudal fold. If not for the French alliance, of '78, organized by

General le Marquis de Lafayette, the fickle force might have succumbed to the strength of Britain's paid army.

So, the various states' militias provided an invaluable addition to the Continental Army. Virginia militiamen contributed much. They saw gritty fighting in the Carolinas Campaign, besides in their own state. Largely, local men served alongside one another. John, Will, Jerimiah, and Matt started out together. Will did not stay with them. Where John left publishing responsibilities to his partners, Will could not break free of the mines. The army needed salt.

Eventually, John relied not only on Will, at the mines, and his partners, at the paper, but on Sarah. The mistress took certain charge of the plantation. Jerimiah, Matt, and he mustered, at camp, with upcountry men. For a while, however, Virginia remained without war.

In time, General Washington lost New York, Britain's most loyal place. But, he took Trenton and Princeton to the southwest. Under General Howe, the British occupied the colonial capitol, Philadelphia, and then under General Clinton, they abandoned it. Significantly, the patriot general, Horatio Gates, defeated General Burgoyne at Saratoga in northern New York. Everyone hailed it as not just a tactical but a great strategic victory, for it convinced France to make an alliance on February 6, '78.

Military life involved Virginia militiamen in routine. Over and over, they drilled and practiced, with intermittent visits home, but saw no action. Ominously, nonetheless, they saw the red tide of war slowly, but surely, roll toward them from the South. General Cornwallis took Savannah. He forced the patriot general, Lincoln, to surrender Charleston on May 12, '80. The capitulation was a big blow to the cause.

That Summer, Colonel Tarleton boldly began taking the rest of South Carolina. Militiamen marched south to bolster the front. Nonetheless, at the Battle of Camden, on an hot August 16, in the pine-wooded hills north of town, in what became a rough fist-fighting skirmish, Colonel Tarleton routed General Gates and mortally wounded General deKalb.

Most upcountry militiamen saw their first real action in that wild melee. Green, undisciplined, and lacking leadership many fled the moving wall of redcoats in a panicked retreat. They gave up Hobkirk Hill and headed into the piney woods. Those who took a stand fell in a slaughter. The embarrassment strengthened the mettle of militiamen more than ever.

Fast on the heels of the Southern Army's northward retreat, Generals Cornwallis and Ferguson bore down, in two columns, right into North Carolina. On October 7, the patriots turned and took a stand, against General Ferguson, at King's Mountain, at the Carolinas' border. The frontier militia reached heights of glory atop that lofty ridge. They badly routed a furious General Ferguson.

On that mountain, Matt Morton met opportunity. He found himself in a position to fight with sniper fire. And, for all his age, he fought valiantly. During the tedious seasons of drilling and practicing, the quick lightweight colored man had chosen to learn to handle a rifle. Rifles proved more accurate than smooth-bore muskets. Though loading the heavy long barrels took time, some agile men excelled at it.

Riflemen came in handy use on flanks. Around the sides of the mountain, yet from unreachable distances, these sharpshooters picked off the oncoming enemy with point-blank accuracy. At the end of that fateful fight, the carnage lay bloodied, smashed, and moaning in misery at the foot of the mountain. Matt never could remember just how many he hit that day. But he always said, "There was a tarnation of 'em. Theys justa kept on a comin'."

John held his ground in the thick of battle. The steep wooded mountainside provided a tactical advantage. In waves, the disciplined enemy charged up, under cover of heavy artillery fire and trees. Jeeringly, patriots shot through the acrid blinding smoke and burning trees. John would later say, "It often got to be every man for himself."

John and Jerimiah never lost sight of each other. They worked as a two-man team. One kept his eyes peeled while the other kept his aimed. Jerimiah believed that's how they stayed alive. He would later say, "It's always betta when mens fight as a team."

Notwithstanding the victory at King's Mountain, General Washington foresaw Virginia's demolition. Wisely, he moved to reorganize the Southern Theater. He appointed General Nathaniel Greene commander of the Southern Department in December '80. At once, Greene's personality made men more confident. He pumped new valour into worn-out ranks.

Audaciously, General Greene divided into two groups to harass General Cornwallis while living off the land. He placed one group under General Daniel Morgan and the other under himself. The radical, General Richard Henry Lee, brought his cavalry up to scout and raid. Thereafter, traditional tactics turned to the unconventional.

The new war tactics proved themselves, providentially. General Morgan killed or captured nearly all of Colonel Tarleton's force at the Battle of Cowpens, west of King's Mountain, in Winter '81. General Cornwallis won a tactical victory, but a strategic defeat, against General Greene, at Guilford Courthouse, at Greensboro, North Carolina, on the Ides of March, when unruly militiamen panicked and retreated to safety. The victory proved hollow for the British because they had extended themselves too far, at that advanced point in the Piedmont, from their base of supply on the coast. Thus, Cornwallis retreated to the port of Wilmington.

By Autumn '81, General Greene had driven the British Army back into Charleston. In the meantime, however, General Cornwallis finally recognized the strategic prize. So little had the redcoats understood the cause while, theretofore, concentrating their hold on the seat of Britain's power, New York.

Although General Clinton refused to depart the good life there, General William Phillips began to focus on the seat of liberty, Virginia. Worse, the untrustworthy patriot turned Tory, General Benedict Arnold, had already invaded the state back in Winter '81. Pointedly, he had plundered thousands of pounds of tobacco stored for shipment to France and Spain. Now, the Dominion had no way to pay for supplies from those allies.

Remorselessly, General Arnold moved inland. He reached Richmond so swiftly that Governor Thomas Jefferson fled west for his plantation at Charlottesville. Simultaneously, General Cornwallis broke out of Wilmington in massive force. At Petersburg, he rendez-voused with General Phillips and Colonel Tarleton plus reinforcements let go by General Clinton from New York. Thus, in May, '81, the awesome British fighting machine stood poised to conquer.

Meanwhile, in the upcountry, Spring's rain summoned Summer's swelter. At the Muddy Creek, in the building heat, doubt added to tension. The newspaper had ceased publishing when the British took Richmond and seized the newspaper building. Plantation mistresses, left alone, depended on the bravery of coloreds and natives for news. They developed an underground means of communication, with the outside world and among one another, through these stealthy messengers.

Sarah had an especial concern for security. Jeremiah's son, Jacob, had espied General Arnold cursing the Chronicle as "a stinking seditious sheet." Trembling while spying crouched behind hay bales, he heard him vow retaliation against its treasonous owners, including Captain Hughes. Would he come to arrest her? Would he burn the plantation? Would he leave women and children out of the retribution, she wondered? She turned to Powhatan Ted's son, Ted Junior, for support.

Powhatan Ted Junior took over like plantation master. He turned the Muddy Creek into a tenable citadel. He organized the boys and men into a contingent of twenty-four hour lookouts. He moved all of the women and children into the house, barns, and stable. The men took up posts throughout the plantation. The house got so packed that the attic, halls, and most every space, except the dining room and front room, became bedrooms.

He assigned every adult weapons and posts at which to use them. Powder kegs were kept handy. The carpenters fenced in the whole area behind the house. All of the dogs got placed in it. The masons built a fake cellar closet in which to hide valuables. Everyone partook in fire brigade drills until the fire-fighting system became efficient.

Thus cloistered, the great extended family group grew even closer. A bond formed among them the likes of which few plantations experienced, neither before nor since. At the beginning and end of each day, everyone partook in a meal from the big dining room. The huge layout reminded them of weekend neighborhood hunt gatherings, weddings, and funerals. Their reminiscence lacked the good times, however. After meals, the plantation gathered around the front porch and lawn to hear music and sing.

One humid evening in that atmosphere of trepidation, the moist muggy air sat motionless. On the lawn, at the end of one sentimental tune, the fiddlers' musical refrain hit its last blissful note. Yet, the melancholy muse of lone harmonica played on into the air. Bacchus could not hold back an onrush of rhythm. His free style spilled out, and drifted forth, far into the silent starry night. Downriver, the mellifluous melody momentarily mesmerized Hermes who meandered along the dark river trail.

Finally winded, Bacchus broke the magical spell. No one moved for fear of losing the feeling. Just as children began squealing, the distant sound of hooves plodding down dirt filtered through the forest. Eyes focused on the dark trail opening. Hermes pulled out of the trees. The whites of his eyes stood out in the darkness.

"It's Hermes," Jemimah softly yelled.

"The boy brings bad news," Pocahontas predicted from sixth sense.

"And fear," Powhatan Ted Junior's wife, Pocacosin, said.

Once out of the dark trail, Hermes kicked his mount for speed across the lawn. He barely allowed it time to stop, before jumping down and running headlong up the big brick steps. The whites of his eyes shone whole, now.

"The Brits is a comin', the Brits is a comin'," the boy grew wilder, while yelling.

Jemimah thrust her head back, propped her fists on her hips, turned up her pink bottom lip, and glared down at the boy.

"I declare, boy. Settle down, now," she demanded.

"I tells y'all, they's is a comin' for sure. A whole big army o' redcoats on horses. An' they's is a movin' fast up the riva. Folks says, they's burnin' plantations as they go," Hermes burst forth excitedly.

The four women went into action immediately. Powhatan Ted Junior put on dark buckskin and rode downriver, on a fast black stallion, to reconnoiter the army's movements. Dozens of hands pumped water into every available tub and jug. The dogs were put up. Doors and windows were bolted. Sentries took their posts. And finally, all lights went out. The plantation awaited a siege.

The next morning, the sun rose, silently. Except for an occasional outburst from one of the innumerous children scattered about the house, no sound pierced the peace. During breakfast, Powhatan Ted Junior walked through the kitchen door full of foreboding.

"Me see hundreds of redcoats, on horses, riding upriver," he announced without emotion.

Jemimah exclaimed, "Glory be. We sure's in for it now."

"Hermes, run tell all the sentries to come in close to the house and be ready," Sarah ordered the boy.

"Yessum, Miss Sarah," Hermes responded rushingly.

"I keeps track a the kids," Jemimah's niece, Little Jemimah, offered.

"Keep them all in the house. Put the big ones in charge of the small ones," Sarah ordered.

"Yessum, Miss Sarah, I sure 'nough will," she fervently responded.

With standby orders thus given, Sarah, Pocahontas, Pocacasin, and Jemimah made the rounds. They double-checked on everyone. Sarah asked all of the men in the stable and barns not to give their lives for the livestock, hay, grain, or anything else. She made sure that someone in the attic kept a constant eye downriver for any horse or footman, whosoever. She impressed the children with the necessity of quiet play and quick obedience. Then, the women gathered around the kitchen table to read aloud, for strength, the pillage scene from Virgil's *Aeneid*, and dreaded the inevitable.

The whole hot day passed. In late afternoon, dinner was served and then darkness came on. Nothing had happened. No advance sentries were sighted. No cavalry. Not even a barking dog. Anxious but tired, all but the lookouts went to sleep.

The following morning, after breakfast, Powhatan Ted Junior rode again. This time he returned posthaste. Winded, he burst through the door.

"Go to attic. See cavalry comin'," he yelled.

A hasty commotion ensued.

"Hush up now," Jemimah shouted loudly. "Youngins, back wheres youse belong.

Everybody gets to their posts. Make hay and make it fast!" she shouted orders.

Powhatan Ted Junior grabbed Sarah's hand and led her to the attic. Jemimah, Pocahontas, and Pocacasin trundled up behind them. Out of the windows, they took in the dreadful sight.

Across the river, through thick green forest, the red-coated cavalry rode. Intently, they strained their eyes to see the massively moving terror until they had to switch to another set of windows. From that vantage point, above the river, they saw the red-coated corps come out onto the open road adjacent to a field.

"They'll set fire to the plantation they's comin' to next, sure as we're lookin' at 'em," Jemimah predicted.

"Hush, Miss Mammy, youse goin' to bring us bad luck sayin' so," old Amos pleaded.

"Don't you tell me to hush, old man," Jemimah shot back.

"Quiet, please," Sarah demanded.

Calm, however, did not return. For within moments, shots rang out behind the house. Everyone in the attic rushed to the back windows to glimpse the ensuing melee. At that point, another shot went off. Commotion intensified.

The kids got to yelling and crying throughout the house. Little Jemimah's shrill shouts made matters more confused. Several dogs barked like mad outside. Snarling, a pack of them rushed to attack the intruders. In a flash, they jumped on the two yet standing, pulled them down in a vicious fight, and mulled them to bloody shreds. The women rushed downstairs and out the back door.

Behind one tobacco barn, they came upon the scene of slaughter. Powhatan Tom stood proudly over four British soldiers, in pioneer dress, prostrate on the ground. One clutched a box of matches in his stiff hand. Blood poured, profusely, in puddles. One yet moaned in agony.

"We gots 'em good," Menalaus said proudly.

"I gots this 'ere one right in the head," Agamemnon boasted.

"Oh, you've all done well," Sarah praised them.

"Yessum. But we gots to bury 'em quick like. Soldiers 'ill be comin' back round 'ere lookin' for 'em," Jemimah said anxiously.

Promptly and unceremoniously, the corpses went deep into the ground in a nearby wood. Powhatan Ted Junior tailed the troop to warn of any whosoever might return in search of their missing comrades. Menalaus and Agamemnon found the stolen raft, on which the arsonists had crossed the river, tied to a low tree under the bank. Lustily, they chopped up its ties and sent its log pieces floating downriver. By nightfall, the plantation regained a measure of composure and calm.

Gradually, during the following days, security seemed to return. After a week's absence, Powhatan Ted Junior came back with the all clear. He described how the British had nearly burned Charlottesville to the ground and captured Governor Jefferson. Then, they headed back to the coast to join up with their forces and fight, what would likely be, the greatest battle of the war.

Outside Yorktown, Virginia, the Continental Army and militiamen prepared for the decisive battle of the war. Win or lose here. The usual tedious practicing and drilling bored no one now.

Not that the most formidable British force of the war excited them. Rather, patriot spirits soared at the arrival of France's fleet, off of the Chesapeake Capes, commanded by Admiral le Comte de Grasse, on August 30, '81. For, if de Grasse were to gain a victory over the British fleet, out there in the open bay, then Cornwallis' army must surrender or starve under siege.

Intense excitement began on the morning of September fifth. At first, terror struck. News of the British fleet's arrival caught the French admiral unprepared. Hundreds of French sailors had deboarded their warships, in landing craft, to ferry French soldiers ashore near the site of olde burned-down Jamestowne. Worse, the tide continued to rise and the wind blew unfavorably. Thousands of men could only watch. For hours, the confused state portended ruin.

Fortuitously, the British admiral, Graves, wore ship and waited for the French to sortie. His was a fatal mistake. Then, he thought to bear down on a course diagonal to Admiral de Grasse. Graves intended to deliver a classic line-of-battle attack.

Just as the gods came down from Mount Olympus, to assist the Greeks at Troy, so too they directed the destiny of liberty at the Capes. A small mistake in flag signals turned the tide of fate. The divine hand. At the British rear, Admiral Hood misunderstood signals and sheared off. The French bore down on the bulk of the British fleet, and thus pounded it into a decided denouement.

Shortly thereafter, the Franco-American military force got a great boost. Generals Washington and le Comte de Rochambeau arrived from the North. Seven thousand French soldiers, fifty-five hundred Continentals, and three thousand Virginia militiamen now faced just eight thousand British. With confidence renewed, the troops strenuously labored to build redoubts and horn-works, dig trenches and saps, plus lay deadly mines.

Vigourous inspiration spread through the ranks. Gallantly, men sortied against the British bastion. During these assaults, drummers rolled and trumpeters blew. Horse and foot soldiers surged forward, into the volley, conveying French and States' flags waving away. Many men proved their mettle and rose to the rank of hero, during those glorious days. John, Jerimiah, and Matt all earned commendations for their valour in the victory. Jerimiah and Matt became, not only war heroes, but free men for having served their country.

Unbeaten, but far from England, General Cornwallis surrendered on October 17, '81. No one felt more jubilant than the honourable General le Marquis de Lafayette. For, he had single-handedly brought in the French, whose navy, obvious to all, made hard-won victory possible.

The auspicious ceremony took place in front of swiftly sketching artists who recorded that memorable day of imperialism's infamy. They exhibited hundreds of ragged colonials marching grandly behind the starred-and-stripped flag, of the Confederation, and blue-coat clad Frenchmen holding the fleur-de-lis flag, of the de Bourbon family, proudly.

For colonials, the victory of liberty over imperialism ended nearly two millenniums of deviation from that tradition, of nascent European culture, that the Greeks established so long ago. The end began in 1607, when the Jamestowne colonists boldly sailed away from security to a self-sufficient life in a new lande. From the beginning, they intended to gain, and then maintain, liberty through tobacco farming. The destiny of liberty became one with that crop.

By 1776, tobacco plantations pervaded Virginia. It would have seemed to many as having been merely a mean to attain wealth. On the contrary, the colony's culture had become one of tobacco. Indeed, the crop defined the very way of life and affected all aspects of it.

Virginians measured time by the natural rhythms of planting and harvesting seasons. The various tasks on plantations were performed according to their relation, in time, to planting and harvesting. Work and leisure times were determined by the crop's own schedule. Since tobacco provided the common crop, all Virginians adhered to that schedule. This timetable held for rural and urban dwellers alike, because the latter's livelihoods depended, more or less, on the rural economy.

Tobacco provided the main mean of economic exchange. Paper money did not exist. Coins existed in just small supply. Those coins that circulated came from Spanish mines in Spain's colonies far to the west and south. Thereby, the supply of coins depended on trade with the Spanish Empire, with which parliament forbade direct commerce, under the various *Navigation Acts*, so as to allow England to monopolize trade with its own colonies.

Moreover, people disliked coins. Their value depended on the current price of gold or silver and weight. However, these factors continually fluctuated. The vagaries of supply and demand kept the price of metals in flux. Also, the phenomenon known as "shaving" caused the weight of coins to dwindle with velocity of exchange. Thereby, many persons who came into possession of coins literally shaved off thin slivers of metal from the edges of their circumferences. Thus, when one came into possession of a coin, one had scant certainty that the weight of the piece equaled its original weight of gold or silver. Therefore, not only did lack of supply limit the number of coins, but uncertainty about their value rendered them an unusual means of exchange.

In addition, tobacco conditioned the economy, itself. The early planters-down had no real choice but to grow tobacco, because parliament demanded that the Dutch tobacco trade, in England, get replaced with an English one. As the demand for Virginia tobacco grew in England, Wales, Scotland, and Ireland, supply responded. Thus, from the inception of the Virginia Colony, tobacco furnished the mainstay. In years when weather conditions caused poor crops, the colonial economy shrank. Likewise, in bountiful years, the economy grew. Therefore, all Virginians were affected by the capriciousness of annual crop production. Truly, Virginia became a tobacco economy.

Moreover, tobacco shaped the political philosophy of Virginians. In effect, that which benefited the tobacco business became a philosophical "good." For examples, the rights to sell tobacco to the Dutch and to sell it at market, as opposed to regulated price, without tariffs, became tenets of the political philosophy of Virginians. Just as the liberty of ancient Greeks followed the premise of self-sufficiency, and the loss of liberty among Romans resulted from their loss of self-sufficiency by dependence on patronage, tobacco maintained the liberty of Virginians.

Wherefore, tobacco, and thereby smoking, emerged as indelible symbols of liberty. King James I turned down his nose at the "unhealthy weed." However, he harbored a hidden political agenda. He meant to create an English Empire in which the government administered trade. He thought to keep colonials dependent on government patronage. He meant to prevent liberty. To prevent the growth of liberty he had to prevent smoking. Notwithstanding the power of his deception, Virginians held, steadfastly, and with noble pride to the culture of smoking.

Add, that their unyielding determination reveals the self-esteem that results from self-sufficiency. In the end, self-governance became their most profound cultural belief. Just as the paternal head of every Greek extended family was an actual king, and just as the English dukes forced King John I to recognize their local armies, so too every Virginian held liberty high.

CHAPTER XXI

THE WAR FOR LIBERTY THROUGH INDEPENDENCE

At the end of the War for Liberty through Independence, colonials tended to doubt the unexpected victory. Theretofore, continual military losses conditioned colonial minds to expect defeat. Everywhere, most everyone thought fighting would recommence.

Sailors kept keen eyes out over the open ocean. Trepidation reminded them that fog shrouds troop ships from sight. Lonely sentries pounded packed earth and gazed abroad the rising rolling swells that smashed steadily onto the olde colonial shore. Soldiers kept their muskets and rifles ready, just in case.

The British Army surrendered to the Continental Army allright, but the redcoats had not been defeated on the battlefield. Rather, colonials won the close victory at sea. The French Navy ran down the British Navy and thus prevented supply lines from England.

In the Battle of Chesapeake Capes, advanced French ship technology gave that fleet greater maneuverability, and speed, than the less flexible opposition. The British Army, trapped on tidelands, with dwindling supplies, unfurled the big white flag. The British Army thus lost by a tactical naval defeat. Englishmen and colonials, both, knew that the Battle of Yorktown was not a strategic military defeat.

And, the mighty British Navy could yet land another army anytime, anywhere.

At Yorktown, the last hangers-on hung around the taverns. Merrily, Continental soldiers and states' militiamen toasted independence long after the admirals and generals had gone. Admiral le Comte de Grasse, General Washington, and the rest had left. The hardy happy men that lingered comprised the main contingent of what remained of the United Forces. Now, they viewed one another, no longer as colonials, but Americans, one and all.

In the victorious colonies, the Franco-American alliance begot confidence. Tremendous celebrations reoccurred for days on end, on town squares and streets. Celebrants, however, neglected to take notice of the French fleet sailing away, to the sugar islands far south. The valorous fleet sailed out of sight. It intended to use its might to escort valuable French West Indies sugar convoys tightly back to France.

Though the olde colonial coast lay ominously vulnerable, at port towns, ships full of formerly forbidden French cargoes sailed jubilantly in. Technologically advanced textile and armament machinery; machine tools of many types; furniture; wine; silk; silver; soap; and perfume filled warehouses and shops. These goods, outlawed by parliament's trade laws since the days of olde Jamestowne Colony, met strong demand, for a while.

In Philadelphia, minters began minting souvenir coins. Methodically, shiny slivers of metal stamped out, from a cast iron mold sheet, and then ricketed up a river of clanging currency. At the other side of the minting plant, packers rolled the brand-new coins into paper cylinders and stacked them tidily. The minters denoted the coins in

Latin: E Pluribus Unum; out of many one. In other words, the several colonies conjoined to make one confederation.

Back in '75, the Confederation Congress established itself in the Latin language. With respect for history and admiration for humankind's achievements, it intended to re-establish the great republican political ideals of pre-imperial Rome. Ironically, however, its political practices adhered more to the traditions of Greek poleis. That is to say, the various colonies, cum states, confederated, to rhetoricize and vote, like Greeks, at Philadelphia.

That logical capitol lay at the center of the colonies. To reach it took a multi-day rough carriage ride from both of the farthest colonies, Georgia and New Hampshire. At war's end, the Confederation disbanded. Thereafter, on the Atlantic coast, self-employed farmers; tradesmen; shopkeepers; professionals; their helpers; and families lived in thirteen separate countries. Each governed itself. Colonials saw their new states as their countries, just as their old colonies had been before the war.

During the 1780's, thirteen states made up the United States. Proudly, the disparate ports, towns, villages, and countrysides held America commonly. And, from Georgia to New Hampshire, two things they all held in common were scarce British currency and pockets full of shiny new state-minted coins. Few ever knew how to calculate exchange values across borders however, because there were thirteen prices.

No matter, Continental Army veterans demanded more of it in overdue pay. Farmers, tradesmen, shopkeepers, and the United States Bank in Philadelphia, besides war bond creditors, waited for payment too. They had lent the army coins, livestock, crops, craft works, and shop goods during the war, in exchange for the disbanded confederation's bills of credit. Unfortunately, some bond holders, without foresight, had sold their credit bills early, during the war, to merchants, for scarce goods. They sold for less than they had paid.

Later, a post-war economic boom drove up commodity prices and profits. The value of such items as cows, pigs, chickens, horses, mules, oats, hay, ale, flour, tents, and blankets, on which the amounts of those credit bills had been calculated, rose in price too. So, the value of credit bills, at par, rose. The early-sellers thus lost their opportunity for gain. Chagrined, they demanded that state governments mint more coins so as to raise crop prices.

The poor financial understanding of these, largely rural, short-sellers, threatened the precarious new economic liberty. Generally, town folks knew better. They knew that the more coins, the more inflation. Not to say that town folks have anything on farmers. Just that farmers were unaccustomed to trading. Time proved the town folks right. Through the '80's, massive production of the various states' coins caused first, postal rates to soar, then inflation became unbridled.

Inflation actually compounded the early-sellers' demands for more state minting plus funding of the confederation's war debts. They were impatient once and once again. Beginning in the '80's, they began vociferously demanding more state coins. Eventually, they became known as Anti-Federalists.

Long-term investors, along with the avaricious merchants who bought credit bills, from early-sellers during the war, saved their credit bills. It did not matter whether they were farmer or banker, countryman or townsman. These economically savvy citizens expected the Confederation Convention to meet again, issue new bonds, and therefrom fund coins to replace long-vanishing British currency. They criticized state coins as inflationary. Beginning in the '80's, they began vociferously demanding confederation coins. They became known as Federalists.

Seven years passed between the surrender in '81 and the submission of a constitution in '88. Wherethrough that time, coins came back into plenty, as, reluctantly, the states funded their coins by taxes instead of bonds. The new coins, made of solid gold and silver, paid for cargoes off of ships. Yet, one could hardly cross state borders with them. For, unlike the old British coins, they did not get issued in uniform denominations. Thus, business began to boom again but by barter basically.

Meanwhile, throughout the land, states enacted libertarian laws. For one, under the *Virginia Statute of Religious Liberty,* in '86, the Protestant Anglican Church transformed into the Protestant Episcopal Church. Thereby, vestries transformed into townships. The Church's political influence waned.

The burgesses moved the capitol to the upcountry, permanently. Coastal Cavaliers had farther to travel now. In addition, the radical burgesses abolished primogeniture and entail. Moreover, they argued and voted on a bill to abolish slavery. It became known as the *Freedom Bill.*

Anti-Federalists defeated the *Freedom Bill* by a narrow margin of votes. They yet smarted from opportunities foregone on credit bills. As said, during the war, they had become confused, about political economy, and foolishly sold their confederation bonds early. After the war, they became confused again when bond values rose, and demanded state minting. In '86, the political economy confused them, yet, again. They did not intend to reduce their capital worth. So, they voted against slave freedom and good economic sense.

No matter how viable the arguments, they would not understand, that generally, they paid more to support a slave, for a lifetime, than they would pay a freed slave his wages for labor. This was so, because slaveholders supported slaves during unproductive slow seasons, work slow-downs, childhood, old age, illness, and disability. All they understood was the amount paid for the slaves some, usually many, years ago and the amount spent feeding, housing, clothing, curing, entertaining, and training them since.

Moreover, Anti-Federalist thought that slaves helped make farming competitive in the face of booming Federalist commerce. According to this economic thinking, the loss of slaves only compounded war losses. Liberty loving planters and professional men argued, without success, against the economics of slavery.

Thus, on that fateful day, at the small statehouse in the new capitol town, Richmond, on that bill for freedom; Federalist did something that had traditionally been considered against a southern statesman's code of honour, they compromised, with Anti-Federalists. The monopolistic merchantilist slave trade would be abolished instead of slavery itself. Although no one present saw it, Nathaniel Bacon's hundred year old spirit rose up from that hero's grave to haunt the halls of the house.

So, with the exception of slave war veterans, government denied freedom. Fortunately, some private men, planters, did not deny their slaves the liberty of Virginians. Notwithstanding freedom denied, they transferred the tradition of liberty to some slaves. For, although tidewater

Anti-Federalists defeated the *Freedom Bill*, some planters parceled out farmland to slaves while others sent them to towns to become tradesmen. In that way, some slaves begot liberty.

Virginians knew the difference between freedom and liberty. They knew Greek and Roman history and philosophy. They knew, for example, that Aristotle had been a slave without freedom. Nonetheless, he had liberty because he owned a farm that his owner, King Philip, father of soon to be great, Alexander, gave him.

Other states followed Virginia's move against the slave trade monopoly, with exceptions. Rhode Island and South Carolina continued the slave trade with African chiefs, for a while. The war had merely interrupted the British Africa Company's monopoly markets at Newport and Charleston. Therefore, on the *Freedom Bill*, the issues of both freedom and liberty were left to slaveholders to decide for themselves. Revolution aside, the imperialistic legacy of empire remained in the economics of slavery. Where else would it rear its ugly head?

If military victory meant liberty for everyone, then it meant land for everyone. For, without the one, the other is lost. This maxim holds especially true in farm country, where even tradesmen strengthen their liberty through ownership of shop buildings. To the landless, a war for liberty through independence meant a war for land. And as for soldiers, they had fought for, and wanted to get paid in, frontier wilderness acres.

Fortunately, the *Treaty of Paris*, in '83, transferred the western wilderness from Great Britain to the victorious colonies. Now, thousands prepared to remove west. The British Army and its native allies, however, saw the wilderness otherwise. They remained reluctant to vacate wilderness forts. Remorselessly, that army thought to draw the Canadian border farther south safely beyond the southern perimeter of Great Lakes area forts.

Into that wilderness, for nearly two hundred years, French fur traders had foraged. Since the fifteen hundreds, fur traders trekked from fort towns, with packhorses, to trap animals in the awesomely vast wilderness. The thick forests, majestic mountains, and valleys through which they walked humbled some in the eyes of God. Nature, however, emboldened others to be like a god.

In the wild place, confidence grows. It finds one staring boldly into the brown eyes of circumspect natives, who approach close, along deeply winding dark forest trails. Traders negotiated with natives cross-legged on the ground, at wigwam villages. As a habit, they gave them gifts of jewelry, whiskey, guns, and powder. In turn, and in time, the natives signed treaties with the French Army.

French officers, soldiers, traders, and braves shared the lonely wilderness until the World War when British forces wrested the West away from the French. Thereafter, the French abandoned their forts to redcoats. Gone, the fleur-de-lis waving in windy forlorn places.

With firm resolve, resolute French traders went farther west. Beyond the Mississippi lay the Missouri River. They trekked far from the redcoats' reach. Slowly, truculently, eastern natives began to trade with the British. And, English speaking people displaced French ones at familiar fort towns.

The new-begotten wild wilderness rolled west from the Allegheny Mountains. Beyond those rugged peaks lay raw country. Farmland in the minds of would-be pioneers. The natives, in that imposing place, remained steadfastly with the British, however. They tended toward unfriendly.

Savagely, they bloodily brutalized explorers, traders, trappers, and especially pioneers. Indeed, the preferred word for natives had long been "savages" in Britain and Europe. Now, more than ever, they lived up to that name. Although the treaty of '83 made the West a part of the United States, de jure, it left the wilderness in British and native hands, de facto.

As for the natives, they became increasingly alarmed about pioneers. Back in 1608, the Great Powhatan, Wahunsunakok, did not begrudge Captain Smith the marshlande on which Jamestowne sat, regardless of what his actions may have seemed. Notwithstanding the wily olde chief's attraction to English culture, Powhatan landes extended no farther than the foothills.

West of the Powhatan Confederation, tribes began forming alliances against the English long ago. At various times, these mutable alliances included the Iroquois, Huron, Illenois, Delaware, and Shawnee. Tribes to the south, beginning with the Shawnee, held loosely to the alliances. They included the Cherokee, Chattahochie, Choctaw, Chickasaw, and Creek.

The weaker side of the confederation began with the Shawnee and tribes to their south. Caintucky and the South lands were the tribes' farming and hunting grounds. These grounds included all the vast wilderness bordered by the mountains, the Ohio River, and the Gulf Sea to the mighty Mississippi. The stronger side of the confederation comprised the northern tribes. They saw the Great Lakes as their farming and hunting grounds. These grounds included all the vast wilderness north of the Ohio to Canada.

However, to get a true idea of the frontier, one needs think back an hundred years before the war, in the first instance. In those days, it could not be denied, the natives dealt easily with the less intimidating Dutch than was the case with both the French and English. Eventually, the natives aligned with the French because, like the Dutch, they came in unintimidatingly small numbers. Through an hundred years time, British colonists crammed the seaboard colonies in large numbers. Therefore, only with the intention to prevent farther growth of British settlements did natives reluctantly align themselves with their former foe, the British Army, and the monopoly fur trade.

Heretofore then, describes the newly independent colonies, on their coasts and frontiers, in their villages and towns, and throughout their countysides, at the end of the hard-fought War for Liberty through Independence. After the confederation disbanded, the states began to disunite. Colonial borders became economic and political barriers.

Two political parties, of sorts, began to form on opposite sides of the economic argument between federal and state coinage. Inflation drove prices up. Long-denied French products rose in supply, and then fell in price.

Notwithstanding the states' close-won victory in war; British sailors patrolled the sea lanes while her soldiers kept a firm hard hold on the wilderness. With tongue in cheek, they surrendered the West but refused to vacate the Great Lakes forts that protected the lucrative fur trade monopoly. Meanwhile, Britain's savage allies policed the wilderness with bloody brutality. Nonetheless, a few brave pioneers, began to remove west with wary resolve.

CHAPTER XXII

THE SPIRIT OF '76

The spirit of '76 sent pioneers west. To find that spirit, pioneers harked far back. Over one hundred years had passed since 1676, when Nat Bacon's keen sense of justice, prompted him to lead frontier planters in heroic revolt, against imperial monopolism. Those liberty loving rebels set their sights on the British Africa Company's shipping monopoly. In the rebel planter's unforgettable speech, he rose against its blocking out British indentures and transporting Africans into Virginia. One decisive man dared take action against the replacement of British indentures, on the quays, with Africans. However, he failed in his endeavor to remind the government of the liberty of Englishmen. Imperialism, and its private sector twin, monopolism, continued to thrive in the slave trade.

Heroism notwithstanding, during the century or so that led up to the war in 1776, parliament passed many more laws than liberty allowed. In fact, fifty years after the original colonists constructed Fort Jamestowne, the first navigation act began regulating colonial trade. Periodic additions to the acts regulated trade with continually growing constraint. Shipping restrictions, price controls, and taxes became more and more onerous. Of course, when taxes rose, prices rose. Just as, when taxes fell, prices fell.

In addition, parliament granted monopolies in businesses such as shipping. In the face of this increasing parliamentary patronage, kings and queens could only protect their power by, understandably, granting monopolies themselves. As a result, the growth of government constrained commerce, trades, and farming. Twice, since the Puritans first laid down restrictions, in the 1650's, colonial tobacco, rice, cotton, indigo, hemp, and grain crops hardly covered the costs of getting them to market. Farmers with foresight fallowed fields oftener.

In 1763, when Great Britain won the frontier from France, the most unjust law, in the minds of many, came when parliament granted a fur trade monopoly on the whole huge West, that the British people had just wrested from the French in hard-won war. Worse, the British Army buckled down at the several Great Lakes forts to enforce the prohibition. Settlers were blocked out, by law, by the army, and in a short time, by the army's native allies, who kept the terms of treaties through the terror of tomahacks.

However, natural law cannot abate itself. That law states: prohibitions always abet black markets. Indeed, the axiom held true in the market for frontier land, too. A black market in it grew greatly under puritanical parliamentary prohibition.

After the War for Liberty through Independence, the Illinois-Wabash Land Company, in defiance of royal proclamations, purchased land, from natives, on both sides of the wide Ohio River valley. The company's stockholders included French diplomats serving in America, and six signers of the *Declaration of Independence*. Four, of those six, came from Maryland and two from Pennsylvania.

No one had been surprised when Maryland refused to sign the *Articles of Confederation*, at Annapolis in '75, until states with western land, especially Virginia, ceded their claims to the confederation. Of course, Maryland delegates knew that land cessions would validate Illinois-Wabash Company claims.

However, the deed had already been done. Decades earlier, Virginia claimed the frontier wilderness that began somewhere in the midst of her mountains. Virginia's longstanding claim to both sides of the wide Ohio River Valley sat on her status as a commonwealth; whereas Pennsylvania's western border sat, immutably, on that colony's status as a grant to Lord Penn.

In other words, Pennsylvania's borders could not move west with its people, because King Charles I had granted a described parcel of land to his Cavalier patron, Penn, as reward for his political support. As for Maryland, she did not border the frontier. Rather, she sat wedged betwixt Pennsylvania and Virginia.

Naturally then, Virginia incorporated the northwest frontier into its Allegany County. The Old Dominion insured her claim by undertaking military expeditions, beginning in '78. By those expeditions, the frontier saw fighting during the war. Virginia militiamen fought hard and won against the British and their native allies.

It was after all, land mainly, that motivated most men. Virgin frontier soil motivated Virginian land speculators and militiamen to induce the burgesses, in '78, to send out the self-supporting Colonel George Rogers Clark Expedition. That expeditionary force aimed to validate the Commonwealth's claim against the Illinois-Wabash and other land speculation companies.

By such expeditions, the rowdy frontier fought the war. Militiamen hunkered down hard in rough country. Valiantly, Virginian's secured the whole of the Northwest by war's end. That wilderness territory encompassed more land than the Dominion herself. It was, perhaps, the greatest strategic victory for the least expenditure of men and arms in all history.

Over the war Winter of '78-9, big burly rough red-haired Colonel Clark, led determined men, in flatboats, down the fast-flowing Ohio River, from near Point Pleasant, all the way to the Cumberland River delta in Illenios country. That delta land lay deep in the wild west. There, they banked the boats and marched, bayonet and rifle armed, on French inhabited villages starting with Vincennes.

Unexpectedly, not a shot needed to be fired. Frenchmen were no Loyalists. Colonel Clark and his men won them over easily. The militiamen then took Kaskaskia and Cahokia in the same manner. However, holding those French towns meant meeting up with the British Army when it would come out of its fort, at Detroit, to drive the Virginians back east across the high mountains.

Daringly, Clark breathed in deeply, and announced to all willing men, both Virginian and French, that he would attack Hamilton's force at Fort Detroit. Shortly, with additions to the ranks from la Belle Riviere, to the south, the military expedition gained enough courage to cross flooded bottomlands. Undaunted by Winter's wetness, shivering soldiers trucked through mud and muck. Tiresomely, they held their heavy rifles, for hours at a time, high above deep slippery sucking slush.

With aching arms, and tense with fear, the soldiers waded on. Always anticipating ambush, every eye and ear looked and listened, intently, for the sudden flight of birds and the sight of bright feathers. At the end of the treacherous march, scalps intact, they attacked the formidable Fort Detroit with bold risk. That decisive day, blinding canon fire killed some militiamen while bullets blew others apart.

But, in the end, Virginia implemented her pre-war charter claims to the Northwest Territory.

The Clark expedition's success allowed the Continental Congress to break the impasse among the states in '80. The majority of representatives thus settled on a western land plan. States' representatives agreed that any western lands ceded to the Continental Confederation, by the various states, would be, "settled and formed into distinct republican States, which shall become members of the Federal Union, and shall have the same rights of sovereignty, freedom, and independence, as the other States."

The congressional mandate thereby established a libertarian union; the likes of which had not been seen since the glorious time of ancient Greece. Indeed, not since 876 B.C., whereat the very first Olympics, the several Greek poleis came together, in mutual self-interest, to conjoin themselves, had the culture of liberty asserted itself so propitiously.

As for history's second libertarian union, Virginia and Pennsylvania made up its first members. North Carolina, Georgia, and New York joined secondly. Then, with Maryland, South Carolina, or New Jersey they made up a majority of the thirteen colonies. Thanks to Virginia's leadership, one by one, western states eventually would add to that quorum.

Late in the war, in June, '82, another expedition, this one under Colonel William Crawford, walked into a stealthy trap, that revealed the strength of the British Army's pugnacious diplomacy. In a bloody red-squirting slaughter, loyalists and natives ambushed marching militiamen near Fort Sandusky, in Ohio country. Fast, out from behind thick trees and brush, menacingly whooping and brightly painted braves ran up behind marchers, with tomahacks held high. Expertly, the warriors sliced the sharp flints down into the backs and necks of unprepared soldiers.

Hastily, the expedition formed ranks and otherwise barricaded itself. Stiff with fear, the men fought for their very lives, and a few flashes of memory, but failed to keep either one. At the end, a grotesque scene of carnage lay strewn about the dirt trail when the last man standing shot off his final bitter rifle load.

More attacks came, forthwith. Not since the Ottawan, Chief Pontiac, rebelled against Britain, had the frontier seen violence and bloody slaughter so voracious. Over the Summer, vengeful natives raided deep into western Pennsylvania and Virginia. In the heat of August, loyalists and natives routed a relieving force of militiamen at Fort Bryan's Station out in the Caintucky Bluegrass. Yet more loyalist and natives routed another relieving force at the Lower Blue Licks, nearby. Bloody Caintucky.

In Autumn of that year, Colonel Clark avenged the dishonor of scalped and mutilated militiamen and pioneers. This time, instead of marching humbly into the wilderness, he rode valiantly at the front of eleven hundred mounted riflemen. The confident force rode high above the forest floor, their horse's hooves pounding down determinedly, and the sun's bright glare glistening off of bayonets. Colonel Clark took the vengeance of outrage as he routed Shawnee and burned their villages near Chillicothe, in Ohio country.

Almost as soon as the grey smoke and red embers of battle died out, thick white snow covered the blackened villages. The following Spring, Great Britain gave up the West by the treaty that settled the war. Betrayed by parliament, the

British Army retreated into the Great Lakes forts that it had once wrested from the French during the First World War. Its native allies fell back to remote villages.

And so, the great gates to the wilderness stood ajar but not open. Indeed, those heavy gates would not fully open for an hundred years. Nonetheless, pioneers would push through them. For, many would remember how their ancestors had planted themselves down on its westward-moving edge. Pioneer tradition taught them that wilderness gets tamed by planting down in it, not by waiting for an army to make it safe. Liberty is for the self-determined. Although natives never stopped attacking settlers who settled down too far west, the greatest lovers of liberty never stopped taking the risk.

The first to step foot, into the new future, on those trails that the Virginia Militia had tramped, went alone. The fearless few, who first went west, caught the last stealthy sight of war. Not so, those who came later. They caught just a glimpse.

Generously, the legacy of Virginia's military success devolved upon her heir, the United States. For, in '80, the Dominion agreed to cede the West to the new republic. The first Continental Congress had agreed that new republican states would get created from the wilderness. The colony once known as the Virgin Lande envisioned her legacy in Caintucky Country. Caintucky would be Virginia's wilderness. Indeed, Daniel Boone, was tramping down a trail there, already.

Four years after the war, longstanding Federalist's efforts to form a quorum of states, finally succeeded. A Second Confederation Congress, made up of mostly new representatives, from the various states, met in convention. The conventioneers drew up a constitution and cautiously deemed it to be suitable as law for a new land.

At the convention, Virginia and New York led a vote to allow a New England pattern of settlement in the Northwest in exchange for New England joining a federation. Although New England had no West, Puritans would not allow a Cavalier culture there. Settlers would live in villages, around churches, and walk to their small plots of farm fields at towns' edges. Caintucky, and south of there, however, would get settled like Pennsylvania and Virginia. Settlers would live on their homesteads, farms, and plantations.

Before the Second Confederation Congress even convened, its representatives called voters to polling places to elect a federal government. Liberty loving Englishmen, at heart, they enthusiastically voted in the best class of men because they deemed them to be the best qualified to govern. The majority cared not for candidates who made promises of patronage. Rather, they held to the tradition of paternalism. Thus, for the most important office, the presidency, overwhelming numbers went to the wealthy Virginia planter and war hero, General George Washington.

The first president, Washington, appointed his Continental Army aide-de-camp, the Federalist, Alexander Hamilton, of New York, as Treasury Secretary. Adept at economics, he founded, in the commercial capitol of the federation, Philadelphia, the Bank of the United States. It replaced Robert Morris' Bank of North America, located there. Hamilton established the bank to issue interest bearing bonds to the public in exchange for their gold and silver specie.

Thereby, he settled the years-long debt funding disagreement that had been, in the first instance, the impetus for the formation of the two political philosophies. His action fell on the side of funding the minting of federal coins, as opposed to funding the minting of state coins. Anti-Federalists, led by State Secretary, Thomas Jefferson, agreed to allow those coins to fund states' debts, but only in exchange for moving the political capitol southward to a rural area. His was a small demand. And, one that would witness the capitol annex parts of, both, Maryland and Virginia, de facto, one unfortunate day.

In addition, the president, commander-in-chief, moved to train seasoned Continental Army soldiers anew, for frontier fighting, and began making big plans for the building of forts in the wilderness. On June 1, '89, the president consummated a propitious peace treaty with the natives. For, in the treaty, he laid down principles for future relations with the tribes. These principles were: first, native lands must always be guaranteed by treaties; second, the federal government will regulate trade between pioneers and natives; third, punishment will be meted out to either natives or pioneers who attack the other; and fourth, natives will live under independent governments of their own.

As for the natives, they broke some of the alliances that they had previously made with the British, though not all of them, and consummated new ones with the United States. The British Army, pugnacious to the end, strengthened fortifications at the several Great Lakes area forts. The president, in response, sent General Arthur Saint

Clair, Governor of the hard-won Northwest Territory, to northern Illenois country, to build the first fort.

Again, like Colonel Crawford and General Braddock before him, Saint Clair's exploration met a spurting blood bath on November 4, '91. Two years later, under General "Mad Anthony" Wayne, a heavily armed army avenged General Governor Saint Clair, at the Battle of Fallen Timbers, near the southwestern shore of Lake Erie. At the end of fighting that decisive day, both British rifles and Canadians lay strewn about the field as evidence of Britain's complicity in savage native raids. Thereafter, a few tribes north of the Ohio River caved in to the population boom. And, pioneers began to trek into a swath of, now safe, land south of the great lake in Ohio country.

CHAPTER XXIII

BACK AT THE OLE PLANTATION

Many Continental Army soldiers and states' militiamen waited so long to get paid in wilderness land that they grew too old to go west. By the time military successes provided some protection to pioneers, nearly two decades had passed. Their sons, out of others, rode the wooden wagon and mule trains out of shady mountain glens into the glare of a brightly shining sun.

Posthumously, the post-war generation flowed through mountain passes to populate Caintucky and Ohio countries. The Revolutionary War generation thus passed the close-won legacy of victory onto their sons, daughters, nephews, nieces, and cousins. The younger generation reaped the fruits of the older one's labour. They were the heirs of liberty.

From the mustering out at Yorktown, when those war-weary veterans rode and walked away from the powder-blackened bloody battlefield, with their backs bent by burdens and their heads hung low by humility, the legacies of war went with them. They were humbled for all they had seen. Yells and sickening screams, bleeding, and maiming haunted their minds. Their muddy ripped rucksacks carried the burdens of camping. Their hearts carried the horrors of war.

They, themselves, carried away more than the legacy of liberty through political independence. Older soldiers and militiamen hauled the legacy of hard-won political honor.

They had fought the war for political liberty. Younger ones, mainly, hauled the legacy of hard-won wilderness land. They had fought the war for the frontier.

The legacy of those republican veterans ended over one hundred years of mercantilism. Hard fought, they returned to their plantations, farms, homesteads, trades, and professions. Hands that had turned hardy handling guns, once again took up leather reins, wood-handled tools, and quill pens, so as to be ready when crop and livestock prices would rise from recession. In towns, villages, and throughout the countryside, they lived for liberty in livelihoods.

While a remnant army remained in uniform to guard the states' uncertain independence, civilian militiamen mustered every few months. They would be ready when needed again. For that purpose, in towns, they built barracks, and in countrysides, camps. To the rhythmical beat of drums and blowing of flutes, they paraded proudly, in homespun uniforms, along the streets of towns and villages. At the sides of those streets, packs of people jammed together waving flags with wild abandon. Patriotic crowds cheered. And, miles outside of those towns and villages, in forests, militiamen camped, and practiced.

Virginia militiamen took the preponderance of credit for victory on the tidewater flats at Yorktown. Without dispute, that credit was due them. At that decisive battle, they fought to finish a war that Virginians had begun. They also fought out of self-defense to defend their own invaded country. Indeed, according to fate itself, the war had to be won there or it would have been won nowhere. Satisfied, volunteer soldiers rode and walked away from the battlefield, together. Afterward, they remained a militia force to defend the new state. Eagerly, from tidewater to mountains, militiamen mustered.

Upcountry militiamen mustered at camps they put down off of forested dirt roads on creeks or riverbanks. At one such remote woods, up in the far reaches of fast-rushing rivers, in the shady Appalachian Mountains, where the terrain turns rough, and men live close to nature, one company of upcountry militiamen camped. In a river valley, up on a broad bank, they pitched their tan canvas tents close by one another.

Although officer's tents sat separately at the right flank, officers intermingled as equals among the non-commissioned men. Upcountry society had always been egalitarian, as much as men can be equal, anyway. The wilderness awed them all.

They tethered horses together on long thick hemp rope lines that were tied tightly around tree trunks. The high-roofed mess tent, with its smokestack sticking out, went up at the rear, and off to the side, right next to the river. No one had to be told that the latrine was downstream.

Each morning, for a week, the company drilled up and down the narrow dirt road that followed the river. After marching and shouting for a few hours, the men would hone their already expert shooting skills. After a while, some would take off to hunt down game in the surrounding forest. Others would lay traps for game, at shallow spots on the river, where wild animals waded in to drink.

Late in the days, the men roasted fresh meat and broke out bottles of whiskey and wine. Everyone would get to sitting around an aromatic campfire. Serious card games ensued. After a few hours, the music of flutes and fiddles flew far into the dark forest, up and downriver, until a merely dim sound of melody faded away far distant.

On a weekend morning, the company awoke in a cool wet mountain mist. No one roused too readily. Within an hour, a few men made their ways to the river's edge, removed their night shirts, and moving fast, washed up in the cold water. Then, just as quickly, they dressed and took the task of hunting for brunch.

Game that season were crowded together more than usual. Recent Spring floods had sent animals foraging onto higher ground. So, upon a rock ledge, above a portion of flooded riverbank, where a clear view over the wooded slopes below provided an advantage, one militiaman balanced himself.

Slowly, and with deliberate sureness, the captain took aim at game gathered together in his sight. Firmly, he gripped his rifle. The varnished wooden butt lodged up in the tight pit of his arm. He pulled his elbow, slightly, back to a new position. The muscles in his finger tightened around the trigger. The scene sat still. Then, in just an instant, his eyes met those of his prey. For a few moments, hunter and prey stood motionless. Only breathing could be heard. The prey twitched. The hunter pulled the trigger.

In a stampede of stomping hooves, and thick mud clods, splattering against surrounding tree trucks, the startled herd ran off. Except for the one. He lay behind. Buckshot blown, blood flowing, and bellowing forth for his final breath. Briskly, the man holstered his rifle and began making his way around the rocky ledge to the thick green meadow below.

"'Twas a sure shot, captain," a nearby soldier shouted out.

"Good aim, captain," loudly echoed a husky voice from above and behind them.

Once down in the meadow, under the deceptive shroud of pine branches that had prevented the prey from sighting him soon enough, he slowly approached the poor shocked animal. His fellow soldiers followed after him. Its once gushing red blood was beginning to ebb now. A clot had begun to form. The deer's head, on the cold ground, tilted slightly toward the direction of flight. Its wide eyes gaped. Its body quivered.

Four of the men bent over and each reached for a leg. Grunting, they lifted and dragged the dead deer back to camp. There, on the ground, they skinned the animal, removed its entrails and inedible body parts, and then skewered it onto an iron rod for roasting. Soon, the smell of smoking meat swelled up out of the pit.

While brunch roasted, another day got underway. It was a Saturday. So, the soldiers lounged about, read, and played games. By mid-afternoon, the moist mountain air began to blow a hard steady rain. Best friends huddled together in one another's tents. The heavy canvas tents became saturated and sagged under the heavy weight of water. Roofs and walls flapped heavily in the wind.

The wind blew stronger by night. In the captain's damp darkly lit tent, he lay wrapped in a dry warm wool blanket, on a canvas cot, with his hands clasped behind his head. The sound of fiddlers fiddling wafted, through the loud rain, from a nearby tent. His tent roof and walls wrapped tightly around his thoughts. A brief breeze blew. The candle flame flickered, momentarily. The tent roof flapped and smacked hard a few times. The breeze blew off. His mind wandered back to morning. Once again, he gazed into the stricken face of the dead deer. Deep within his mind's eye, he saw the faces of many deer that he had killed through his years.

This time, somehow, out here at the edge of the frontier, the killing seemed different. He sensed that, likely, the startled eyes had never seen a white man. They hesitated a moment too long, to take the time, to take in the strange sight. One mistaken moment. A lifetime for a moment, in the wild wilderness.

Both the World War and the War for Independence had come and gone during his long life. He remembered the first war, when colonial militias sided with the British Army against that of the French, and their native allies, for the wilderness. He thought about the second one, when colonial militias fought the British Army, and what had become their native allies, for that same wilderness. He took in a deep breath of it. His chest pushed up, and his thought felt the thick overwhelming weight of that westward-rolling wilderness. His head turned in its direction. He doubted.

A few days later, on the long eastward ride from camp, down the Appalachian slopes, across the valley, and toward the Blue Ridge, the soldiers slowly began to sense contrariety creeping in upon them. Whether from ahead or behind, they did not know. Ahead lay their homes. But, behind lay the lure of wilderness. The long row of double-breasted riders remembered many rides they had ridden together, through forests, in formations like this one, to bivouacs and battles. Yet, as the rough riders turned to confirm their thoughts in the faces of their fellows, they saw instead the innocent faces of younger men among themselves. Every muster, it seemed, more recruits joined the ranks. Now, less war veterans rode.

A remote homestead in the hills broke their thoughts. The hardy homesteaders stopped to wave, broadly, as they toiled on their patch of cleared land walled in by wilderness. Within a few miles, another homestead appeared off the road. Within hours, they had passed several more.

By the middle of the day, the company caught up with the eastward-moving rain. They pulled on their canvas coats and secured the hoods. They kept moving. Rain rushed at their faces and into their eyes and noses. The water weighed down the wilderness with the aroma of wetness. The horses stepped with purpose to keep their big bodies balanced on the muddy road. The lightened food wagon gave teamsters an awkward handle, as it slid from side to side, on the slick surface. By late afternoon, soaking wet and straddling squeaking saddles, the road widened and, at sojourns, farm fences appeared aside its wide gulleys.

In the foothills, clearings spread up hillsides to abut forest borders. Cattle, horses, mules, sheep, and goats, grazed in fenced pastures. Post-and-rail fences ran along hills to barns of varying sizes and shapes. The whitewashed walls of the biggest barns stood in contrast against the dull wooden-walled and drab-roofed ones. Farms with painted barns had houses to match.

By late afternoon, the riders reached the Great Valley Road junction at the village of Lexington. From there, the road continued over the Blue Ridge, into the upcountry, and along the James River to Richmond. The junction marked the turn-off point for some frontier militiamen. They would take the Valley Road north, for a while, before crossing the Blue Ridge toward Charlottesville. In the morning, the riders would split up. Tonight, they scouted a campsite, at the edge of the village, and built a big roaring fire. They pitched the tents and a dark night set in.

Being the biggest place on the Great Valley Road, the village of Lexington welcomed travelers everyday. Weary riders rested at its inns. Some of the men made ready to ride in to a tavern. A few made plans to ride through Liberty University. They thought to send their sons there, and not William and Mary, when that day would come. In mountain country their boys would be. Tired but eager, many men took to their mounts, yet again, and headed into the village. Most of the militiamen, however, got into their bedrolls.

In the morning, the camp awoke to irritating drizzle. The soldiers fought off sullen moods. Another wet hard day's ride lay ahead of them. With few words, they ate fat-fried eggs with toasted and buttered bread, along with coffee. Those that took the Valley Road bid the rest goodbye and rode off. The remainder headed down the Richmond Road.

Captain Hughes led the men down the Richmond Road. At the end of that second day, the riders descended out of the mountains. On the third morning of the long ride home, men began reaching their neighborhoods. They would turn off in pairs, or alone, onto roads that led to their plantations. Those whose plantations sat on the river needed only turn onto their own roads. By the end of the day, twenty-three men pitched ten tents on a bank of the Rockfish River, near its flow into the James.

Next morning, the bright sun began breaking out of its cloudy barrier, intermittently. The river road stretched forth in front of them like a wide unraveled ribbon. It wound through woodlands, past plantation's pasturelands and croplands, and through villages. The riders began passing other horsemen and wagons more and more. The ranks thinned down as riders turned off the river road.

The captain's own plantation lay a short ride ahead. He had been sensing a melancholy among the men. Unconsciously, their paced had slowed. He turned his head around to them and yelled out loudly.

"We'll come to my place soon. Y'all stay there tonight," he invited them.

"We'd be glad to, captain," they heartily agreed.

An hour later, the remaining riders rounded a lengthy bend in the river. At a clear point on the riverbank, they wearily dragged up their heavy heads and focused their eyes into the distance, to see any sign of their destination. Way ahead downriver, through thick tracks of forest on both banks, across broad rolls of farm fields tucked, like kneaded buns, into one another, they could just make out the old plantation house.

"Sure 'nough captain, there's your place, yonder," one man yelled out.

"I see it," another shouted. "Now let's get there."

Suddenly, from out of the brush, a pack of barking and howling dogs came rushing toward the riders. Once upon the horsemen, they came to a fast firm stop, and almost growled before they recognized their master. Overwhelmed, the dogs moped about in embarrassment but simultaneously wagged their tails wildly, sniffing around all the while, and then began howling again, in a friendly way. The riders rode on behind them. The dogs caused the horses to pick up speed to keep up the pace. Within a few minutes, they were at a trot.

The riders crossed the Muddy Creek upstream. Cautiously, the horses stepped through deep water on slippery rocks. On its opposite side, the forest opened up into pastureland. The dogs, anxious to reach the stables, upset a big slow-moving herd of goats. Bleating and blathering loudly, the muddy goats crowded in on one another. The whole commotion disturbed the horses.

Heading on, the dogs led the horsemen through cow pastures. For a long way, they rode through hundreds of black-and-brown-spotted cows whose bulls roared out warnings to those who dared disturb the security of the flock. Ahead, at the flat edge of a woodland border, on a curve of the creek, sat whitewashed pig sties. There, they entered the plantation road that climbed at a reluctant rate through groves of fruit trees, and then rounded down, easily, pass coloreds and natives' houses. Pass the quarters, it rolled on toward the barns, paddocks, and stable.

The captain led his men toward the front porch. The warm wet sunny lawn caught a cool breeze blowing off the river. The big old rambling white wooden house glistened in the sun. The wide big brick porch sat in shade.

As the horsemen rode onto the thick green expanse of lawn, more dogs, along with children, poured out of seemingly nowhere. They ran, barked, and hollered around them, eager to meet the men and get attention. The horses and militiamen found themselves within an uproar. They would be the focus of attention until bed time.

Meanwhile, the boys and girls shouted up questions at the dismounting riders, grabbed reins to hold their horses for them, and yelled at one another in a general ruckus of commotion. The dogs tried every way they knew to get petted. Entreatingly, they approached one militiaman after another with their heads down and tails wagging, enthusiastically.

"Who are y'all?" Powhatan Ted Junior's young son, Powhatan Teddy, squinted up.

"Where'd y'all come from, anyhows?" Jacob's little cousin, Jedidiah, shouted.

"We come from way down yonder," one humored militiaman offered as he bent over, picked the boy up high in the air, shook him to-and-fro, and then placed him back down on the ground.

His action caused other kids to try to get picked up and shook by the men.

"Y'all goin' to stays 'ere tonight?" the captain's younger son, David, inquired with a face full of intense hope.

The captain grabbed him, with a broad grin, and answered, "That's right Davie, the Muddy Creek is puttin' up the Virginia Militia tonight."

At his announcement, the hoard of children and dogs began yelling, shouting, barking, and howling even more.

Powhatan Ted Junior approached, from behind the house, and walked with sure steps up to the horses. Around the crown of his head sat a leather headband etched with Powhatan insignias. Around his neck hung beads of various bright colors. His slick black hair blew behind him. He stopped short of the captain's horse. His face betrayed the wisdom of the ages that lay hidden in his long lineage. He was Powhatan Tom's first cousin, Powhatan Ed's nephew, Powhatan Ted's son, Brave Eagle's grandson, Deerslayer's great-grandson, Moose Hunter's great-great-grandson, and a Powhatan royal.

The captain greeted him loudly so that all of the men could catch the brave's name.

"Powhatan Ted, how goes the plantation?" he asked.

"Plantation going good, John," he answered assuredly. Will be long growing season this year, methinks," he added.

"No problems to report?" the captain inquired.

"I manage plantation during war. Now, I manage when you muster," Powhatan Ted Junior answered with certainty.

Just then the front door opened wide. Jemimah stepped onto the porch, followed by the captain's daughter, Mary, holding Jacob's cousin, Jasamine, in her arms. A stern look came to Mammy's face, as she turned up her pink lower lip, threw her head back, placed her fists on her hips, and yelled, "What in tarnation's causin' all this 'ere commotion?"

Rushingly, Jedidiah, leaped halfway up the steps to answer her.

"Ta ginia militia, granmammy," he squealed out wriggling and grinning gleefully.

The captain's older son, William, stood close by Jedidiah.

"Dad's home, Mammy" he yelled out with a grin. Then, he turned and trotted toward his saddle sore, weak-legged, exhausted father, who had just put his brother down onto the ground.

The captain grabbed him solidly and greeted him, "Billy, my boy!"

Jemimah, now on the lawn, taking in the scene with a big smile, while waiting for a pause in action, spoke out.

"Well tarnation, Mista John, we supposed to feed all these 'ere hungry men on such short notice?" she demanded with an unhidden huff.

"I am truly sorry, Mammy, mam. We militiamen are imposin'," he apologized.

Jemimah relented, just a little.

"Well," she offered, coyly.

"It would not be gentlemanly of us all to impose on the hospitality of the Muddy Creek, mam," one militiaman demeaned himself with a slight bow.

Another one stepped forward and interjected gallantly. He placed his hat on his chest, and bowed.

"We'd be obliged of it, mam," he cajoled her.

Slowly, Jemimah pulled in her thick bottom lip. She looked down, then up quickly.

"Well, allrights," she said. "But its goin' to take some cookin' up," she added loudly as she lifted her skirt, turned, and began to ascend the steps. Then she paused, looked back, and added louder, "An' glory be, do y'all need washin' up 'fore comin' in the house, cause it ain't springtime I'm a smellin'."

Jedidiah ran back up the steps to hold the door for his granmammy.

The militiamen responded, in unison, with, "Thank you, mam."

In good cheer, the men, with much assistance from the boys, led the horses to the paddocks. The wide wooden stable doors stood wide-open. Inside, native and colored men, in cotton shirts and denim trousers, were working with horses. Captain John greeted the stablemen and introduced his militiamen all around.

The soldiers placed their horses into the interconnected paddocks, removed saddles and bridles, then stored their gear in the stable. The captain instructed a few of his men to climb the loft ladder and use the pitchforks to throw hay out the loft door. He instructed others to wheel some oats out to the bins. He instructed yet a few others to take turns pumping water into the trough. Finally, he made sure, himself, that the horses had salt licks.

With the horses settled in, the captain led the men, rucksacks in hands, to the back of the house, where Jerimiah and his teenage son, Jacob, met them with baskets full of towels, wash rags, and bars of soap. Jerimiah led the group, boys following, to the creek. There, the men washed vigorously on a rocky bottom in two and three feet of flowing cold water.

Upon the group's return to the house, they entered through the rear door into the back hall. Jerimiah and Jacob led them up the back stairs to the boy's big dormitory room. Jerimiah stopped and stood in the middle of the room, with his hands turned out, perplexedly.

"They ain't near 'nough beds in this 'ere room for y'alls. But, we sure 'nough had plenni o' guests 'fore, an' we got the beds, an' beddin'. We gots to haul some o' those canvas cots an' beddin' up 'ere," he thought out loud, as he turned to begin the task.

Soon, the dormitory became crowded with both beds and cots. They had to be placed side by side, along both long walls, to accommodate them all. The men, and boys, would have to enter them from the bottoms.

Meanwhile, downstairs in the front room and library, with the doors wide-open to conjoin the rooms, the men pulled chairs together and sat down to drink and smoke. Jacob, who had proudly donned a burgundy wool vest and white cotton gloves, because they made him feel like a butler, adeptly served whiskey, wine, and cold water, along with pipes, tobacco, and native weed from silver trays that he manned, with a proud smile, at the sideboard. The captain showed off his book collection. At a square table in the corner, six men began playing cards. Several children took seats in the other soldiers' laps, and beseeched them for stories about the wilderness and war.

Cooking and setting up the dinning room had been keeping all of the women working, since the militiamen arrived. After dark, that April evening, they finally served dinner. The plantation was capable of laying out a fabulous feast on short notice. In the dining room, crystal, china, silver, and cotton napkins sat in high piles on a sideboard. Fat round pork roasts oozing out juice, steaming thick dark gravy, mashed yams covered in raw honey and walnuts, green beans with sliced mushrooms and onions mixed in, besides thick chewy wheat rolls and butter occupied platters and bowls, all kept hot by candle flames, on the table.

Everyone filled their own plates and found seats, in the front room, library, and den. Walking around balancing plates and bowls filled with food was a cautious endeavor. Kids handled their plates and bowls with extra balanced care under Jemimah's keen eyes. On any other night, this twilight hour would have brought their bath and bed time.

Slowly, the evening wound down. All of a sudden, some of the kids became so sleepy that, one by one, they sequestered laps, chairs, and even floor space on which to fall asleep. That day was the most exciting they remembered in a while. They slept soundly as Jacob, Bacchus, and a few soldiers happily played fiddles and flutes at the far side of the front room. Those so inclined danced. In the dining room, Jerimiah, Powhatan Ted Junior, Powhatan Tom, and several soldiers played hard at cards until the early hours.

In the morning, after a breakfast that rivaled dinner, the soldiers stood about the back lawn thanking the captain's wife, Sarah, the coloreds, and natives for their great hospitality so long that the Spring sun moved over the shade trees. It was only the discomfort of young heat that forced them onto their waiting mounts and down the river trial. On the broad lawn, dejectedly, the children, dogs at their sides, watched the soldiers ride away, until they were out of sight down the river trail. They longed to follow them into the forest. Many would one day.

CHAPTER XXIV

THE LEGACY OF LIBERTY

Growing up on a plantation was its own world. Every other plantation and any village were someplace else and a long walk away. Days and weeks could go by without ever leaving the place nor seeing anyone from somewhere else. There were weeks when months went by without ever going anywhere nor greeting anyone. The countryside was thick with forests.

Sometimes on Sundays, families rode to church. Otherwise, monthly on weekends, neighbors gathered for roasts or barbeques, depending on the season, at one plantation or another in the neighborhood. At those times, play was more fun than usual. And sooner or later, it always got wild and rough.

In Winter, youngsters put in plenty of time in the pine-paneled plantation schoolroom. Generally restless, they sat long hours, without play, on hard wooden chairs at heavy tables. They pushed through assignments, with fat round lead-filled dark red-painted pencils, on brown paper, that always held some splinters in varying shapes and sizes. Many hours of childhood were consumed sitting at those tables facing tutors. For the rest of their lives, one memory they would never forget would be the view of the front of that school room, where the new red, white, and blue flag stuck out from high up on the wall, attached to a varnished wooden pole, tipped with brass, over the painting of General President Washington.

Underneath the flag, a broad black heavy-framed chalkboard hung bolted onto the single plastered and painted wall in the room. On the right and back of the room, the pine-paneled walls held maps of Virginia including its Old Northwest and Caintucky territories; North America; and Europe with the British Isles; along with framed paintings of upcountry heroes Patrick Henry, James Mason, James Madison, and Thomas Jefferson; that were painted from live subjects by talented Powhatan Tom. In addition, there were drawings of Homer; Hesiod; Herodotus; Thycidedes; Eurypides; Socrates; Plato; Aristotle; and his pupil Alexander, besides posters that portrayed the chemical elements; biological parts of the body; laws of physics; and great buildings of history, including the Temple of Apollo at Delphi; the Acropolis at Athens; and Parthenon at Rome. Notwithstanding such a dramatic convergence of two cultures, ancient and modern, the scene the students would remember best was the view, out of the four high windows aligned in a row, and down to the flowing wild river yonder.

To get to be twelve years old was the time to get to. That was, mainly, because most kids expected to be big enough to ride a horse by then. Riding a horse, and having a horse by twelve, was a right of passage on the plantation. As one-year olds, children learned to walk. As twelve-year olds, they learned to ride. After a few years of riding, it became like second nature. The best horsemen were admired for more than horsemanship. They were admired, not just for having mastered a skill, but for the intelligence and character that went with the mastering. Horsemanship was somewhere up there with shooting a gun, or predicting the weather when it came to status in the upcountry. Horses, themselves, taught the children something, too. Horses taught the kids how to love. And, all of them came to love their horses the same as they loved their dogs.

At hunting, whether on horseback or foot with rifle, younger boys kept up with older ones and all ages of men. A hunting party would start out from the stable, after spending some time sitting around getting gear and rifles ready. For about half an hour, hunters followed varnished wood post-and-rail pasture fences that rolled away from the stable, and nearby barns, like a border into another world. Once beyond pastures, they headed down along wide hedges that bordered the edges of farm fields. By the time the hunters were walked out, they reached distant woodlands that surrounded the plantation.

In those shady shadows, unsuspecting and unwary, wildlife roamed in bountiful numbers. Hunting game down did not take much determination except, maybe, in cold weather. Cleaning up the animals required more work than hunting them down. Hunting game, cleaning it, and hanging it in the smokehouse was not considered real work anyway.

Actually, hunting down foxes on horseback was considered sport. Hunts were hard run and fast-moving. Neighbors rode their horses to a hunt gathering, at one plantation or another, on most Saturdays except in Summer. The excitement of a hunt wore out the day. Afterwards, there would be a roasting party, with fast-fiddling fiddlers, that spread throughout the host house.

Whether the morning brought sun, rain, wind, or snow nothing would stop a hunt once it were organized. The gathering of horses and riders began slowly at a designated stable by mid-morning. An hour or so before noon, the hunt master took his mount. Within a few minutes, all hunters had their mounts in hand.

As the hunt neared readiness, horses became hard to hold as a dozen dogs barking, all around them, could cause such a disturbance that they would become agitated. That only added to the growing excitement. Then, finally, the trumpeter blew the horn. The whole packed-in rumpus intensified. And, they were off, at once, in a massive pounding of hooves.

Childhood and teenage years passed reading, writing, and reciting in the school room, handling horses at the stable, hunting in the woods, and in or on the water. Where the Muddy Creek met the James River was generally considered to be the best spot on the whole plantation during hot Summer days. The carpenters on the plantation had built the plank board dock real big and sturdy. The length of it accommodated not only tobacco and grain barges but rowboats, canoes, and swimmers, too. The upstream side began at water more than deep enough to swallow a high plunge. For that purpose, the heavy hemp rope hung from a thick oak branch grown out a good way over the creek.

In the boathouse, varnished canoes carved out of tree trunks sat upside down and ready for rowing out onto the river. Once the boys on the plantation where big enough to row the canoes, they began to venture across the river. On the other shore, they banked the canoes and hiked on the packed-dirt river road or, to make it more like an exploration, through the forest along the shore. Going upriver, the first place they came to was the Mason plantation store.

The store was an amazing place. The storekeeper crammed more merchandise within its walls than anyone could walk around and look at in a whole hour. Upon one wall hung painted container tops and other colorful souvenirs of salt, soda, powder, and such brands as there were. Another long wall sat covered with tall thick cases containing shelves that reached up to near the ceiling. On the bottom shelf, above closed cabinet doors, sat square glass jars filled with chewy and hard sugarcane candy. The jars were just the right height for staring into.

In addition, the store held rolls and rolls of sewing cloth, including Scottish clans' plaid flannels with multi-colored crossbars; burgundy-colored flannel; dark colors of plaid and plain wools; bleached and unbleached cotton; and indigo-dyed denim, besides thread; needles; scissors; leather belts, boots, and shoes of all sizes; thousands of candles; pine boxes packed full of soap; shiny wood-handled razors and toothbrushes; smooth polished pipes; iron pots, pans, utensils, and nails; glass panes; hemp rope; and tools of all types for all needs of which one could think. Even that wasn't near all of it.

The plantation store was the nearest thing to a town for a long ways around. Planters, farmers, and homesteaders throughout the neighborhood traded their tobacco, on credit, for merchandise at the Mason plantation store. Every now and then, a traveler would come along looking for directions, something hot or cold to drink, depending on the season and time of day, besides a place to rest awhile. Sure enough, by the time anybody got there, they would be tired, and sometimes sore, from traveling far through the forest trails.

They would seat themselves, informally, at the several tables and chairs in the front of the store for pleasant breaks of drinking, smoking, and conversing. The larger farmers around the neighborhood would send their coloreds to the plantation store, in a wagon, instead of making the tedious trip themselves. Generally, they sent the slaves to purchase supplies, post a letter, and pick up mail. On any given weekday, a few of them might be gathered at the tables that sat together to the one side of the front door. It was their habit to keep to themselves at the tables on the one side, as opposed to the other side, at which, it was generally understood, smaller farmers kept to themselves. Coloreds from big farms felt themselves to be of a class separate from small farmers. When they did come up and talk to one another, they were friendly enough, nonetheless. Virginia was, after all, a country of equality of opportunity.

After the boys from the Muddy Creek Plantation would tarry a few hours at the plantation store, looking curiously at everything, and talking to everyone, they would start heading back to the river and the banked canoes. Hikes to, and from, the Mason Plantation took the greatest part of a day. And, if they lingered long enough, then sooner or later, mostly on Saturdays, they might meet up with other boys. That would keep them even longer.

The older they became, the less enthusiastic they were about hiking on foot. As teenagers, they would just as soon take off on rides up or downriver. Of course, horses got them farther than canoes. And, they were always wanting to go farther.

Rowing and riding away from the plantation, made the boys feel a deep down, hardly describable, sense of risk that was really nothing more than the terror of adventure. In their minds, they always looked back. For, to be sure, life on the plantation was its own world, and the new union of states aside, Virginia was its own country. It had always been their country. And, beyond her lay other countries.

Somehow, from secluded memory, from stories the old folks told, the boys and girls, knew all of this. They had a sense of history. They had a sense of living within history. They had a sense of themselves, too. They had an even stronger sense of family. They knew all of their ancestors, and thus they knew all of their cousins, close and distant alike.

Unlike their ancestors, they were not British. They were Virginians. Here, they had no king. Nor were there titled royals, at all. Their prime minister was the president. And, leaders claimed to be equal, in regard to opportunity, anyway. Perhaps, that is as equal as men could ever be. No matter, for of opportunity there was plenty. In fact, the United States was most famous, not for equality, but for being big. A big bountiful land. And, it was vastness that drew young men and boys away from home.

While rowing a dugout canoe upriver, against the current, four boys strong, one warm Saturday, Dave turned around to his older brother, behind him, and wondered aloud about just that.

"Jus' how big are these 'ere United States, anyhow, Bill?"

He knew Bill did not have the answer anymore than he did not have the answer. But he knew Bill would answer the question another way. And, in so doing, his brother would tell him what he wanted to know.

"They're bigger than any place in this whole world," Bill answered loudly from behind him.

"Do ya think anybody could ever see the whole place? Explorin', I mean." he asked.

"Maybe. First, you'd 'ave to trek across the rough ole mountains full o' bears, and then drift yourself down the Ohio River to the mighty Mississippi. After that, you'd roll right on into Louisiana and out to sea, if ya didn't stop yourself," his brother answered.

Dave squinted his eyes and strained to see as far ahead as he could.

"That would be a trip to behold," he imagined out loud.

"You bet, and ya wouldn't even 'ave seen half o' the place," Bill added.

Both boys wandered, through their own images of the wilderness, for awhile. They knew that it went far west. What they really wanted to know, however, was how far they would ever go.

The sixth generation on the Muddy Creek Plantation grew up in the same way as their father, grandfather, great-grandfather, and great-great-grandfather before them. Their great-great-great-grandfather, Jesse Hughes, was already grown when he came to the virgin lande. He had grown up on his father's lande in the English-Welsh borderlandes. As a young man, he planted himself down, on the riverbank at the muddy creek, here in remote Powhatan wilderness. The plantation was his legacy.

Successive generations handed the place down, many times over. Yet, Jesse's spirit never left the lande. His spirit stayed behind him, in memory. From somewhere behind the ancient stand of thick towering trees, on the breezy bluff, under a stone slab, from the graveyard, the olde man had been keeping guard over his lande for two centuries now.

Jesse gave Chief Wahunsunakok muskets, gunpowder, a compass, and bugle on an expedition, with the bolde

Captain Smith, from Jamestowne to Werowocomoco. In exchange, Wahunsunakok gave him the lande, initiated him, and adopted him as a werowance, into the Powhatan Tribe. In addition, the cautious chief placed him under the magic spell by sprinkling powder on him. Under that spell, harm would come to neither he nor his progeny, in the Confederacy, under threat of certain revenge.

True enough, after two centuries, no harm had dared come to visit Jesse's descendants. Even though there were times when they did not sleep soundly in the still darkness of night, they had never been awakened by bright shining tomahacks. After Wahunsunakok died, his younger brother, the vengeful Opekankano, never torched the vulnerable wooden barns, big stable, house, and cabins. Nor did he make prize of scalps, as he had done farther downriver. During the French Wars, truculent Shawnee, from the West, never came over the mountains and torched without warning.

Several years had passed since British General Benedict Arnold marched his malicious men up the James River aiming to burn out plantations at the heart of the rebellion. The redcoats torched, even up, to the far reaches of the river, where it narrows to a small stream, and homesteaders produced no crops to feed patriot soldiers and their horses. The carnage spread all the way upriver, on both shores. The British Army burned down hundreds of barns, stables, and houses. But not the Muddy Creek.

On that mean march, the theft of gold, silver, livestock, crops, and of womens' chastity was without precedent since the Dark Ages, before Charlemagne, when few dared venture outside castle walls for fear of encountering robber barons. The invaders stole livestock and crops, gold and silver, for army and personal use, respectively. They took women for the use of both.

That memorable day, the women in charge of the plantation; whilst the men marched in the Southern Campaign through South and North Carolina, then into tidewater Virginia; thought hard and acted courageously. They determined it best to shoot any soldier who stepped onto the place since troopers meant to torch, not just steal. So, the colored and native men shot soldiers dead in their treacherous tracks. Their heroism saved the plantation home that day.

The ole plantation. It lived on, under the iron cloak of the magic spell. The place had a life of its own. It grew with the passage of time. The generations themselves were lucky to live to be all of an hundred years old, but the land lived longer. Generations of planters were just caretakers of the land.

Since that damp Spring day when Jesse, John, Moose Hunter, and Brave As Bull reached this riverbank in far wilderness, and planted themselves down in that remoteness, the plantation had grown to abut its neighbors' borders. At first, there was just a cabin, shed, and some fenced pasture on cleared lande where the house, stable, barns, crop, and pasture lands now stood. Nearly two hundred years later, the surrounding massive wilderness, up and downriver, had given up trees to plantations, farms, and homesteads. Now, a neighbor farmed not far away.

The plantation produced thousands of tons of tobacco and grain, plus livestock, annually. The craft shops made it self-sufficient in barges, boats, wagons, tools, leather, gunpowder, glass, furniture, cloth, candles, soap, whiskey, wine, and all of its genuine needs. The fifth generation inherited responsibility for land that provided a livelihood for hundreds of persons and supplied thousands more. The scope of production had grown prolifically. It was nothing less than a wonder to behold at harvest time.

Captain John's tenure as caretaker of the land lasted through both the second war against France with her native allies, and the rebellion against England that followed that great World War. He witnessed two wars, besides two decades of peace before, and two after them. His generation fought France for the West and then England for independence.

His brother-in-law, Will Morton, and he, founded the salt mining enterprise. It was the first major mining business, in the British Empire, founded with a monopoly grant from neither parliament nor king. Along with a few other partners, he founded the Richmond newspaper. That libertarian press was Virginia's first upcountry newspaper. In his militia company, he fought in the Southern Campaign right up to the surrender at Yorktown. During the last several years, he lived out deep recession yet, through efficiencies, prospered somewhat, nonetheless.

Captain John grew up with a sense of home that itself had grown. For, unlike his ancestors, he saw himself more a Virginian and less an Englishman. As a boy, he was English. As a man, he became a Virginian.

Sitting back slowly into the creaking folds of a dark-brown leather armchair, on the big broad brick porch, and gazing out over the rolling river, as he drew purposefully on his pipe, he fell freely into deep thought about the country he had come to know so well, Virginia. The draw of his pipe's pungent aroma slowly put him in a trance-like state. His thoughts moved through the politics, to the economy, then society, and finally into the very culture of his country.

The culture of his country, he knew, was one of liberty. For, it was a country where most men were self-sufficient in farming, trades, or professions. And, those who yet were not, sought to be so.

The soothing smell of his pipe reminded him that tobacco made that culture possible. It was, after all, the demand for tobacco, back in England, that made agriculture profitable in the colony. His reflective mind expanded even more with every draw. He began to understand more poignantly, than theretofore, how tobacco made liberty possible.

As he had at the graveyard, that warm morning, back in '76, like deja-vu, intuitively, he sensed that tobacco and liberty are inseparable. Then, again, the thought grew in his mind like a developing dawn. He began to sense that smoking is a whole culture in itself. That was the reason King James was so against smoking whence it began. For, its popularity provided Virginians' liberty, and thus independence from government.

Tobacco, and the culture of smoking, had made possible the liberty of Virginians in the early years of the colony. Now, after the war for liberty through independent government, tobacco, and the whole culture of smoking, had made possible the liberty of Americans everywhere, whether Virginian or not. His thoughts turned to the future of the culture of smoking. Was it strong enough to maintain that precious liberty against resurgent monopoly and imperialism? The war was won. Or, was it?

Just then, the screen door slammed shut.

"Yessa, when it's this warm in May, sure 'nough means they's heavy rain a comin', an' cool 'hind that," Jerimiah observed, as he walked onto the front porch and felt the contrast from within the house where Winter's cool hung on.

"We'll 'ave a rough night, allright," John agreed, as he studied the rain clouds rushing over the rough river.

"A bad one's a comin' sure 'nough. I smells it," Jerimiah added.

The voices of the two men drew Bill, out of the front room, where he was consumed in Edmund Burke's distinctions between English and French views of liberty in *Reflections on the Revolution in France*. It seemed, to him, that the French were confusing liberty with freedom.

"The stock are startin' to make their ways in," the boy observed through the blowing wind. "Even the ornery ones oughta head in tonight," he added.

"Yessa, it sure 'nough smells like a bad one comin'." Jerimiah paused. "But, I ain't seen nothin' yet like the storm o' '89. Thunder just a smackin' right up 'hind ya." Jerimiah shot his hands out, swiftly, and smacked them together loudly. "An' bright white," he grinned.

John remembered, "Yes, that was a rough one. Thought somethin' would catch fire for sure. Old Zeus pitched his big bolts down hard that night."

"We might get hail, allright," Bill added, with a just discernable assumption of authority.

Just then, Jedidiah came hurtling around the side of the house, holding a leather ball, tightly, under his clenched arm, and running as fast as he could, across the big lawn, toward the river trail. Another boy, his cousin, Hector, ran hard on his heels. Their eyes caught those of the men, and they froze fast, at once, in their tracks.

Jerimiah stood up with a scowl, slapped the side of his thigh, and yelled out loudly at them, "Hey, hey, you boys be goin' out by the barns, a runin' like that."

"Yessa," the boys barely had time to shout out, of the corners of their eyes, before they were beyond sight.

Bill turned and stepped to the sideboard, that sat against the front wall, behind the group of armchairs and small tables, on the porch. He lifted a sweating silver pitcher and poured out a glass of iced-down tea. He sensed the intentions of the two men near him. He poured out two more tumblers for his father and butler.

The captain, yet somewhat preoccupied in thought, only half noticed the cool drink coming his way. He heard the boys playing from somewhere nearby, and his mind wandered. Their laughter traveled through the distance disrupted only by the blowing breeze.

The captain turned distractedly toward the direction of the barns. His mind moved into a scene from one warm Spring day, the recollection of which was new to his memory. From deep within his mind's eye, he saw himself chasing his older brother, James, across that lawn, as hard as he could.

Unexpectedly, an indistinct feeling, ever so distant, of something akin to doom, struck his sixth sense. Instinctively, he turned back to focus on the rolling dark clouds and whistling wind, once again. At that moment, a burst of breeze blew, through the trees, rustling leaves as it went. His eyes fell on the rough river.

The sunken sensation deep within him struggled to speak, "The Virginian way o' life, it has been said, is more prosperous, over all, than anywhere in the world." A pause allowed pride in country to make itself felt. John continued, "That is, where one considers ways o' life besides just material wealth."

"What other ways o' life are you thinkin' 'bout, dad?" Bill asked.

John so much wanted his son to comprehend the magnanimity of his legacy. For, the maintenance of liberty would soon be his generation's responsibility. In an attempt to convey that nobleness to the boy, he answered slowly and with preponderant thought.

"This land has provided not just material wealth, but a whole way o' life, that except to a limited degree in England, men 'ave only been able to dream about since ancient times in Greece and Rome. Virginian farms and trades provide its countrymen with livelihoods. That independence is prerequisite for liberty. As a young man, I saw planting life grow so prodigiously as to provide the impetus to fight for more than economic liberty. My generation fought the war for independent government and thus political liberty, too."

Bill thought he understood, "The land provides more than material wealth then. It provides the liberty of Virginians."

"Sure 'nough, without this 'ere land, ain't none of us would 'ave liberty, because we'd all be workin' for someone else," Jerimiah keenly understood.

"I would like to think that this land will provide liberty to my descendants, Jerimiah's, and Powhatan Ted's, forever," John continued.

"You have doubts, John?" Jerimiah sensed.

"Lately, I'm beginning to 'ave doubts about the future o' liberty in Virginia, and indeed, throughout our new states. We fought the mean, marching through mud and muck, gettin' shot at, bloody war for liberty. And, don't get me wrong. I'm not holdin' any regrets. But now, after all that shootin', killin', burnin', and ridin' sore through rain, sleet, snow, and misery, liberty is getting lost.

"How's it getting lost, dad? We only just won it," Bill queried confusedly.

"I know what happen to liberty," Powhatan Ted Junior answered Bill, as the screen door slammed shut behind him, and he sat down in an empty seat. "Not enough land for so many to have it," he remembered his own father's words of wisdom. "My father say, someday the land be so full of folks plantin' down, there not be enough land for all to have liberty."

Jerimiah concurred, "Sure 'nough, even as far upriver as Richmond, the country's growin' so full o' folks comin' from somewheres else that they's crowdin' the town up wid themselves. Like, they all don't sees one anotha. They's all lookin' for land, or a trade shop, but they ain't 'nough land and shops for 'em all. That's hows cum they's payin' to live in someone else's houses and laborin' for nothin' but wages. Why, they's might as well be slaves."

John changed position in his chair so as, subconsciously, to gain attention and began again, "Methinks, most folks, when they think 'bout these 'ere united states, whether they know it or not, are thinkin' 'bout an opportunity to gain liberty. Thirteen hundred years of serfdom and slavery have passed since the ancient days of liberty. The Roman Empire, the Dark Age, and Middle Age, have passed through history, each in their turn. Nowhere in Europe, Britain, nor America is opportunity so great as 'ere in this land o' villages, farms, woodlands, and wilderness. The Virginian way of life was founded on liberty in livelihood. Nonetheless, I fear that our liberty has seen its greatest day, because there are too many comin' to America, too fast, to gain it."

Bill did not want to hear words of gloom and doom about his young innocent country. Impulsively, his hands tightened around the thick arms of his chair, as he attempted to refute his father, "The West is really openin' up, now. Folks take Dan Boone's road into Caintucky, regular. There's plenny o' land for liberty out there."

"If people keep coming, then even West not be enough land. It fill up too. Just like East," Powhatan Ted Junior predicted.

"It seems hard to believe that this huge continent could ever fill up," Bill thought out loud.

"Natives know. West fill up fast, like East," Powhatan Ted Junior retorted.

Bill could not let go of his dream.

He continued, "Vice President Jefferson talks about a future in which everyone has liberty. He has a dream. He envisions an America of farmers."

John spoke confidently to his son, "I have talked with him, on occasion, at the tavern in Richmond, and at plantation gatherings, here and there. I can tell you, son, his vision has a firm root in sagacious foresight, allright. For years, he has been voicing his view that New York businessmen will come to dominate the other states' economies, politics, societies, and even cultures, because Federalists continue to maintain strong ties to the mighty British Empire."

Jerimiah added loudly, "New York is the centa of imperialism in the whole federation. The place neva did become independent. Why, I rememba the end o' the war. New York was the last place the Brits were willin' to lose."

John continued, "To counter the imperial power of New York commercial interests, Jefferson maintains that farmers should dominate the government. Thus, his land of farmers, and, he would add, tradesmen in their own shops."

"Well, then he thinks that everyone can get land," Bill held to his belief.

His father shifted, uncomfortably, in the old leather chair.

Then, he responded, "Good 'ole Tom believes that the way to strengthen liberty is to extend the vote to all the landless newcomers. That way, according to his reasoning, New York businessmen will be unable to monopolize political power, because the very large number of voters will prevent their monopolizing it."

Powhatan Ted Junior answered Bill's question, "Mister Jefferson sees plenty land in West, for meantime. Sees Louisiana land for later."

"Louisiana! Wow. That place goes on forever," Bill exclaimed.

"That what natives thought before Englishman came," Powhatan Ted Junior corrected him again.

John continued to contemplate Jefferson's thoughts, uneasily.

He continued, "Methinks, perhaps Tom is mistaken about the relationship between liberty and democracy, however. The Greeks were the first, in history, to practice not only liberty, but democracy. Since we are establishing a democratic republic in the Greek tradition, we would do well to know their history so as not to repeat any of their mistakes."

Bill became impatient. He interrupted, "What mistakes did the Greek republics make, dad?"

John responded patiently, "When they extended the vote, Greeks began voting for patronage. That habit eventually enslaved them."

Bill asked eagerly, "What types of patronage did Greek office holders give voters in exchange for votes?"

His father answered, "Land reform, at first, and eventually when land was gone, just jobs. Jobs rowing in the merchant fleet; jobs applauding or booing at the theatre; jobs voting yae or nae at court trials."

Jerimiah finished John's logic, "If landless men become voters, then they'll vote for land. When there's no mo land to give way, they'll votes for jobs. Then, the mo folks votin', the less their vote 'ill be worth, and the less they'll get for it. Why, in Rome, folks gots nothin' but bread and circuses for all their votes."

John allowed a few reflective moments to pass.

He resumed his discourse, "Greeks voted out the oligarchs, the large farmers, because they offered nothing but good government. They voted in the tyrants, a few wealthy men, because they offered land reform and jobs."

"Sure 'nough fooled them," Jerimiah shot out.

John finished, "I predict that the more democratic we become, the more power will vest in the few wealthiest men, such as the tyrants of old Greece. New York businessmen will, indeed, dominate the states. Just that which Tom Jefferson seeks to prevent with democracy. He foresees the problem, allright, but his well-intentioned resolution will bring it about."

Bill understood, "Too much democracy leads to tyranny."

His father shook his head slowly, "That's right son. And, eventually slavery. Let's not forget Hesiod's wise words in the *Theogony*, his book about the creation of the Greek world, like our biblical book of Genesis. He wrote,...and then the gods gave Greeks kings, for justice; because kings give the best justice; since their interests are the same as those of the people."

Jerimiah's intuition spoke, "You ain't gonna be enslavin' white folks, now. No sir. Ole Jefferson's farmers 'ill be

fightin' a war against New York for independence one day."
He looked up, thoughtfully, and grinned. "Yessa, anotha
war for liberty thru independence. It'll be the whole South
agin' the whole North. Two countries. E pluribus duo."

On that far-reaching insight, the men pondered for a
lengthy minute. Then, the first, almost faint, rumble of
thunder roared in the far distance. A strong chilly gust blew
boldly against their faces. And, for a fleeting moment, they
felt the presence of time itself, as if it had stopped, for just
that instant, in that year, seventeen ninety-nine.

John's dire prediction that American democracy would
go down the Greek way took a big step, in that ill-fated
direction, when Vice President Jefferson became president.
After that momentous year, at the turn of the nineteenth
century, the vote did indeed get extended to the landless.
The oligarchy, of sorts, that had been governing the United
States, men such as Washington, and Jefferson himself,
would soon be displaced by tyrants, of sorts. That is, men
who promised patronage for votes.

The captain was a member of the Revolutionary War
generation. All his life, he heard and read arguments
building more resolute until '76, when right out rebellion
brought war. Whether he were at home, neighbors, tavern,
or church, native treaties and taxes were all the talk. As a
boy, and throughout his life, the captain's favorite hero was
Nat Bacon, rebel planter. The red, white, and blue rebel flag
had hung in his dorm room window at college. Now it hung
in the boy's big dorm room, upstairs. For his fellows and
he, the honor of rebellion had followed the loss of liberty,
in a natural way.

At the end of those hard-fought years, on the battlefield
at Yorktown, he found himself standing at attention, as the

English Army band played, "*The World Turned Upside Down*." That day, he witnessed nothing less than the surrender of colonialism. Since then, he witnessed the colony transform into the state of Virginia. Then, he witnessed the creation of the United States. Lately, however, he thought he was witnessing reaction against that hard-won victory. The Continental Army and states' militiamen had fought the war for liberty. Instead, they seemed to have gotten democracy.

Liberty was his generation's legacy. At his death, his *Last Will and Testament* made that legacy law. His older son, William, who loved the land and lived outside, inherited the plantation and his partnership, with the Mortons, in the salt mines. The bulk of the fortune was thus his by the tradition of primogeniture. True, the rebellion had brought an end to both primogeniture and entail. Nonetheless, government sometimes ends traditions that have enduring value to people. John believed that the tradition of primogeniture would maintain liberty so long as the family remained together. For otherwise, to divide the land would mean its eventual loss through multiple divisions. He could thus foresee that economies of scale, in planting, must be practiced for the plantation to provide perpetual liberty to his progeny. The new democracy conflicted with liberty. His younger son, David, who skillfully edited the newspaper, inherited his partnership in it. Politics and publishing were that boy's growing passions. He held powerful traditions deep inside him. For his daughter, Mary, he left a large dowry, beginning with the silver. And so, the legacy of liberty devolved unto the next generation.